Of Caves and Shell Mound

Of Caves and
Shell Mounds

Edited by
Kenneth C. Carstens and Patty Jo Watson

The University of Alabama Press

Tuscaloosa and London

Copyright © 1996
The University of Alabama Press
Tuscaloosa, Alabama 35487-0380
All rights reserved
Manufactured in the United States of America

The paper on which this book is printed meets the minimum
requirements of American National Standard for Information
Science-Permanence of Paper for Printed Library Materials,
ANSI Z39.48-1984.

Library of Congress Cataloging-in-Publication Data

Of caves and shell mounds / edited by Kenneth C. Carstens and
Patty Jo Watson.
p.   cm.
Based on a symposium of the Southeastern Archaeological
Conference held in Tampa, Florida, 1989.
Includes bibliographical references and index.
ISBN 0-8173-0805-9 (alk. paper)
1. Big Bend Sites (Ky.)—Congresses.   2. Mammoth Cave
National Park (Ky.)—Congresses.   3. Indians of North
America—Kentucky—Green River Region (River)—Antiquities—
Congresses.   4. Excavations (Archaeology)—Kentucky—Green
River Region (River)—Congresses.   5. Caves—Kentucky—
Green River Region (River)—Surveying—Congresses.
6. Kitchen-middens—Kentucky—Green River Region
(River)—Congresses.   7. Watson, Patty Jo, 1932—   Congresses.
I. Carstens, Kenneth Charles.   II. Watson, Patty Jo, 1932-
III.   Southeastern Archaeological Conference.
E78.K3034   1996
976.9'8—dc20   95-20772
                                                    CIP

British Library Cataloguing-in-Publication Data available

To Louise M. Robbins:
Colleague and Friend in the
Caves and at the Shell Mounds

Contents

Figures

Tables

Preface

Kenneth C. Carstens

IN 1989 I organized a symposium for the Southeastern Archaeological Conference in Tampa, Florida. The symposium was titled "Twenty-six Years along Kentucky's Green River: Papers in Honor of Patty Jo Watson." Although a participant of the symposium herself, Watson did not know the symposium was being held in her honor until she was seated among other symposium participants.

At the symposium papers were presented by Ken Carstens, Guy Prentice, Bruce Manzano, Jan Hemberger, Philip DiBlasi, Ken Tankersley, Gail Wagner, Cheryl Claassen, Christine Hensley, Valerie Haskins and Nicholas Herrmann, and Patty Jo Watson, followed by discussions provided by Cheryl Munson, Mary Lucas Powell, and Vincas Steponaitis.

The purpose of the symposium (and of this book) was twofold. First and foremost, I wished to bring together friends and researchers associated with Patty Jo Watson to honor her for the work, friendship, and guidance she so willingly gave to her students and colleagues throughout 30 years of work along Kentucky's Green River. A more academically oriented goal of the symposium was to bring together papers addressing past and current research taking place in two areas along Kentucky's Green River that have been associated with Watson: Mammoth Cave National Park (MCNP) and the Big Bend (shell mound) region of Green River.

Very positive comments from those in attendance followed the symposium, including, "Why don't you bring the papers together and publish them?" Carstens and Watson agreed. Watson further recommended the addition of chapters by Bill Marquardt, Mary Kennedy, Mary Lucas Powell, and David Dye to round out the contents of the present volume. Owing to severe press of other commitments, Marquardt was unable to join us, and Manzano agreed to pull his paper, but other papers by Kennedy, Powell, and Dye were included.

The book that came together as a result of the symposium contains fourteen chapters, divided topically into two archaeological areas associated with Watson's work along Kentucky's Green River: Mammoth Cave National Park and the karstic areas surrounding it (chapters 2–7) (Figure P-1) and the Green River Big Bend (shell mound) area (chapters 8–12) (Figure P-2). Dye's chapter provides a regional perspective on riverine adaptation in the Midsouth, and Watson's

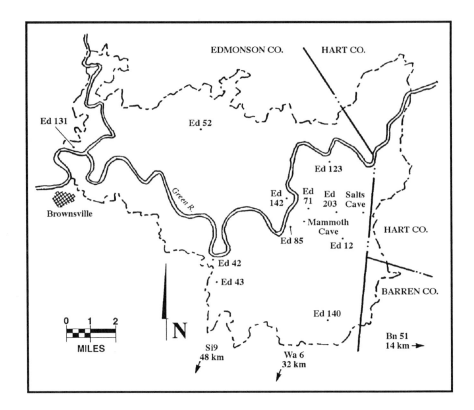

P-1 Various Archaeological Sites in Mammoth Cave National Park

concluding chapter (chapter 14) ties the Mammoth Cave and the Big Bend research areas together (Figure P-3).

Chapter 1, by Munson, examines Kentucky's archaeologically significant
Green River region, the importance of Watson's archaeological research to that
area, and the impact Watson's work has had on our understanding of prehistory
in the Green River region.

Chapter 2, by Carstens, represents a summary of his doctoral research in
MCNP conducted between 1973 and 1975. His work addresses the Park's prehistoric culture history. In particular, Carstens describes the technoenvironmen-
tal characteristics of the cultures from which the specialized Late Archaic–Early
Woodland cave activities developed.

The chapter by Guy Prentice (chapter 3) carries forward from Carstens's
work in MCNP. Prentice, working in MCNP between 1987 and 1990, added
more sites to the data base and sampled a wider range of prehistoric (and historic) sites. His work provides the most detailed understanding of MCNP prehistoric cultures currently available.

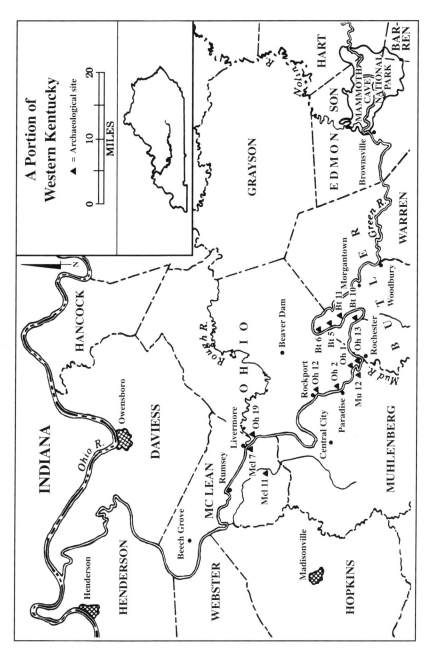

P-2 Green River Big Bend Area. *Source:* Based on a map by William H. Marquardt. Used by permission.

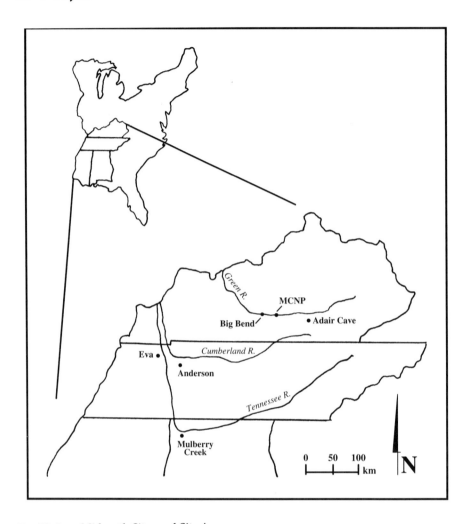

P-3 Various Midsouth Sites and Site Areas

Ken Tankersley (chapter 4) examines the special nature of prehistoric mining activities in the big caves of MCNP and in particular the mining of renewable mineral resources (mirabilite and satin spar).

In chapter 5 Philip DiBlasi discusses several newly discovered mud and
cane charcoal drawings in Adair Cave, Salts Cave, and Mammoth Cave that appear to be considerably different from (and older than) previously described
protohistoric artwork (Faulkner 1988; Faulkner, ed., 1986; Faulkner et al. 1984).
DiBlasi recognizes a Late Archaic–Early Woodland artistic tradition.

Chapter 6, by Mary Kennedy, presents a thorough discussion of 35 radiocarbon determinations from Salts and Mammoth caves. Kennedy makes comparisons among the various radiocarbon laboratories, kinds and types of

possible contamination, and the temporal and spatial variations present within the radiocarbon sample retrieved from Salts and Mammoth caves.

The last chapter in the cave section of the book (chapter 7), by Jan Hemberger, draws principally from three caves in the Central Kentucky Karst and examines management problems, laws that protect caves, and the role public education can play.

Gail Wagner's chapter (chapter 8) centers on methodological concerns relevant to paleoethnobotanical studies in the Shell Mound area. In her study, Wagner takes a retrospective look at, and reevaluation of, pioneering botanical studies initiated by Watson and her associates.

Chapter 9, by Christine Hensley, focuses on the importance of studying archaeological collections made during the Works Progress Administration era in the Green River Shell Mound area. Although archaeologists today are pressured to excavate their own data, Hensley, who examines archaeological materials from the Read shell midden (15Bt10), demonstrates that valuable information can be gleaned from studying older collections.

In chapter 10 Valerie Haskins and Nicholas Herrmann review the bioarchaeological literature associated with shell mound archaeology and provide further insight into the bioarchaeology of the Read shell midden.

In chapter 11 Mary Lucas Powell contributes an examination of health and disease in Green River Archaic populations.

Chapter 12, by Cheryl Claassen, calls into question previous interpretations of archaeological shell from the shell mounds. Claassen opens new avenues for shell mound research with her innovative ideas and observations about Archaic shell-fishing societies.

Chapter 13, by David Dye, examines riverine shell mound adaptation in the Midsouth at the Eva, Mulberry Creek, and Anderson sites. Dye notes that an increased exploitation of riverine aquatic species led to an intensive occupation of floodplain habitats in the Midsouth.

The last chapter (chapter 14), by Patty Jo Watson, details her interests in the caves and shell mounds of Kentucky's Green River, refers to the work she and her colleagues have accomplished since 1963, and forecasts future studies in the two geographically different, but related, Green River areas.

One of the reviewers of a draft version of this book questioned why the chapters in this book, especially those dealing with the Shell Mound area, would precede the long-awaited shell mound book by Marquardt and Watson. Owing to a series of delays—primarily the fault of the project directors, Marquardt and Watson—a detailed report of the Shell Mound Archeological Project is not yet available. Many of the report's components are completed in final draft manuscripts, however, and have been consulted by several contributors to the present volume. References to those manuscripts are noted in the present text as "author, in prep." The manuscripts themselves are with the Shell Mound Project documentation files at Washington University in St. Louis, where the preparation of the final publication is taking place.

Archaeological research along Kentucky's Green River by Watson and her associates has had considerable impact on our understanding of prehistoric life-ways in the Eastern Woodlands, as indicated in part by the present volume. Those of us who have had the privilege of working with Patty Jo Watson, and her interdisciplinary research teams, have been fortunate, indeed. Whether above ground or below, growth in knowledge *and* friendship have long been a hallmark of this research. Thanks, Pat!

Acknowledgments

T HE ARCHAEOLOGICAL research described in this book took place throughout the last 30 years. Many people and many agencies facilitated our research efforts during that time.

Work in the Mammoth Cave area was administratively supported by officials from the National Park Service, Mammoth Cave National Park, and the Cave Research Foundation.

While working in the Big Bend area of Green River, we received valuable support from people from the community of Logansport, Kentucky, especially the late John L. Thomas and Waldemar and Ethie Annis.

A special thank you is extended to Cindy Lawson and Richard Mjos for their computer and artistic skills, respectively. The staff at the University of Alabama Press, especially Judith Knight and copy-editor Marie-Josée Schorp, provided much assistance and many helpful suggestions.

This manuscript was prepared primarily during Carstens's one-semester sabbatical granted him by Murray State University. Additional funds in support of this project were provided by Peter Whaley, director of Murray State University Committee on Institutional Studies and Research, and by Joe Cartwright, dean of the College of Humanistic Studies. Grants from Washington University, the Cave Research Foundation, the National Geographic Society, the National Endowment for the Humanities, and the National Science Foundation have been awarded to Watson in support of our research. Permission for Christine Hensley to access and study the Works Progress Administration collections at the University of Kentucky came from the University's Museum of Anthropology, directed by Dr. Mary Lucas Powell. The index was prepared by Kathleen Tucker. Last, we would like to thank Dr. William H. Marquardt for allowing us to use his line drawings for Figures P-2 and 9.1.

To these people and agencies, we wish to express our most sincere gratitude and appreciation.

KENNETH C. CARSTENS AND PATTY JO WATSON

Of Caves and Shell Mounds

1 | Introduction

Cheryl Ann Munson

WHETHER IT IS called the Central Kentucky Karst, west-central Kentucky, or the western coalfields of Kentucky, the region under study is archaeologically best known simply for the Green River drainage of Kentucky—and principally for the shell mound and cave sites in the central portion of this drainage.

My view of the chapters in this volume and of Green River archaeology is mostly idiosyncratic, that of an archaeologist looking in from an adjacent region. Like most "outsiders" seeking information for related research, much of what I have learned about the archaeology of the Green River region has come from presented papers and published articles. But in limited ways, I have had the chance to be directly involved in Green River archaeology, and this gives me a special perspective on the course of research over the last several decades. One study involved recent surveys in Salts and Mammoth caves with Patrick Munson, Ken Tankersley, and others and the opportunity to carry out fieldwork with Patty Jo Watson (Munson et al. 1989). Although this work grew out of research questions developed from investigations in Wyandotte Cave, Indiana (P. Munson and C. Munson 1990), it led to reconsideration of previous studies and to new observations and interpretations concerning the materials, procedures, and antiquity of the prehistoric mining of cave minerals in the Green River region. My other research was a series of surveys and test excavations of open-air sites in a section of bottomlands and uplands along the lower Green River, near its junction with the Ohio. This was a cultural resource management project conducted in 1987 and 1988 for an Indiana coal mining company. Because the lower Green River section is archaeologically little known in comparison with the central section, I reviewed the literature and unpublished records for the better known central section and became more familiar with the work of Patty Jo Watson and other researchers. Perhaps for this reason, Ken Carstens asked me to be a discussant at a symposium on Green River archaeology held at the 1989 Southeastern Archaeological Conference. The essays presented then make up most of the chapters in this volume.

The 1989 symposium, titled "Twenty-six Years along Kentucky's Green River," was held (coincidentally) 26 years after Howard Winters began a reconsideration of the wealth of previous descriptive work conducted by William Webb (1946, 1950a, b) and others during the New Deal era at Green River shell mound sites. Winters's (1963, 1968, 1974) new views of Late Archaic settlement models and trade cycles stimulated many archaeologists. At the same time, Patty Jo Watson initiated work along Green River that has led to greater insight on many topics. The years of her involvement in cave and shell mound research from 1962 to the present represent three phases of research. Each phase has had a different perspective, but all reflect Watson's approaches to understanding the past.

The first decade was focused on the archaeology of Salts and Mammoth caves. Watson (chapter 14) says that this work began simply and with an emphasis on "time–space systematics." Probably so, but the basic approach of what, where, and when were quickly expanded to include why. Although researchers discerned much about prehistoric cave exploration and the extraction of minerals, they early recognized the importance of the cave environment for producing direct evidence about human subsistence and early horticultural economies. Soon anthropologists with other specialties (e.g., ethnobotany) and scientists in other fields (e.g., palynology) joined Watson to explore the potential of the well-preserved cave deposits more fully. In addition, they applied the then-new technique of flotation long before it became widely used to recover carbonized seeds and other small-scale remains.

Monographs on the archaeology of Salts and Mammoth caves (Watson, ed., 1974; Watson et al. 1969), along with a host of other contributions by various scholars, represent the culmination of this first phase of Green River research. The researchers established that the Early Woodland cavers—who procured salts and other minerals during seasonal forays—were indeed horticulturalists. In the fall, Early Woodland peoples consumed seeds of cultigens then believed to be of tropical origin (squash/gourd), seeds of native cultigens (including sunflower, chenopod, and sumpweed), and hickory nuts. Pollen analysis revealed that in late spring/summer, these fall-harvested plant foods were also eaten as stored products, along with ripening maygrass seeds and various fruits.

The second phase of research, from 1972 to 1982, was directed toward pre–Early Woodland economies and the origins of the plant food subsistence profile seen in the cave deposits. This required a move outside Salts and Mammoth caves to known sites of the antecedent Late Archaic of the Green River. Bill Marquardt joined Watson, and their work became known as the "Shell Mound Archaeological Project," or SMAP (Marquardt 1972a, b, 1974; May 1982). Research outside the caves also involved survey and testing of pre- and post–Early Woodland sites in the immediate karst region (Carstens 1974, 1980). Watson and Marquardt conducted a series of new excavations in the Carlston Annis and Bowles shell mounds. Additional specialized studies expanded the research program. Geoarchaeology, chert sources, microstratigraphy and site formation processes, reconstruction of paleoenvironments, site distribution modeling, and assessment of occupational seasonality were incorporated into the SMAP, adding greatly to studies of chronology, artifacts, and plant and animal remains. Other researchers at this time fixed new attention on the Green River shell mound human skeletal series, which were collected during the New Deal era. Their analyses of the curated collections brought new insights on paleodemography, paleopathology, and paleonutrition (see chapters 10 and 11).

The second phase of Green River research, although more directly focused on a central theme and involving more data categories than the first, did not produce all the desired results. Among the sought-after early cultigens, squash was identified in several excavated shell mounds and sunflower in one, but the Late Archaic deposits of the central Green River lacked evidence on early cultivation of native species of chenopod, maygrass, and sumpweed, producing instead an abundance of remains of wild (or moderately tended) plant foods dominated by hickory nuts.

Concurrent with the SMAP and other second-phase Green River research, a substantial amount of work took place on Middle Archaic, Late Archaic, and Early Woodland sites elsewhere in the Midwest and Midsouth: at Koster, Napolean Hollow, Pabst, Carrier Mills, and other sites in Illinois, at numerous sites in the Normandy Reservoir and in the Little Tennessee River drainage in Tennessee, and at Cloudsplitter Rockshelter in Kentucky. Smaller-scale investigations took place at Late Archaic burned-rock midden sites and other open sites at Patoka Lake and Lake Monroe in southern Indiana. Although these studies showed the importance of hickory nut procurement during the first five millennia B.C., they produced evidence of various early cultigens at different times and in different places. No single, broad geographic pattern of early horticultural trends emerged, leading recent reviewers to see "generally parallel, but distinct co-evolutionary histories for native cultigens" (B. Smith 1987:37) or "multiple pathways" to plant food production (Fritz 1990).

Various results of the second phase of Green River research were presented at symposia in 1979 held at a meeting of the Society for American Archeology and at the Southeastern Archaeological Conference. Other results have been published as articles or incorporated in dissertations, but much is soon to come out as a series of edited papers (Marquardt et al., eds., in prep.). Questions about early horticulture along Green River remain important, as do the only slightly better known whats, whens, and whys for other regions. Indeed, the SMAP narrowed the chronological window for these questions by producing a suite of radiocarbon dates. As a result, we now know that questions about early agriculture along Green River must address the period bracketed by the Late Archaic and Early Woodland, which is sometimes referred to as the "Terminal Archaic," 2000 to 1000 B.C.

The third phase of Green River study, beginning in the early 1980s and continuing to the present, has involved new researchers and broader research themes, but also efforts by individuals and agencies to protect and manage cultural resources. Beyond their shared geographic focus, these investigations are linked in many cases by specialist studies and a renewed concern with time–space systematics—the empirical approach employed so successfully in Watson's first phase of work. Some studies (e.g., Haskins 1995; Haskins and Herrmann 1989) expand on the attention given to the curated New Deal era collections, whose research value has recently been assessed and enhanced (Milner and Smith 1986a, b, 1988). Other studies target previously uninvestigated types of sites, such as burned-rock (or dark earth) middens, which are being included in models of river valley settlement (Hensley 1994) or are directed toward archaeological resource protection (e.g., the Shell Mound Archaeological District, National Register of Historic Places [Hockensmith, Sanders, and Pollack 1985]). Still others highlight new problems in the traditional research settings, a back-to-the-caves and back-to-the-shell-mounds approach (e.g., Haskins 1988; Hensley-Martin 1986; P. Munson et al. 1989).

It is hard for me to predict the course of future research along the Green River (and a new phase of study would probably not be immediately recognized by an outsider), but I am especially optimistic on one front. The steps taken by Charles Niquette (1984), Watson, and others to protect archaeological sites in the central Green River drainage from destruction due to coal mining have helped to bring about a required program of archaeological assessment and mitigation of mine impacts. Previously, mining consumed vast tracts in the Green River drainage with no attention to archaeological resources, but now thousands of acres in the hinterlands and the tributary drainages are being investigated, and some significant sites have become the subject of detailed excavations (e.g., Niquette 1991; Schenian 1987, 1988, 1990; Sussenbach et al. 1990). Such efforts should allow archaeologists to develop a fuller picture of human adaptation in the region by making it possible to integrate the wide array of sites found on the landscape with the better known shell mounds and cave sites.

Although many third-phase studies are still in progress, initial research results have begun to appear in dissertations, presented papers, and published articles. Other results make up chapters in this book. Each chapter was stimulated in some way by the work of Patty Jo Watson; together they provide a tribute to the enduring—and continuing—contributions of her Green River research.

2 | Toward Building a Culture History of the Mammoth Cave Area

Kenneth C. Carstens

THE CENTRAL KENTUCKY Karst is located primarily in south-central Kentucky's Mississippian Plateau physiographic region. This is an area consisting of deeply bedded limestones and associated karst (including cave) features. The region extends north into Indiana, south into Tennessee, and west to the Kentucky portion of the Cumberland River; it lies south of the western coal field region (Quinlan 1970). Within the north-central area of the Central Kentucky Karst is Mammoth Cave National Park, a region of about 21,342 ha. The region has long been known primarily for containing the world's longest cave system, but for several decades the professional archaeological community has also been aware of important prehistoric organic materials in the Central Kentucky Karst (Carstens 1980; Watson 1966; Watson, ed., 1974; Watson and Carstens 1975, 1982; Watson et al. 1969). Between 1973 and 1975 I conducted archaeological investigations in and around Mammoth Cave National Park to locate a temporal sequence of rockshelter/cave vestibule sites collectively spanning the prehistoric culture history of that archaeological region. My work (Carstens 1974, 1975a, b, 1976, 1980; Watson and Carstens 1982), now supplemented and complemented by Prentice (1987b, 1988, 1989, 1994), was important because it was the first since Nels C. Nelson (1917, 1923) to provide information about prehistoric economies giving rise to Archaic and Woodland horticultural activities in this karstic region.

Among earlier accounts of the prehistory of the Mammoth Cave area are writings by Rafinesque (1824) and various reports of "mummified" (actually desiccated) Indians (Meloy 1971) from several surrounding caves. Rafinesque's 1824 entry "shellmounds along Green River and mummies in caves" both highlighted and foretold of future archaeological studies for the region.

The first detailed reporting of cultural resources from the Mammoth Cave area were foreshadowed by Col. Bennett Young (1910), who wrote what might best be described as a "guide" to the antiquities of Kentucky. But it was the massive collections of organic and inorganic prehistoric artifacts obtained from Salts Cave by F. W. Putnam for the Peabody Museum and materials donated to the American Museum of Natural History by John Nelson, Mammoth Cave guide, that brought about the first systematic archaeological study of the Mammoth Cave region by Nels C. Nelson between 1916 and 1923.

Nels C. Nelson was the first person to conduct and report results of archaeological surface studies and excavations in the Mammoth Cave area (1917, 1923). Known primarily for his excavations in the Vestibule of Mammoth Cave, Nelson obtained additional collections for the American Museum of Natural History by conducting surface reconnaissance and excavations throughout the area of present-day Mammoth Cave National Park.

Unfortunately, Nelson's work was largely ignored by fellow archaeologists. Even the additional discovery of another "mummy" in 1935 (Meloy 1971; Pond 1935, 1937) added but short-lived interest to the significant archaeological potential of the Mammoth Cave area. In retrospect, it might have been disinterest in the cave archaeology of the Mammoth Cave region that contributed to preserving some sites throughout the area. Archaeological methods of the 1920s to 1950s often included total site excavation.

During the late 1950s and early 1960s Douglas W. Schwartz conducted a series of studies in Mammoth Cave National Park and vicinity for the federal government (Schwartz 1958a–h, 1960a, b, 1965, 1967; Schwartz and Hanson 1961; Schwartz and Sloan 1958, 1960a, b; Schwartz, Sloan, and Hanson 1960). Schwartz inventoried previously reported sites (i.e., C. Moore 1916; Nelson 1917; Funkhouser and Webb 1928; Young 1910), surveyed portions of major trunk passages within Mammoth Cave for archaeological materials, reported previously unrecorded sites, and test-excavated several sites located in the Nolin and Rough River areas north of the park.

In spite of the aforementioned work, no chronicle of the culture history for the park region had been developed prior to Watson's work in the late 1960s (Watson, ed., 1974; Watson et al. 1969). According to Watson (ed. 1974), her work during the early 1970s in the Mammoth Cave area had two major purposes. She wished to describe systematically and to explain the aboriginal utilization of the cave system and to document the prehistoric diet of the Late Archaic and Early Woodland cave explorers as preserved within human paleofecal specimens from that cave system (Watson, ed., 1974:xv). It was Watson's intent to gather data bearing on the development of horticulture that would help answer important questions anthropologists ask about the origin of food production and its role in cultural evolution. More specifically, Watson wanted to know what sort of local economy gave rise to the horticulture and whether it developed indigenously or as a result of ideas or seeds derived from elsewhere (ibid.).

Having apparently documented the presence of cucurbit and other early horticulture through excavations on nearby Archaic Green River shellmounds (Crawford 1982; Marquardt 1972a; Marquardt and Watson 1974, 1976; Watson 1985b) and through excavations and collections from within the Flint-Mammoth Cave system (Watson, ed., 1974; Watson, et al. 1969), Watson's research group wanted to understand the cultural context within which plant domestication originated and the impact it may have had on indigenous populations of the Central Kentucky Karst. In 1974 I began to gather data to construct a culture history of the Mammoth Cave region that would examine prehistoric economies diachronically, thereby attempting to answer some of the questions posed by Watson's research (Watson, ed., 1974:xv).

The Green River Survey

Thirteen major areas of Mammoth Cave National Park and two locations outside the park were surveyed and studied systematically between 1974 and 1976. During that time a combined total of 58 archaeological sites were located or verified. Open sites—although necessary for the ultimate success of the project—were not pursued for the study because of difficulties in obtaining "open-ended" federal survey and testing permits. Instead, rockshelters, caves, and overhangs were sought, because no federal permits were necessary to hike throughout the park area and observe and record cultural materials exposed in the drip lines of these site types.

Surface collections were not made from the sites (again, because of delays in permitting), although descriptions of each site's surface contents were recorded, photographs were taken, and outline drawings of "type" artifacts were made. On the basis of the known age range for the "type" artifacts found, it was possible to order 26 of the sites in a sequence ranging from Paleoindian through Mississippian cultural traditions. Eight of the 26 sites were then selected (GRS #'s 15Ed29, 15Ed52, 15Ed42, 15Ed43, 15Wa6, 15Ed56, 15Ed62, and 15Ht30) for test excavation on the basis of best representation for the culture historical sequence of the region and the probability of also containing economic data fitting into Watson's (Watson, ed., 1974; Watson et al., 1969) previous work. Of those eight sites, four were selected for further study and extensive testing: 15Ed52, Blue Spring Hollow Rockshelter (GRS-12); 15Ed42, Patch Rockshelter (GRS-18); 15Ed43, Owl Cave (GRS-19); and 15Wa6, Crumps Cave (GRS-21) (Carstens 1980).

Results

The excavation of four sites (Owl, Patch, Crumps, and Blue Spring Hollow) provided a temporal context collectively spanning Early Archaic through Mississippian cultures. This 8000-year record was supplemented by descriptions of artifact types found on the surfaces of other sites located during our Green River Survey (GRS). A preliminary cultural outline for the Central Kentucky Karst region was thus made available for later modification and refinement (Table 2.1).

The Paleoindian period is poorly represented in the park. Only two Paleo projectile point types were recovered between 1973 and 1976 during the survey: four Quad and one Cumberland. All of these were found out of context, either

Table 2.1. Technoeconomic Culture History of Excavated Sites in the
Central Kentucky Karst

Site	Horizon	Cultural Period	Subsistence Orientation	Projectile Forms	^{14}C Years, B.P. (not corrected)	Ceramic Types
15Ed52	II	Mississippian	Diffuse	Madison		Rough River Series Baytown Plain Bell Plain McKee Island
	I	Late Woodland	Diffuse	Levanna Copena Adena	820 ± 80 UGA-1838	Rough River Baytown Plain Burnished Ware
15Ed42	Ib	Middle Woodland	Focal	Baker's Creek Adena	1425 ± 100 UGA-1837	Rough River Wright Check Stamped Mulberry Creek
15Wa6	II, level 4	Early Woodland	Diffuse	Turkey-Tail Buck Creek Adena	1920 ± 150 UGA-1839 2365 ± 95 UGA-1840	Rough River Series
15Ed42 15Wa6 15Ed43	Ia I II	Late Archaic	Diffuse	Buck Creek Merom		
15Ed43	I	Middle Archaic	Focal	Cypress Creek Side-notched		
15Ed43	I	Early Archaic	Focal	MacCorkle		
15Ed62	NA	Paleo	Unknown	Quad Cumberland		

Source: Modified from Carstens 1980.

on the surface (15Ed62) or associated with artifacts from a context that was as-
signable to other periods of prehistory (e.g., at 15Ed42 and 52). Other than indicating the limited presence of Paleoindian materials in the Mammoth Cave
region, the few projectile points found during this study offered little new information about Paleoindian culture in the Eastern United States.

Three of the four sites excavated contained cultural deposits characteristic
of the Archaic: 15Ed43, Owl Cave, Horizons I and II; 15Wa6, Horizon I from
Crumps Cave; and 15Ed42, Horizon Ia from Patch Rockshelter. The estimated

temporal duration for these cultural horizons, as interpreted from typed projectile point forms, is 7000 to 1000 B.C.

Various different ecological zones were used throughout the Archaic by the park's early inhabitants, and several notable differences and similarities were present in the numbers and types of zones exploited.

Early to Middle Archaic occupations are represented in Horizon I of Owl Cave. Four environmental zones were exploited by the occupants of this site between 7000 and 3000 B.C. Only one zone was exploited intensively, the transitional forest edge, as chiefly reflected by the remains of deer in the archaeological assemblage (which varied between 83% and 85% of the faunal remains identified). Some collection of hickory nuts is also evidenced (21% to 64% by weight of all botanical specimens). Projectile point types present at Owl Cave within the Early and Middle Archaic deposits include MacCorkle, Cypress Creek, and a small side-notched projectile form (Lamoka-like?).

Three different sites contain overlapping evidence for the Late Archaic to Early Woodland transition: 15Ed43, Horizon II, Owl Cave; Horizon I; 15Wa6, Crumps Cave; and 15Ed42, Horizon Ia Patch Rockshelter. Cultural deposition within each of these horizons is primarily Late Archaic (ca. 3000 to 1000 B.C.).

The subsistence economy throughout the Late Archaic at these sites remained focally oriented, varying between 49% and 83%, toward the exploitation of white-tailed deer. But, seven different environmental zones in the Late Archaic, instead of only four as in the pre–Late Archaic, were exploited. In other words, it appears that a more diffuse economy was pursued from these sites during the Late Archaic, although deer exploitation remained the focal subsistence activity. Hickory nut exploitation continues to occur, too, but with greater variation (17%–64%); locally available walnuts (10%) supplement hickory nut collection in Horizon I of Crumps Cave (15Wa6). Also present is a change from side-notched and bifurcated-based projectile forms to very small side-notched (Merom) and barbed-stemmed (Buck Creek) projectile types.

The Early Woodland horizon at Crumps Cave (Horizon II, level Four, ca. 800 to 100 B.C.) exhibits a continuation of deer exploitation and an increase in the number of environmental habitats exploited. The use of hickory, walnut, and acorn also increases slightly. No projectile points were found within this horizon at Crumps Cave, although contracting stemmed projectile forms appear at other sites in the park area.

The earliest recorded ceramics for the park area include a locally typed, limestone-tempered ware, Rough River cordmarked (Schwartz and Sloan 1958). The origin of this ceramic type and its morphological relation to other Early Woodland ceramics is not currently known.

Horizon Ib at Patch Rockshelter (15Ed42) overlaps with the terminal Early Woodland Period and continues into the late Middle Woodland (ca. 500 B.C. to

A.D. 500). Subsistence pursuits within this horizon return to focally based environmental zone exploitation. Only three habitats were exploited: open woodland, transitional forest edge, and riverine (Green River).

The Middle to Late Woodland period occupancy of the Patch site (Horizon II) represents a distinct focal economy as marked by the prominence of deer exploitation. In addition, several ceramic types are present (Rough River Series, Mulberry Creek Plain, and Wright Checked Stamped). Also present are expanding-base projectile point forms (e.g., Baker's Creek).

Late Woodland subsistence economy at Blue Spring Hollow Rockshelter (15Ed52) is focal for Horizon I. The principal use of this site was hickory nut processing, as evidenced by numerous nutting and milling stones, storage pits, and a thick greasy midden laden with charred hickory nut hulls. Deer hunting and the opportunistic collection of many box turtles from the local riparian woods supplemented the diet for the Late Woodland period.

The Mississippian occupants of Horizon II at Blue Spring Hollow also used the site focally. Instead of hickory nuts, their interest centered on deer hunting as evidenced by the dominance of small, straight, and concave-base projectile points, and the physical remains from the hunt. Some box turtles were also collected to supplement the diet. Both Late Woodland and Mississippian groups used the bow and arrow, which appears in a relatively late context for the park area (probably post-A.D. 900).

In addition to Rough River limestone-tempered ceramics in the Late Woodland horizon, shell-tempered Bell Plain and a clay- and limestone-tempered Baytown Plain occur in the Horizon II, Mississippian, occupation. The Blue Spring Hollow ceramic sample, like that from other sites within the park area, was small in both size and number. It is possible that the rough and broken terrain of the park area may not have been conducive to using ceramics, the local people opting instead for less fragile and more durable baskets, wooden, hide, or *Cucurbita* sp. containers. Although present throughout the Woodland and Mississippian cultural sequences, ceramics do not appear to have played a major technological role in nonopen sites of the Central Kentucky Karst.

Summary and Conclusion

My work between 1974 and 1976 concentrated on the verification of previously reported sites and the discovery of new sites for the Mammoth Cave portion of the Central Kentucky Karst (Carstens 1974, 1975a, b, 1976; Watson and Carstens 1975). Several sites were extensively test-excavated to provide a cultural sequence of the Central Kentucky Karst region and to document local economies that gave rise to the use of domesticates previously reported by Watson (Watson, ed., 1974; Watson et al. 1969) from Late Archaic/Early Woodland cave contexts.

The analyses of the technoeconomic cultural systems from the excavated sites reveal several significant trends that need to receive additional investigation, but it is important to note that *no evidence* of horticultural activity was found within any of the sites excavated in the described sample. Unlike Salts and Mammoth caves, where evidence of plant domestication has been documented, our excavated site sample contained no evidence of plant cultivation (Wagner 1976, 1978).

Why is there an absence of plant domesticates at the small-cave and rockshelter sites? Were these sites used only seasonally? Is it a function of cave size or use by nonhorticultural groups? Were smaller caves and rockshelters used for special purposes that excluded the use of cultigens, or did our earlier research at Salts and Mammoth caves place too much emphasis on the presence of domesticates found in the large caves? If domesticates were important to local inhabitants, why is their presence unrecorded at other cave sites in and around the immediate vicinity of Mammoth Cave? And, why is there an absence of plant domesticates within the cultural horizons of those sites within the park that postdate the Archaic tradition? (One would assume that some evidence of plant domestication would be present within Woodland and Mississippian horizons of the excavated sample because of their presence in Early Woodland paleofeces in Salts and Mammoth caves.) Although I asked these questions fifteen years ago (Carstens 1980), they remain unanswered today, but progress toward elucidating them is being made (Prentice this volume, 1994).

In 1976 Cleland proposed a focal-diffuse model of cultural evolution. His model may have some bearing on solving the origin of plant husbandry activities in and around the Central Kentucky Karst region. However, to apply his model fully, information about the complete seasonal round/settlement systems characterizing the relevant time periods must be known. My work was unable to provide this information. More recent research by Hensley (1987, 1992, 1994) and Prentice (1987b, 1988, 1989, 1994) at several open Late Archaic/Early Woodland "base-camp" sites may yet provide the answer to our many questions about the context of early plant use in the Central Kentucky Karst.

3 | Site Distribution Modeling for Mammoth Cave National Park

Guy Prentice

IN 1989 THE National Park Service concluded a three-year archaeological survey project in Mammoth Cave National Park, Kentucky. Directed by the author, the project's accomplishments included the discovery of 93 previously unrecorded prehistoric sites and 7 isolated finds, revisitation of 63 previously known sites, hand test excavations at 14 sites, and backhoe excavations at 2 other sites (Prentice 1988, 1989, 1990). Added to the previous work of Watson (1966; Watson, ed., 1974; Watson et al. 1969), Carstens (1980), Schwartz (1958a–h, 1960a, b, 1965), Beditz (1979, 1981), and others, we now have a better understanding of the range of sites that occur in the Mammoth Cave area, the manner in which these sites are distributed across the landscape, and the kinds of activities that occurred at these sites.

Physical Setting

Mammoth Cave National Park is divided into southern and northern halves by Green River, which runs east to west through the center of the park. The southern portion of the park lies within the Central Kentucky Karst portion of the Pennyroyal Plateau, and the area north of Green River lies within the Chester Upland of the Western Coal Field. The Chester Upland is formed principally of Mississippian and Pennsylvanian age sandstones and limestones, and the Plateau is composed mainly of Mississippian age limestones.

The two major limestone beds outcropping in the park are the Ste. Genevieve and Girkin formations. It is from the Ste. Genevieve limestone that the bulk of the locally used chert was obtained prehistorically and used to make tools. In the upland areas north and south of Green River, these limestone beds are capped by the Big Clifty sandstone formation. It is the Big Clifty sandstone layer that produces the majority of rockshelters in the park. In the Chester Upland area north of Green River, the Big Clifty sandstone formation is overlain by the Haney limestone formation, the Hardinsburg formation (sandstone), the Glen Dean formation (limestone), the Leitchfield formation (shale), and the Caseyville formation (conglomerate sandstone). The Caseyville Formation is another sandstone layer within the park in which rockshelters occur.

For purposes of biotic study, the topography of the park can be divided into four different categories: the upland ridges, the upland valleys, the floodplains, and the bluffline areas. This division is based on differences in elevation, ground slope, soil types, and vegetative cover. The upland ridges cover 9182.92 ha, making this zone the largest topographic section, comprising 44.65% of the park. In contrast, the upland valleys are relatively small, comprising only 6.56% (1348.84 ha) of the park. The floodplains and the bluffs make up 6.66% (1370.71 ha) and 42.13% (8664.78 ha) of the park area, respectively. North of Green River, the uplands can be characterized as wide ridges into which tributaries of Green River have made deep incisions to form bluffline areas. South of Green River, the uplands consist of wide ridges separated by deep valleys resulting from the dissolution and breakdown of underlying limestone formations subsequent to breaching the caprock. Surface water in this portion of the park is typically lacking. Rainwater runoff is quickly channeled into limestone caverns beneath the surface. The difference in surface water availability between the Mississippi Plateau and Western Coal Field is very pronounced, with a near absence of surface streams south of Green River and a dendritic drainage pattern north of Green River.

The bluffline areas of the park, with their steep slopes and overhanging cliffs, contain a variety of rockshelters and cave openings for which the park is well-known, particularly Mammoth Cave. From the base of the blufflines to the banks of Green River and its tributaries lies the floodplain area. Green River is deeply entrenched within the floodplain, its steep river banks exceeding 3 m in height in many areas. The Green River floodplain is quite narrow in this portion of the state with a maximum width in the park of only 400 m.

Vegetative communities within the park correspond closely with the topographic zones: Oak-Hickory forests characterize upland ridges; Cedar-Pine mixed with grasslands characterize upland valleys; Maple-Beech forests occur in bluff areas; and Sycamore-Box Elder communities typify floodplains. Within the four major vegetative zones, smaller microbiomes may occur where the faunal and vegetative resources vary according to local soil types, water drainage, and temperature differences due to solar exposure (Faller 1975). The most noticeable of these microbiomes are the remnant hemlock forests that occur in the bluffline areas of the Chester Upland.

Soils in the upland ridge areas are typically deep, sandy, acidic, easily eroded, and generally limited in agricultural potential (Carstens 1980:51–52; Latham 1969). The Oak-Hickory forests associated with this topographic zone (Table 3.1) are dominated by oaks, hickories, and yellow poplar (Ellsworth 1934; Faller 1975). Other plant species associated with this zone include black tupelo, black walnut, dogwood, sassafras, sourwood, Carolina buckthorn, mountain laurel, hazelnut, farkelberry, black haw, and blueberry. Prehistorically, American chestnut (*Castanea dentata*) would have been present in significant numbers (Braun 1950; Faller 1975).

Table 3.1. Characteristic Plant Species
within the Major Natural Forest Zones

Oak-Hickory Forests

Dominant tree species
  Black oak (*Quercus velutina*)
  White oak (*Quercus alba*)
  Chinquapin oak (*Quercus muehlenbergii*)
  Pignut hickory (*Carya glabra*)
  Shagbark hickory (*Carya ovata*)
  Northern red oak (*Quercus rubra*)
  Yellow poplar (*Liriodendron tulipifera*)
Associate tree species
  Scarlet oak (*Quercus coccinea*)
  Post oak (*Quercus stellata*)
  Southern red oak (*Quercus falcata*)
  Black tupelo (*Nyssa sylvatica*)
  Black walnut (*Juglans nigra*)
  Dogwood (*Cornus florida*)
  Sassafras (*Sassafras albidum*)
  Sourwood (*Oxydendrum arboreum*)
  Carolina buckthorn (*Rhamnus caroliniana*)
  Mountain laurel (*Kalmia latifolia*)
  Hazelnut (*Corylus americana*)
Understory plants
  Farkelberry (*Vaccinium arboreum*)
  Serviceberry (*Amelanchier arborea*)
  Black haw (*Viburnum prunifolium*)
  Blueberry (*Vaccinium* sp.)

Maple-Beech Forests

Dominant tree species
  American beech (*Fagus grandifolia*)
  Sugar maple (*Acer saccharum*)
Associate tree species
  White oak (*Quercus alba*)
  Northern red oak (*Quercus rubra*)
  Yellow poplar (*Liriodendron tulipifera*)
  Chestnut oak (*Quercus prinus*)
  Slippery elm (*Ulmus rubra*)

(*continued*)

Table 3.1 (*continued*)
  Shagbark hickory (*Carya ovata*)
  Bitternut hickory (*Carya cordiformis*)
  Pignut hickory (*Carya glabra*)
  Mockernut hickory (*Carya tomentosa*)
  White ash (*Fraxinus americana*)
  Mountain laurel (*Kalmia latifolia*)
  Witch-hazel (*Hamamelis virginiana*)
  Bigleaf magnolia (*Magnolia macrophylla*)
  Umbrella magnolia (*Magnolia tripetala*)
  Pawpaw (*Asimina triloba*)
  Persimmon (*Diospyros virginiana*)
Understory plants
  Spice bush (*Kalmia latifolia*)
  Viburnums (*Vibernum* sp.)
  Wild hydrangea (*Hydrangea arborescens*)

Sycamore-Box Elder Forests

Dominant tree species
  Sycamore (*Platanus occidentalis*)
  Box elder (*Acer negundo*)
  River birch (*Betula nigra*)
  Black willow (*Salix nigra*)
Associate tree species
  Slippery elm (*Ulmus rubra*)
  Winged elm (*Ulmus alata*)
  American hornbeam (*Carpinus caroliniana*)
  Yellow poplar (*Liriodendron tulipifera*)
  Hackberry (*Celtis occidentalis*)
  Red maple (*Acer rubrum*)
  Black cherry (*Prunus serotina*)
  Wild plum (*Prunus americana*)
  Honey locust (*Gleditsia aquatica*)
  Red mulberry (*Morus rubra*)
  White ash (*Fraxinus americana*)
  Witch-hazel (*Hamamelis virginiana*)
Understory plants
  Spice bush (*Kalmia latifolia*)
  Grapes (*Vitis* sp.)
  Blackberry (*Rubus* sp.)
  Cane (*Arundinaria* sp.)

Soils in the bluffline areas are more variable, primarily as a result of localized surficial geology and ground slope, but can be generally characterized as shallow, rocky, and unsuitable for agriculture. The Maple-Beech forests associated with the bluffline areas are dominated by American beech and sugar maple (Ellsworth 1934; Faller 1975). Secondary tree species include oaks, hickories, yellow poplar, slippery elm, white ash, mountain laurel, witch-hazel, bigleaf magnolia, umbrella magnolia, pawpaw, and persimmon. Other plant species associated with this zone are spice bush, viburnums, and wild hydrangea.

Soils in the floodplain areas are Quaternary in age and can be characterized as well-drained to somewhat poorly drained alluvium, slightly acid to neutral, and suitable for agriculture (Carstens 1980:51; Latham 1969). The Sycamore-Box Elder forests associated with the floodplain areas are dominated by sycamore, box elder, river birch, and black willow (Ellsworth 1934; Faller 1975). Secondary tree species include slippery elm, winged elm, American hornbeam, yellow poplar, hackberry, red maple, black cherry, wild plum, honey locust, red mulberry, white ash, and witch-hazel. Understory plants include spice bush, grapes, blackberries, and cane.

Notably, the major vegetative communities currently existing in the park have been altered from the "natural" state that existed prior to the arrival of Euro-Americans in the late 1700s (Prentice 1993, 1994). Diseases introduced by Europeans such as chestnut blight and Dutch elm disease, forest fires, selective lumbering and land-clearing practices for agriculture and grazing have modified the makeup of the various vegetative communities. The best example of this is in the upland valleys where nineteenth- and early twentieth-century land-clearing and farming practices have produced a successional forest of cedars, pines, and grasslands. Some evidence suggests that the pre–Euro-American vegetative communities in these upland valleys consisted of a forest dominated by oaks and would have been similar in composition to Faller's (1975) "Mixed Woods" category, which includes white oak, southern red oak, northern red oak, black oak, chinquapin oak, and mockernut hickory (Carstens 1980:60; Wagner 1978).

The prehistoric distribution of the vegetative communities in the area has not been studied in detail, but generalizations can be made based on the existing archaeobotanical and limited pollen data. Present ideas hold that the correlation of vegetative communities with the major topographic zones outlined has been a relatively stable one since the Hypsithermal, roughly 5,000 to 6,000 years ago (Carstens 1980:59–60; P. Delcourt and H. Delcourt 1981; Prentice 1994; Wagner 1978; Watson and Carstens 1982:24). Prior to this time, the vegetative regimes were considerably different, reflecting the major global warming and cooling trends that followed the last ice age (see P. Delcourt and H. Delcourt 1981).

The Mammoth Cave National Park Archeological Inventory Project

The National Park Service's recent archaeological survey of Mammoth Cave National Park was divided into three field seasons, or "phases," beginning in 1987 with the first phase consisting of shovel testing in randomly selected areas in the uplands and bottomlands in the park (Prentice 1988). The second phase consisted of pedestrian surveys of the bluffline areas (Prentice 1989). The third phase consisted of test excavations at selected upland, bottomland, and bluffline sites (Prentice 1990). These investigations were conducted under the aegis of the Mammoth Cave National Park Archeological Inventory Project (MCNPAIP). During the MCNPAIP 1,594 shovel tests were excavated in 28 randomly selected shovel test blocks encompassing a total area of 78.04 ha in the uplands (ridges and valleys) and 30.30 ha in the bottomlands. Randomly selected survey units along the blufflines encompassed a total of 1,359 ha, or 16% of the total 8,665 ha of bluffline area in the park. These investigations have produced six major kinds of prehistoric occupation sites: (1) large rockshelters; (2) small rockshelters; (3) large multicomponent upland scatters on the ridge tops adjacent to Green River; (4) small upland scatters located away from Green River, usually near small tributary confluences, springs, and ponds; (5) large bottomland sites located near the confluences of major streams with Green River; and (6) small bottomland sites on natural levees and elevated portions of the floodplain away from major tributaries. Another type of open-air site, chert extraction sites, was also identified during the survey.

Rockshelter Sites

The MCNPAIP surveys of randomly selected units along the blufflines resulted in the recording of 416 overhang locations in the selected survey areas. Fifty-one of these overhangs produced prehistoric cultural materials and were classified as prehistoric rockshelter sites. These sites range in size from just a few square meters to over 500 m^2 and span the time range from late Paleoindian to Historic. As noted, rockshelters occur along the exposed portions of the Big Clifty and Caseyville sandstone formations. Overhangs principally occur where the average ground slope exceeds roughly 5 degrees (in other words, along blufflines) and where ground contours make bends or turns. Large rockshelters occur with greatest frequency at the heads of hollows.

Evaluation of the survey data collected at all overhangs both occupied and unoccupied within the sampled bluffline areas indicates that rockshelter site selection was not random. The hypothesis that overhang size was a factor affecting site selection was evaluated by first estimating floor areas for all overhangs using the formula, floor area = 1/2 (length × width), then grouping the 418 over-

Table 3.2. Distribution (by percentage) of Natural Overhangs
and Occupied Rockshelters by Size Class

	1	2	3	4	5	6	7	8	9	10	11	12	13	14
O	44.7	25.5	8.4	7.2	2.9	1.7	2.2	1.0	0.5	0.2	3.1	0.7	0.7	1.0
R	3.9	15.7	11.8	11.8	15.7	3.9	2.0	2.0	0.0	2.0	13.7	5.9	3.9	5.9

O, Natural overhangs; R, occupied rockshelters.

hangs into 14 size classes developed on the basis of data gathered during the
project. The first ten overhang classes were grouped on the basis of successively
increasing increments of 10 m^2. Class 1 overhangs had estimated floor areas of
less than 10 m^2, Class 2 overhangs had floor areas between 10 and 20 m^2, Class
3 overhangs had floor areas from 20 to 29.99 m^2, class 4 from 30 to 39.99 m^2, etc.
The next three classes increased in increments of 100 m^2 (e.g., Class 11 = 100–
199.99, Class 12 = 200–299.99, and Class 13 = 300–399.99 m^2); all overhangs with
formulated areas greater than 400 m^2 were assigned to Class 14.

Plotting the distribution of all overhang size classes by percentage (Table
3.2; Figure 3.1) produces a reversed "J" curve indicative of fewer numbers of
overhangs in each of the successively larger class sizes, as one might expect. This
is the natural universe from which the prehistoric inhabitants of the area selected their rockshelter sites. If the prehistoric selection of overhangs for occupation was random, one would expect a similar reversed "J" curve to result
when occupied overhangs are similarly plotted. Instead, one finds a bimodal
distribution indicating a selection for overhangs in the 10 to 50 m^2 range and in
the 100+ m^2 range.

When one looks at the numbers and types of artifacts collected from the
occupied overhangs according to class size (Table 3.3), one is led to the conclusion that large overhangs were preferred site locations and were occupied more
frequently and longer than smaller overhangs. Typically, large rockshelters (100+
m^2) are multicomponent, with a larger range of artifact types (including projectile points, hoes, hammerstones, scrapers, cores, blades, pottery, and plant-pro-
cessing stones such as metates, pestles, and hominy holes). Excavations at the
large rockshelters commonly uncover storage pits and significant quantities of
charred nutshell, wood, and other floral materials, deer and other animal bone,
freshwater mussels, and many kinds of chert tools and debris, and human burials (only female burials have been found thus far). All of these pieces of evidence
point toward the conclusion that the activities conducted at these sites were
quite varied and were probably performed by members of both sexes. Of particular note is the overwhelming evidence that rockshelter sites were utilized
almost exclusively in the fall and winter and that nuts, deer, turkey, and other
animals were the primary resources exploited at the time of site use (Carstens

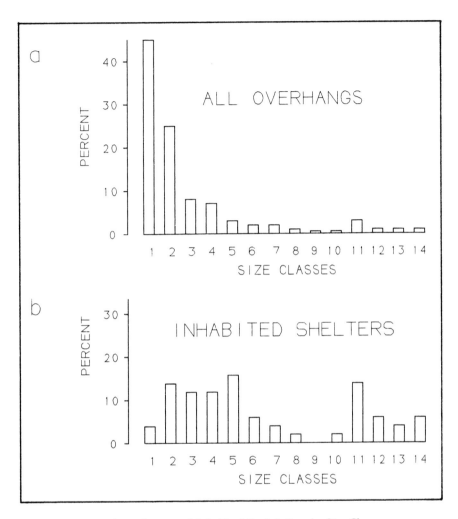

3.1 Distributions of Overhangs and Inhabited Rockshelters by Size Class

1980; Prentice 1994; Wagner 1978). Assuming that the archaeological assemblages are true reflections of the range of activities pursued at each site, and that shelter size generally correlates with size of inhabiting groups, there is reasonable evidence to conclude that large rockshelters were primarily fall and winter occupations with large shelters occupied by individual household groups (Prentice 1994), perhaps extended families or small bands.

In contrast, smaller rockshelters (less than 50 m^2) typically exhibit little more than a few scattered chert flakes, an occasional projectile point or two, and maybe a pottery vessel fragment. Often when diagnostic artifacts are recovered, they can be assigned to a single time period. There are, of course, small shelters that evidence multiple occupations, but these are a minority and usually exhibit

Table 3.3. Some Attributes of the Prehistoric Rockshelters Located during the MCNPAIP Bluffline Survey

Class	Size Site Number	Components	Number of Known Present	Pottery Present	Number of Artifact Hominy Hole on Surface	Vandalism Types Observed or Looting
1	157	1	No	No	1	No
1	178	1	No	No	1	No
		Mean = 1			Mean = 1	No
2	164	3*	Yes	No	1	No
2	187	1	No	No	1	No
2	191	1	No	No	1	No
2	198	1	No	No	1	No
2	200	1	No	No	2	No
2	209	1	No	No	2	No
2	869	1	No	No	1	No
		Mean = 1.3			Mean = 1.3	
3	100	1	No	No	3	No
3	168	4*	Yes	No	7	No
3	180	1	No	No	2	No
3	190	1	No	No	3	No
3	210	1	No	No	3	No
3	868	1	No	No	2	No
		Mean = 1.5			Mean = 3.3	
4	102	1	No	No	3	No
4	174	1	No	No	1	No
4	186	1	No	No	4	No
4	196	1	No	No	1	No
4	208	1	No	No	2	No
4	211	1	No	No	1	No
		Mean = 1			Mean = 2.2	
5	99	1	No	No	2	No
5	155	2	No	No	5	Yes
5	166	2	No	No	2	Yes
5	167	1	No	No	3	No
5	184	1	No	No	5	No
5	194	1	No	No	1	No

(continued)

Table 3.3 (*continued*)

5	199	1	No	No	2	No
5	207	1	No	No	2	No
		Mean = 1.3			Mean = 2.8	
6	95	4	Yes	No	9	No
6	101	3	Yes	No	3	Yes
6	172	1*	No	No	2	Yes
		Mean = 2.7			Mean = 4.7	
7	192	1	No	No	6	Yes
7	195	1	No	No	2	No
		Mean = 1			Mean = 4.0	
8	870	1	No	No	2	No
		Mean = 1			Mean = 2.0	
10	98	1	No	No	4	Yes
		Mean = 1			Mean = 4.0	
11	43	3*	Yes	No	4	No
11	54	1	No	Yes	3	No
11	171	5*	Yes	No	9	Yes
11	189	4	Yes	No	10	No
11	202	1	No	No	3	Yes
11	204	1	No	No	3	Yes
11	871	1	No	No	1	No
		Mean = 2.3			Mean = 4.7	
12	97	3	No	No	3	Yes
12	197	1	No	No	5	No
12	867	1	No	Yes	1	Yes
		Mean = 1.7			Mean = 3.0	
13	25	1	No	No	1	No
13	206	1	Yes	No	5	Yes
		Mean = 1			Mean = 3.0	
14	24	2	Yes	No	5	Yes
14	44	4*	Yes	Yes	5	Yes
14	866	1	No	Yes	5	Yes
		Mean = 2.3			Mean = 5.0	

*Number of components based on test excavations.

only a few occupations, often greatly separated in time. Excavations conducted at these sites have in the main produced no subsurface features such as pits and scant floral and faunal remains. It is probably safe to say that small rockshelter sites represent short-term occupations by a relatively few individuals who performed specific tasks. The high frequency of broken and whole projectile points at these sites would suggest that small, predominantly male, hunting parties were the principal users of these sites.

Size alone does not, however, predict whether an overhang was occupied. Of the 24 largest overhangs within the bluffline survey areas, 16 (67%) were occupied. Of the eight (33%) remaining large overhangs that did not exhibit prehistoric occupations, six had very wet floor conditions, and one was located in the middle of a steep bluff, making access to it extremely difficult. Habitability and accessibility were, it would seem, factors that sometimes led potential occupants to reject some large overhangs as habitation sites.

Evaluation of such single factors as direction of exposure, rocky surface conditions, and accessibility have not shown any significant selection for, or against, shelter use based on these factors alone, although there appears to be a slight preference toward southern and western exposures (Table 3.4; Figure 3.2).

Open-Air Sites

The MCNPAIP identified four major kinds of prehistoric open-air habitation sites: (1) large multicomponent upland scatters on ridge tops adjacent to Green River; (2) small prehistoric upland scatters located away from Green River, usually near small tributary confluences and springs, or surrounding the few natural ponds that occur on the upland ridges south of Green River; (3) large bottomland sites near the confluence of major streams with Green River; and (4) small prehistoric bottomland sites on natural levees and elevated portions of the floodplain away from major tributaries. A fifth type of open-air site, chert extraction sites, was also identified during the survey. These specialized extraction sites occur in the upland valleys south of Green River along gentle slopes at elevations of roughly 335 m (700 ft) above mean sea level. These areas represent locations where weathered surficial Ste. Genevieve and Girkin limestone formations have deposited chert nodules in abundance. Raw chert is also available for easy exploitation along blufflines of Green River, especially in the larger hollows, where Ste. Genevieve limestone is exposed. Some of the larger open-air bottomland sites, located near the larger hollows, such as Hollow Creek (15Ed142), may also have been used as chert extraction localities (Prentice 1993:441–42).

Like the dual division of rockshelters into large and small, a division of open-air sites into large and small seems equally appropriate. Large upland sites consist of multicomponent artifact scatters located on large ridge tops immedi-

Table 3.4. Distribution (by percentage) of Natural Overhangs and Occupied Rockshelters by Direction of Exposure

	N	NNE	NE	ENE	E	ESE	SE	SSE	S	SSW	SW	WSW	W	WNW	NW	NNW
O	6.7	2.4	11.8	1.7	10.3	2.4	9.1	2.6	8.7	4.8	8.4	2.4	10.3	2.4	13.2	2.4
R	2.0	6.0	9.8	3.9	0.0	19.6	9.8	5.9	3.9	9.8	5.9	3.9	9.8	2.0	3.9	7.8

O, Natural overhang; *R*, occupied rockshelter; *N*, north; *NE*, northeast; *E*, east; *S*, south; *SE*, southeast; *SW*, southwest; *W*, west; *NW*, northwest.

ately adjacent to Green River in areas where access to the river bottoms is relatively easy. The large hollows that border Green River apparently provided the most commonly used avenues of access between bottomlands and uplands. One large upland site that diverges from this pattern is 15Ed203, which is located almost 3 km from Green River on a ridge adjacent to Adwell Springs. The availability of this perennial water source no doubt influenced the selection of this ridge as a place for repeated occupations.

Periods of known occupation span Early Archaic through Mississippian at the large upland sites, but excavations at these sites have failed to produce any subsurface features. Despite the lack of adequate subsistence data from undisturbed archaeological contexts from upland open-air sites, there is enough evidence to conclude that fall hunting and nut harvesting were the primary activities pursued there. First, there are the vegetational and pedological characteristics of the uplands. Dominated by oak-hickory forests, the uplands are the primary source of the valuable acorn and hickory nut resources that are ubiquitous within the archaeobotanical record. Oaks and hickories occur in significantly lower numbers in bluffline and floodplain areas. Nut harvesting (and presumably site occupation) during the fall would have occurred extensively in the upland and immediately adjacent bluffline areas. The upland areas are also generally poorly suited for agricultural purposes. Generally poor in nutrients, the soils in the majority of these topographic situations also erode easily. Extensive soil erosion associated with farming was a significant problem encountered by the original park developers in the 1930s, and large erosional gullies still scar much of the upland areas. Second, "nutting stones" or stone mortars/metates have been recovered from at least one of the large upland sites (15Ed123) and would appear to support the hypothesis of nut harvesting being a major activity at these kinds of sites. Third, there are enough ethnohistoric examples of eastern Native American subsistence practices (Reidhead 1981; B. Smith 1975; Swanton 1946) to conclude that, in all probability, hunting, especially for deer and turkey, would have been a major activity during the period of nut mast availability. This is supported by the frequent occurrence of projectile points at large upland sites (Manzano 1989, 1990). Although absence of subsurface features at the upland

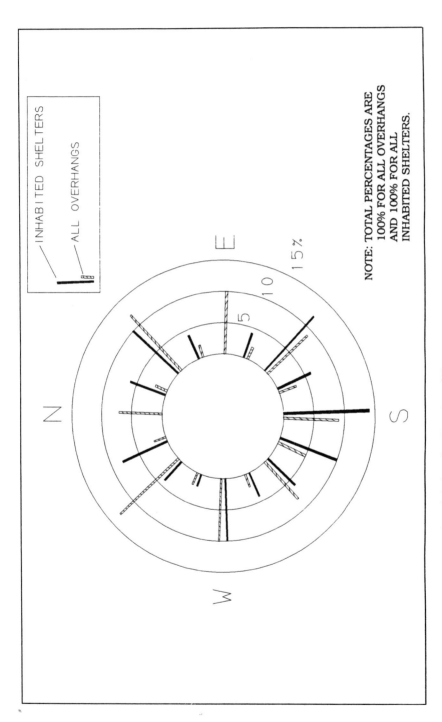

3.2 Distributions of Overhangs and Rockshelters by Direction of Exposure

sites may simply be a result of inadequate sampling, currently it is believed that the absence of features is probably indicative of less site permanence at large upland sites than that observed at rockshelters where features do occur.

Small upland sites contrast with large upland sites not only in size but also in location. Small upland sites are typically located away from Green River, usually near seasonal streams, springs, and small ponds, in areas where access to Green River is more difficult. These sites often consist of little more than small lithic scatters. Excavations at small upland sites have also failed to produce any subsurface features. Like their larger-size cousins, these sites appear to have been of short duration but, unlike larger sites, were not places of repeated occupations, although some of the scatters around the upland ponds (e.g., Beaver Pond and Hawkins Farm sites) appear to have been frequently selected as habitation spots.

Large and small upland sites have their counterparts in the bottomlands. The large bottomland sites are located near the confluence of major streams with Green River where there is easy access to the uplands and sizeable floodplain areas for occupation. Smaller bottomland sites are typically further removed from the major streams on small natural levees and ridges. Like their upland counterparts, the differences between the two bottomland site types appear to be mainly of repeated occupation at large sites, versus infrequent occupations of the smaller site locations. In both the large upland and large bottomland site types, easy access to adjacent upland and bottomland zones and the Green River appear to have been primary factors influencing site location. Such a settlement pattern allowed site inhabitants access to multiple resource zones (river, floodplain, bluffs, and uplands) with a minimum of travel time and effort.

Floodplain sites are somewhat more problematical to interpret given a lack of good subsistence data from the majority of them. Only the small Dry Creek site (15Ed131) has been excavated sufficiently to conclude that it probably represents an Early Mississippian hamlet or homestead and that its inhabitants raised maize, harvested nuts, fished, and hunted deer and small mammals (Prentice 1994). At face value, this site would appear to have had a summer and fall occupation. The possibility that it was occupied year round is currently not appraisable, but given its floodplain location, it is unlikely that it was occupied during the spring.

The Green River floodplain is a hazardous place to live at certain times of the year, particularly spring. Inundation of the entire floodplain in the park, despite water-control measures (i.e., dams), is a nearly annual occurrence. Studies of the modern flood patterns in the Mammoth Cave area (National Park Service 1991:21) show that water levels reach approximately 139 m (456 ft), or 10.6 m (35 ft) above normal pool level (421 ft) at approximately two-year intervals. Given the frequency of flooding in the spring, it is unlikely that extended occupations would have occurred there during this time of the year.

Given the seasonal flooding pattern along this portion of Green River, it seems reasonable to conclude that sites on the floodplain would have been largely vacated during the period of heavy spring rains. It appears logical to infer that occupations in the park area during the spring were probably situated at higher elevations where flooding of the river would not have posed a problem. Some rockshelters, located along blufflines adjoining Green and Nolin rivers and well above floodstage, may have been occupied during the spring as were large upland sites immediately adjacent to the floodplain.

When open-air sites occur on the floodplain, they generally appear on small natural levees or on the large alluvial/colluvial fans associated with major tributaries of the Green and Nolin rivers. These locations reveal a concern with the hydrological factors found on the floodplain and apparently a preference for those areas providing easier access to the uplands through tributary hollows. The greater availability of chert resources near the larger hollows may also have been a factor influencing more extensive utilization of these large floodplain sites.

Explaining the Settlement Patterns at Mammoth Cave National Park: Taking a Wider Perspective

An earlier emphasis on simply identifying and inventorying cultural resources in Mammoth Cave National Park came to an end in 1961 when Patty Jo Watson and her associates initiated their work in Mammoth Cave area archaeology (Benington, Melton, and Watson 1962). As a result of their work in the caves at Mammoth Cave National Park, we are in a better position to evaluate: (1) the adoption of horticulture during the Archaic; (2) the shift during the Late Archaic/Woodland periods from a hunting and gathering economy to one that relied considerably on domesticated plants; (3) prehistoric mining activities within the cave systems of the park; and (4) changes in prehistoric ceremonial practices during the Archaic and later periods. This wealth of information is due in large part to the data gathered during excavations in the Vestibule and interiors of Salts Cave (Watson 1966; Watson, ed., 1974; Watson et al. 1969).

Perhaps the most significant results of the work of Watson and of her colleagues in Salts Cave is the information gathered concerning prehistoric dietary practices and the early domestication of plants in the Green River area. Yarnell's (1969, 1974a, b) analysis of the plant remains recovered from the paleofeces taken from the cave, the intestinal contents of the desiccated human remains known as Little Al, and the Salts Cave Vestibule flotation samples indicate a diet high in hickory nuts (*Carya* sp.) and starchy seeds—sunflower (*Helianthus annuus*), marshelder (*Iva annua*), goosefoot (*Chenopodium* sp.), maygrass (*Phalaris caroliniana*), and amaranth (*Amaranthus* sp.).

Although Watson's work in Salts Cave provided valuable information regarding the adoption of Late Archaic and Early Woodland horticultural practices, these practices were in relationship to a very specialized range of activities, especially the extraction of cave minerals (see Tankersley, this volume). How representative it was of general life-styles of the prehistoric cavers was left unanswered. In an attempt to address this question, Watson and her colleagues initiated additional work in the Big Bend area of Green River in what was to become known as the Shell Mound Archeological Project.

Located roughly 60 km downstream from Mammoth Cave, the Big Bend area of Green River is significantly different in topography and has a greater range of archaeological site types from what is found in the Mammoth Cave area. Here the floodplains are expansive, more than 2 km (1.2 mi.) wide in places. The area and sections of the river downstream are possibly best known archaeologically for the "Shell Mound Archaic" sites (e.g., Indian Knoll, Carlston Annis, and Read) that were first investigated by C. B. Moore (1916), and extensively excavated by Webb and Haag (Webb 1950a, b, 1974; Webb and Haag 1939, 1940, 1947). More recent excavations directed by Marquardt and Watson (1983a, b) have added archaeobotanical information to the faunal and lithic data gained from these earlier investigations.

While shell midden sites are common in the Big Bend and lower stretches of Green River, they are exceedingly scarce upstream in the Mammoth Cave area. Excavations at the shell midden sites have contributed greatly to views currently held by archaeologists regarding the social organization, exchange systems, and subsistence practices of the mid-Southeast during the late Middle and Late Archaic periods (Jefferies 1990; Rolingson 1967; B. Smith 1986; Steponaitis 1986; Thieme 1991; Watson 1985b; Winters 1968, 1969, 1974).

Investigations at Indian Knoll (15Oh2) under the direction of Webb in 1939 as part of the Works Progress Administration (WPA) produced 1,178 burials and more than 55,000 artifacts (Webb 1974:122, 137). Indian Knoll had been previously dug into by C. B. Moore in 1915, when he removed a reported 298 human skeletons (Moore 1916). Excavations by Webb at the site recovered Middle Archaic through Mississippian period artifacts. Projectile point types included Kirk (Early Archaic), Big Sandy II/Raddatz (Middle Archaic), Matanzas, Elk River Stemmed, and Ledbetter Stemmed (Late Archaic), and Early Woodland stemmed points (Justice 1987; Rolingson 1967; Watson 1985a; Webb 1974). Pottery collected primarily in the upper 45 cm (1.5 ft) of the site included shell-tempered types (Mississippi Plain, Bell Plain, McKee Island Cord-Marked, Kimmswick Fabric Impressed), limestone-tempered types (Rough River Simple Stamped), and grog-tempered types (Mulberry Creek Cord Marked) (Haag 1974). The major occupation of the site has been defined by Rolingson (1967) as the Indian Knoll phase and has been roughly dated to between 2500 and 1500 B.C., based on artifact typological comparisons and radiocarbon dating (Rolingson 1967; Watson 1985a).

Faunal materials collected at Indian Knoll included deer (97.6% of mammal bone), dog, raccoon, opossum, woodchuck, squirrel, beaver, fox, bear, bobcat, rabbit, skunk, mink, chipmunk, turkey (83.4% of bird bone), goose, turkey vulture, sandhill crane, box turtle, aquatic turtle, drum, and buffalo fish (Webb 1974:334–39). Tools and debris collected by Webb that were indicative of activities performed at the site included fire-cracked rock (hot-rock cooking), hoes (digging, gardening?), pestles, nutting stones, and charred nutshells (nut processing), axes (tree felling), fishhooks (fishing), freshwater gastropod and bivalve shells (shellfish collecting), hammerstones, cores, flakers, flakes (lithic tool production), hafted scrapers (hide preparation), and projectile points, atlatl hooks, atlatl weights, and faunal debris (hunting).

The WPA work at Carlston Annis Mound (15Bt5) in 1939 under the direction of Webb produced 390 burials and a collection of artifacts similar to Indian Knoll in overall composition (Justice 1987; Webb 1950b). Projectile point types include Big Sandy II/Raddatz, Saratoga, Ledbetter, Adena, and Mississippian. Woodland and Mississippian pottery were also recovered. Other common artifact types included fire-cracked rock, hoes, pestles, nutting stones, axes, fishhooks, gorges, freshwater gastropod shells, bivalve shells, hammerstones, cores, flakers, flakes, hafted scrapers, atlatl hooks, and atlatl weights. Faunal materials were dominated by deer with raccoon, fish, bird, and box turtle also present.

As part of the Shell Mound Archeological Project, Marquardt and Watson directed excavations at Indian Knoll (15Oh2), Carlston Annis shell mound (15Bt5), and Bowles shell mound (15Oh13). Marquardt and Watson's and their colleagues' work (Crawford 1982; Marquardt and Watson 1983a, b; Stein 1982) at Carlston Annis demonstrated that the shell mound had been covered by a "shell-free midden" of cultural origin. Both were accretional deposits resulting from the accumulation of soil and plant and animal residues transported to the sites by the human occupants (Stein 1982). Dating of hearths and charcoal levels from various levels in the site indicated an occupation spanning roughly 3400 to 1350 B.C. within the shell midden zone (levels 5 through 20) (Marquardt and Watson 1983a, b). Within this shell midden layer, the most common shellfish species were inhabitants of riffle/run, shallow water environments (Marquardt and Watson 1983a:120).

Of greatest importance, the excavations at Carlston Annis revealed a plant-exploitation pattern different from that found at Salts and Mammoth caves. Instead of a plant assemblage dominated by domesticates, the faunal material consisted primarily of hickory nuts (90%) with minor amounts of acorn, black walnut, and seeds of blackberry (*Rubus* sp.), grape (*Vitis* sp.), honey locust (*Gleditsia triancanthos*), knotweed (*Polygonum* sp.), persimmon (*Diospyros virginiana*), elderberry (*Sambucus* sp.), foxtail-grass (*Setaria* sp.), panic-grass (*Panicum* sp.), wild plum (*Prunus* sp.), cinquefoil (*Potentilla* sp.), cleavers (*Galium* sp.), hazelnut (*Corylus* sp.), and possible sunflower (*Helianthus annuus*) (Crawford 1982). Fragments of squash (*Cucurbita pepo*) rind were also recovered. This, in addition to the large quantity of fish and mussel shell remains contained in the shell mound, indicates that the site was occupied primarily during the summer and early fall (Marquardt and Watson 1983a:330).

Essentially the same plant species in roughly the same proportions were recovered by Marquardt and Watson at the nearby Bowles site, although only 26 taxa were represented. Plant species found at Bowles but not at Carlston Annis were hackberry (*Celtis* sp.), wild bean (*Strophostyles* sp.), wild rice (*Zizania aquatica*), purslane (*Portulaca* sp.), and tickclover (*Desmodium* sp.). Again, a summer and early fall occupation of the site appears to be indicated.

The differences in the artifact assemblages recovered from the shell and midden mound sites in the Big Bend area from the cave, rockshelter, and open-air sites located just 60 km (37 mi.) upriver in Mammoth Cave National Park are indicative of a basic settlement pattern that was established during the later portion of the Archaic and continued through the Mississippian (Prentice 1994). This pattern was based on a seasonal round that emphasized the exploitation of riverine and floodplain resources (primarily weedy plants, fish, mussels, deer, and turkey) in the warm-weather months and upland resources (primarily nuts, deer, and turkey) in the cold-weather months. Once gardening as a means of food production had become established by the Late Archaic, the seasonal round of site occupation and resource exploitation would remain essentially the same for the remainder of known Native American prehistory in the Green River area.

The major economic factors affecting site selection remain relatively unchanged even as the number of domesticated plants (e.g., sunflower, goosefoot, maygrass) continue to increase with time because the primary value of these domesticated resources was probably in the ability to store the seeds for consumption in winter and early spring, the leanest time of the year. Nuts, deer, fish, mussels, turkey, and other naturally available foods continued to be economically important, because they could often be procured and stored in the fall of the year with less effort than their domesticated counterparts and because doing so allowed postponing the consumption of the domesticated crops until later in the year (i.e., late winter/early spring).

A pattern of wild and domesticated resource utilization was thus established by the Late Archaic that resulted in an emphasis on riverine and bottomland resources in late spring to early fall and upland resources in late fall to early spring. This, in turn, resulted in a residence pattern that continued relatively unchanged over 3,000 years and produced an archaeological record typified today by late spring/early fall floodplain sites such as Carlston Annis and Dry Creek and fall-winter sites such as Blue Spring Hollow Rockshelter (Carstens 1980).

The reasons for this basically stable residence pattern have primarily to do with the availability of different subsistence resources and the procurement and storage costs associated with each resource. Site catchment analysis and linear programming models developed to evaluate the least-cost (effort) solution in obtaining an adequate diet using wild and domesticated subsistence resources (Prentice 1994) illustrated that during the spring and summer months, the most productive areas in the Green River valley are the river itself and the floodplain that it crosses. Fish, mussels, various greens, tubers, berries, fruits, and other foods were available at a time when the adjacent upland oak-hickory forests had much less to offer in comparison and at a much higher cost in expended effort. People located their residences near the river where they could take advantage of the distribution of these river and floodplain resources.

With the adoption of gardening as a food production method, the availability of floodplain soils became an even greater factor in the selection of site location. In the vicinity of Mammoth Cave National Park, the narrow floodplains would not have been very conducive to supporting many households practicing this mode of subsistence production. Sixty kilometers downstream, in the Big Bend area where the floodplain reaches a breadth of over a mile, a much greater number of potential garden spots would have allowed a much larger residential population. Extensive and repeated occupations in the Big Bend area in the form of numerous Late Archaic, Woodland, and Mississippian shell mound and midden sites exemplify this choice in settlement location.

As the emphasis on raising domesticated plants increased, presumably reaching its greatest emphasis during the Mississippian, the broad floodplains such as those found in the Big Bend area would have been a preferred locality in which to clear fields and build homes. It comes as no surprise, therefore, that it is in this area of the Green River that the nearest Mississippian mound center (the Annis Village complex) to Mammoth Cave is found (Lewis 1990; Prentice 1994).

Although lacking in the terms of riverine bottomlands, the Mammoth Cave area certainly possessed extensive upland oak-hickory forests, which would have been at their most productive in the fall and early winter. At this time of the year, acorn and hickory masts provided a storable and highly productive resource that also attracted deer, turkey, and other fauna, making exploitation of these faunal resources more efficient. Rockshelters rimmed the edges of the uplands and afforded natural shelter to those who chose to exploit the available deer, turkey, nuts, and other autumn plants and animals. During this time of the year, the narrow floodplain and shallow waters of Green River afforded easier access to the river's supply of fish and mussels and reduced the amount of distance one had to travel to exploit the various resource zones. To take best advantage of the situation, upland sites in the Mammoth Cave area were most often located on the broad upland ridges immediately adjacent to the floodplain or in the bottoms immediately adjacent to a major hollow so that access to both bottomland and upland resources would be easier.

This combination of factors resulted in the settlement patterns exhibited in Mammoth Cave National Park today and helps explain other aspects of Mammoth Cave area archaeology as well. It explains, for instance, why pottery is generally found in such low numbers at the rockshelter and upland sites found within the park. Residence at such sites probably seldom lasted more than a month at a time, making transportation of more than a few pots to these sites burdensome and cumbersome. Production of pottery at these sites probably would have been minimal because ethnographic evidence indicates that making pottery during the cold and/or wet weather months would have been hampered by poor drying conditions (Shepard 1971). What pottery was available would certainly have been transported away from the site if it was not broken during use. As a result, relatively few examples of pottery are found at the rockshelter and upland sites in the Mammoth Cave area.

It also resolves the previously unanswered question as to why domesticated plants, so well represented in Salts Cave and Mammoth Cave, are so rarely encountered in the rockshelter sites surrounding them (Gremillion 1990; Wagner 1978). Rockshelter sites continue to be used by Native Americans as relatively short-term seasonal occupations for the primary purpose of exploiting fall and winter resources of the uplands, most importantly nuts, deer, and turkey. In comparison, the currently available evidence suggests that the use of Salts Cave was heaviest in the spring months (Prentice 1994; Schoenwetter 1974:55; Yarnell 1969:50). This author's analyses of resource procurement costs and seasonal resource availability (Prentice 1994) have shown that a diet high in stored vegetal foods (e.g., chenopodium, sunflower, amaranth, maygrass) would have been a cost-efficient means of obtaining the minimum dietary requirements during the spring of the year. It is not surprising, therefore, that they should represent such a high proportion of the Salt Cavers' diets. The insects, frogs, and so on that Watson (ed. 1974) cites as being evidence of a protein-poor diet among these people probably reflects the consumption of any edible item fortuitously encountered during this lean time of the year in a site location poorly situated to exploit the resource zones that are most productive in the spring: the river and floodplain. Located 2.4 km away from Green River, locally available, spring-season resources would have carried a relatively high cost in production effort. Site catchment and linear programming analyses have shown that it would be much more efficient to live closer to the river, where an adequate diet relying heavily on stored seeds augmented by naturally available spring resources (fish, mussels, deer, turkey, greens, tubers) could be obtained with less effort. Thus, in the spring of the year, it is expected that most habitation sites would be located near Green River where the riverine and floodplain resources would have been more easily exploited. The archaeological evidence corresponds well with this expectation. It also logically follows that it would be at this time of year, when people could subsist most efficiently on a diet consisting primarily of stored plant foods, that persons would spend greater time in non-subsistence-oriented tasks, such as cave exploration. Thus, it is the seasonal round and the scheduling of resource production and consumption that best explains the differences noted for the various site types that occur in the prehistoric Green River settlement system.

Motivated by management goals but also designed to address questions of scientific merit, the MCNPAIP, in conjunction with the previous work of Watson (1966; Watson, ed., 1974; Watson et al. 1969), Carstens (1980), Tankersley (1989), Munson et al. (1989), Wagner (1978), Schwartz (1958a–h), Pond (1935, 1937), and others, has provided the park and the archaeological community with an invaluable basis for studying human–land relationships. Approached with different research goals in mind, each attempt to understand these relationships has furthered our knowledge regarding past subsistence practices, economy, religion, and social organization. No doubt, this will be the case with future investigations into Mammoth Cave and Green River archaeology.

4 | Prehistoric Mining in the Mammoth Cave System

Kenneth B. Tankersley

MORE THAN 100 years of archaeological investigations demonstrate that the Flint-Mammoth Cave system was explored prehistorically. Indeed, Putnam (1875), Young (1910), Nelson (1917), Pond (1935, 1937), and Schwartz (1960a) illustrate a wide range of perishable artifacts associated with prehistoric caving activity. Watson (1966, 1977, 1985b, 1986; Watson, ed., 1974; Watson et al. 1969), demonstrates that most of this exploration activity was carried out by Early Woodland peoples for the purpose of obtaining two types of cave minerals— gypsum and speleothem salt.

In this chapter I focus on the prehistoric exploitation of speleothem salt, first describing the occurrence of these resources and the techniques used in their procurement. Evidence suggesting that Early Woodland peoples understood that speleothem salt is renewable, and that they took steps to exploit this phenomenon is presented. Finally, the implications of renewable mineral mining in the context of contemporary exploitive patterns in the Green River valley is discussed.

Speleothem Salt Occurrence and Procurement Techniques

Two forms of speleothem salt occur in the Mammoth Cave system— mirabilite ($NaSO_4$ $10H_2O$ hydrous sodium sulfate, glauber salts), and epsomite ($MgSO_4$ $7H_2O$ hydrous magnesium sulfate, epsom salts). Mirabilite has a salty taste and is more common and widespread than epsomite in the areas of the Flint-Mammoth Cave system that were explored prehistorically (Watson 1966, 1977; Watson, ed., 1974; Watson and Yarnell 1966). My discussion concentrates on this resource.

The procurement techniques of speleothem salt varied according to its habit, that is, the shape and relative proportions of the crystals. Mirabilite effloresces as both fibrous and massive crystals (Hill 1976:61–75). If the deposit occurred as delicate cottonlike "whiskers," then speleothem salt could have been brushed into a receptacle with a stiff feather, like those described by Putnam (1875) and Young (1910:316). If the deposit occurred as needles protruding from sulfate-saturated alluvium, then the salt-rich sediment was likely excavated with the aid of a digging stick (Munson et al. 1989; Young 1910:317). If the deposit occurred as a crust or series of flowers, then stone and shell tools were probably used to scrape the salt from the cave walls (Watson et al. 1969:59, 61).

Because of their chemical and textural similarity, mirabilite and gypsum frequently co-occur (Watson 1966:242; Watson and Yarnell 1966:847; White 1969:79–82). In this form, speleothem salt falls from exfoliating cave walls and ceilings. Undoubtedly, large chunks of this material were procured by hand. In its purest crystalline state, mirabilite is soluble and dehydrates when exposed to surface air (Hill 1976:65). Speleothem salt, however, retains its salty properties in most surface environments (Watson and Yarnell 1966:847).

Opportunistic and Systematic Mining

The earliest form of speleothem salt mining was perhaps strictly opportunistic. As the first prehistoric cavers explored the dry upper levels of the Flint-Mammoth Cave system, they would have encountered sparkling white speleothem salt on walls, ledges, breakdown, and alluvial surfaces (Figures 4.1 and 4.2). In certain areas, such as the Snow Room in Mammoth Cave and the area just north of Grand Forks in Salts Cave, the salt is so concentrated that the aboriginal cavers must have literally tasted it in the air as one does today.

It seems reasonable to assume that subsequent salt procurement would have continued to be opportunistic, but also systematic. Assuming a "least cost" mining attitude, speleothem salts located closest to cave entrances would have been procured first, and those deposits located farthest from entrances would have been procured last. Aside from the excitement of exploring the underground world, the exploitation of speleothem salt may have been the early driving force behind the exploration of the Flint-Mammoth Cave system (Watson 1985b:152; Watson 1966:242; Watson et al. 1969:57).

Given the fact that the suite of radiocarbon dates associated with prehistoric activity in the Flint-Mammoth Cave system spans more than 2,000 years (Kennedy, this volume; Watson, ed., 1974:236–37), two archaeological and geological assumptions can be made concerning speleothem salt procurement: (1) speleothem salt regenerates in areas of the cave that were previously mined, and (2) Early Woodland miners noticed this phenomenon.

Some of the mining sites that were stripped of salt one year would have been entirely replenished during the following season. Mirabilite grows relatively rapidly, in a matter of months (Hill 1976:65). This regrowth usually occurs during the damp months of late winter and early spring (White 1970).

Conversely, it seems safe to assume that some of the areas where speleothem salt was procured were never replenished. The micropores of bedrock can clog. Without porosity, sulfate-saturated groundwater cannot reach cave interiors and renew speleothem growth. Also, changes in temperature and humidity can stunt or even prevent the growth of mirabilite. Caves are dynamic geological

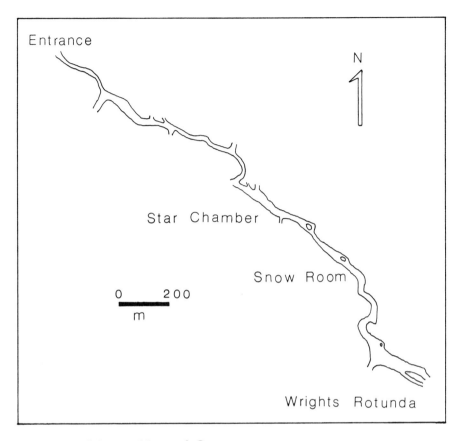

4.1 Main Trunk Passage, Mammoth Cave

features. New entrances fall open and old ones collapse shut. It is quite likely that the upper levels of both Mammoth Cave and Salts Cave displayed changes in humidity as a result of this process.

The stimulus for renewable mineral mining could have come from the fact that some areas of the cave system displayed speleothem salt regrowth and others did not (some areas exhibited prolific deposits of salt, year after year, regardless of the intensity of mining activity).

Renewable Mineral Mining

Evidence that speleothem salt was prehistorically mined as a renewable mineral resource can be found in both Mammoth and Salts caves. Most of this evidence is restricted to areas that display large slabs of breakdown or ledges beneath active efflorescences.

In Mammoth Cave mirabilite deposits are concentrated in various areas of

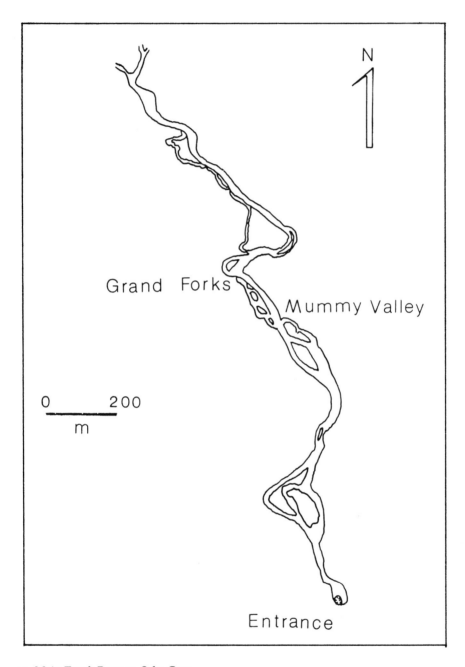

4.2 Main Trunk Passage, Salts Cave

the "main cave" between Star Chamber and Wrights Rotunda. This section of the main cave used to be referred to as the Snow Room by park guides because snow-white mirabilite flakes precipitate abundantly (at least seasonally) from the cave ceiling. A similar depositional environment occurs in the Upper Trunk of Salts Cave between Grand Forks and Club House Valley.

Deposits of mirabilite in these areas accumulate on large breakdown slabs displaying nearly horizontal surfaces. Interestingly, most of these mirabilite-covered surfaces are free of cave debris. I interpret the absence of detritus as evidence for prehistoric "sweeping." Once swept, these surfaces would accumulate clean deposits of speleothem salt that could be seasonally brushed into gourd, squash, or wooden containers.

Ledges beneath wall efflorescences in the Main Trunk of Mammoth, near a feature known as the "Whale," and between Mummy Valley and Grand Forks in Upper Salts Cave show similar characteristics. In these areas, mirabilite has been scraped from the overhanging walls. Although most of these ledges are covered with mirabilite, they are barren of detritus. Again, it is as if they were prehistorically swept to provide a clean surface on which mirabilite could accumulate.

An additional line of evidence for renewable speleothem salt mining may be found in the types and abundance of artifacts that occur in or around ledge and breakdown accumulations of mirabilite. If speleothem salt was recognized as a renewable resource, then we would expect to find gourd or other kinds of containers more abundant in areas where mirabilite regenerates than other parts of the cave system. Unfortunately, these artifacts have been collected from both Mammoth Cave and Salts Cave for more than 100 years (Watson 1986; Watson et al. 1969:10). Although this hypothesis might have been testable prior to historic disturbances, it is unlikely that the current distribution of these artifacts would be statistically meaningful.

I am not arguing that bowls were actually used to catch mirabilite that fell under its own weight during seasonal growth. Nor am I arguing that these containers were used only in the procurement of speleothem salt (see Tankersley et al. 1985 and Munson et al. 1989 for other uses of bowls in the Mammoth Cave system). Rather, I am suggesting that Early Woodland miners may have cached containers in areas where mirabilite regenerated.

Renewable mineral mining is neither a labor-intensive nor a high-risk activity. By taking advantage of the fact that mirabilite is a regenerative mineral, prehistoric miners would have had more time to invest in the procurement of other cave mineral resources, such as the fancy crystalline forms of gypsum, selenite and satin spar (Munson et al. 1989). Indeed, prehistoric gypsum crystal mining appears to have been the most labor-intensive, and apparently hazardous, activity in the Flint-Mammoth Cave system. The extraction of crystals often required miners to scale high vertical cliffs and walk along narrow, sloping, boulder-strewn ledges. In these precarious situations, miners excavated crawl-ways into gypsum-rich sediments overlain by multiton boulders. The remains of an Early Woodland miner was found under one of these boulders near an enlarged cavity in the sediment beneath it (Munson et al. 1989; Pond 1935, 1937).

Implications

I view the mining of renewable cave minerals as an extension of contemporary resource exploitation patterns in the Green River drainage. Abundant renewable aquatic resources may have brought Early Woodland peoples into the Mammoth Cave region. Silviculture, horticulture, and hunting in the adjacent forested uplands exposed these people to the natural entrances of the Flint-Mammoth Cave system (Munson 1988; Watson 1966, 1988).

The obvious questions that arise, however, are, Why did prehistoric peoples first enter the deep recesses of these caves? and, of more importance, Why did they procure renewable speleothem salt?

The answer to the first question may simply be the fact that people have a natural curiosity about the unknown, or more specifically, the unexplored (Watson 1977:148, 1986:21). Caves offer both these qualities. In any case, prehistoric peoples "noticed cave entrances and utilized them frequently and freely to gain access to the world underground" (Watson 1987:36). Archaeologically, this behavior is evidenced by the presence of prehistoric human footprints and fragments of torch charcoal, hundreds, sometimes even thousands of meters from cave entrances (see Watson 1966, 1983, 1987; Watson, ed., 1974; Watson et al. 1969; Robbins, Wilson, and Watson 1981).

The answer to the question, Why was renewable speleothem salt procured? may be found in our current interpretations of the Early Woodland economy. As a result of efficient long-term boiling, the products of hunting, aquatic collecting, and silviculture were more effectively processed; for example, animal fat and nut oils could be consumed while a greater portion of the animal and nut meats were stored (Munson 1986, 1988). Storable wild foods and modest horticultural crops, such as sumpweed, sunflower, and chenopodium, provided populations with an economic basis for year-around settlement (Watson 1989:561). As populations aggregated and increased, so did social stratification, the amassing of nonutilitarian goods, and long-distance trade (Munson 1988:13).

In the Early Woodland economic setting, speleothem salt may have been valued as a preservative, as a cathartic, and as a trade item. While drying and parching are effective means of preserving starchy and oily foods, salt has the additional advantage of being an insect repellent; and insects are an ever-present threat to the nutritional value of stored foods. Thus, the properties of this preservative might have been in demand by peoples who were dependent on stored foods during seasonal shortages (Watson 1985b, 1988).

Perhaps a clue to understanding the importance of speleothem salt as a preservative lies in the Early Woodland paleofeces. Watson and Yarnell (1986:250) demonstrated that the food waste in Lost John's intestinal tract is comparable in general composition to the contents of Little Al's (another desiccated prehistoric individual from the Flint-Mammoth Cave system) lower digestive system and the hundreds of fecal deposits from Mammoth Cave and Salts Cave. Plant foods conspicuously present are chenopodium seeds, sumpweed and sunflower achenes, and hickory nut shell. Although this constellation of fall-harvested plant foods may indicate that most, if not all, of the mining activity took place during the late fall or early winter, all of these plant remains are easily storable, and they could have been trail food anytime during the year, noting also that they co-occur with strawberry and blackberry seeds.

One could also argue, however, that the consistency of Early Woodland food waste suggests a diet of coarse foods. A prolonged diet of coarse vegetable fiber and seeds can lead to constipation. Experiments by Watson's investigative team demonstrated that relatively massive doses of speleothem mirabilite do indeed produce cathartic effects (Watson et al., 1969:58; Watson and Yarnell 1966:846). Additional evidence of mirabilite's medicinal value may be its presence in Little Al's gastric intestinal tract. Apparently, he died from internal hemorrhaging related to a rapid deceleration injury. Little Al ingested mirabilite prior to his death (Tankersley et al. 1994:140).

The extent and magnitude of prehistoric salt mining features in the Flint-Mammoth Cave system implies that some of the mirabilite may have been procured for trade (Watson 1966:242, 1985a). Even if we allow for more than 2,000 years of recurrent seasonal salt mining, the number of prehistoric features implies that more mirabilite was procured than local populations could possibly use for storage or medicinal purposes. The fact that mirabilite has cathartic properties, as well as being a salty mineral, suggests that it would have been valued prehistorically.

Regardless of whether there was a culturally conditioned use of speleothem salt as a preservative, as a cathartic, or primarily as a trade item, the growing body of archaeological and geological data supports Watson's (1987:37) suggestion that "there seems to be a business like and perhaps even commercial use of caves" by the Early Woodland peoples of the Mammoth Cave area.

5 | Prehistoric Expressions from the Central Kentucky Karst

Philip J. DiBlasi

In 1979 a recreational caver exploring a cave in eastern Tennessee found a series of drawings that were immediately recognized as prehistoric mud art. This discovery eventually led to the site's examination by a team of investigators from the University of Tennessee at Knoxville and to the description of a previously unknown Mississippian body of art (Faulkner, Deane, and Earnest 1984:350–61). Eight radiocarbon determinations from inside the passage date from A.D. 465 to A.D. 1605. However, "it is believed that the intensive utilization of Mud Glyph Cave occurred during the Mississippian period, especially around the thirteenth to fourteenth centuries A.D." (ibid.:358). Several additional caves and rockshelters containing petroglyphs that have been assigned to the Mississippian tradition have been described by Faulkner (1988; Faulkner, ed., 1986).

A tradition of Mississippian art and motifs has been identified. However, it has been shown that the majority of prehistoric cave use in Tennessee and Kentucky dates to the Late Archaic/Early Woodland period. Until recently, there has been no art found within caves that clearly date to this early use of caves. Two new discoveries have located both mud and charcoal drawings that appear to date to this earlier period. The first discovery was made in May 1986 while University of Louisville students were participating in a recreational caving event known as Speleofest in central Kentucky. During one of the cave trips they happened upon a mud-floored, upper-level passage measuring approximately 150 m long and 4 m wide. They reported that the floor was covered with incised geometric drawings. In 1987, as a Western Kentucky University class was being shown Salts Cave in Mammoth Cave National Park, another set of drawings was discovered. They had been executed with torch charcoal on a large slab of ceiling breakdown. Examination of these two examples of prehistoric art show that they have several motifs in common and that they differ significantly from the Mississippian motifs described by Faulkner et al. (1984). In this chapter I argue for an earlier tradition of art in caves that dates to the Late Archaic/Early Woodland period.

The Mississippian Motifs

Mud Glyph Cave, Tennessee, presents a situation in which numerous Mississippian motifs can be identified. These motifs include anthropomorphic, herpetomorphic, geometric, "Southern Cult," and various animals (primarily bird) elements (Muller 1986:36–80). Anthropomorphic examples include representations of the human form that range from complete individuals to recognizable body parts. Most frequently the body parts represented are the face and head. Many of the faces include the Eastern Woodlands "Weeping Eye" motif. One individual appears to represent a "birdman" (ibid.:51–56). The herpetomorphic representations cover several meters and have circles or diamonds for eyes. Several of the serpents have possible wings and apparent bird heads (ibid., 1984:56–59). One of the drawings consists of a "horned serpent," which is represented by a zigzag line with a circle for a head and upturned horns (ibid.:50, Plate VII b). Another represents a turtle drawn by altering the print of a bare human footprint. The depression formed by the heel was altered by adding several incised lines, one encircling the depression (forming the carapace) and others that make up the extremities, tail, and head. Another human footprint was altered by the addition of incised lines to form an anthropomorphic face or "human mask" (Faulkner et al. 1984:354, 355, Figure 4). Geometric motifs include the circle, inverted "V," diamond or rhomboid, and ogee. Also noted are simple arcs of curved lines and cross-circles. The "Southern Cult" motifs present include the weeping eye, the bilobed arrow, and maces (Muller 1986:60–62). Animal motifs include owl, hawk, woodpecker, and a possible opossum (ibid.:62–64). Several herpetomorphic motifs appear in Mud Glyph Cave as well as several abstract designs. One such design consisted of "meanders and macaroni drawn with the fingers" (Faulkner et al. 1984:353). The cross-hatching and latticework designs were usually components of larger units such as animals or human figures (ibid.:353).

B. Bart Henson (1986:81–108) describes three sites in the eastern United States where herpetomorphic glyphs are associated with Mississippian motifs. Site 11, Jackson County, Alabama, has a horned snake as well as a spiral and rectangle (ibid.:98). Site 16, Franklin County, Alabama, has a turtle and anthropomorphic and other zoomorphic designs "painted in black" (ibid.:101). Site 30, Washington County, Missouri, has a snake and other zoomorphic designs as well as spirals, a mace, and bilobed arrows (ibid.:106). All of these renderings are on either rock outcrops or rockshelter walls; unfortunately, there are no radiocarbon determinations for these drawings.

Officer Cave and Devil Step Hollow Cave, both in Tennessee, contain anthropomorphic petroglyphs that are similar to the glyphs of Mud Glyph Cave, Tennessee. Notable details are the weeping eye motif and the "toothed mask"

(Faulkner 1988). Radiometric determinations for Devil Step Hollow Cave of A.D. 920 and A.D. 1330 support the contention that these petroglyphs are Mississippian (Faulkner 1988).

One of the most distinctive characteristics of the Mississippian Period art described by Faulkner is the naturalistic and realistically drawn figures, particularly when compared with the glyphs found in Central Kentucky. In addition, many of the motifs can be found on Mississippian ceramic, copper, and shell art.

The Late Archaic/Early Woodland Motifs

Four caves are now known in the Central Kentucky Karst that contain glyphs: Adair Glyph Cave, Mammoth Cave, Salts Cave, and Smiths Grove Cave (the latter has not yet been published about and is not discussed here). Glyphs in Mammoth Cave and Salts Cave contain drawings in charcoal from burned cane torches. Adair Glyph Cave contains drawings incised on a mud floor passage. As in the glyphs described by Faulkner, there are distinct stylistic similarities among the three sets of drawings, but all three differ from those described in Tennessee.

The glyphs found in Adair Glyph Cave, more than 1 km from the entrance, consist of geometric patterns, primarily zigzags, chevrons, and cross-hatching. These drawings are incised at a large scale in the damp mud of the floor. Preliminary examination of the passage indicates that the incising was carried out with a pointed or sharp-edged object such as a stick, small fragment of breakdown, or the edge of a freshwater mussel. In fact, a freshwater mussel was found near the entrance to the passage. The mussel appears worn, as though it was used to draw in the stiff mud. The glyphs appear to be executed with some care, they do not overlap, and the individual elements are fairly symmetrical.

It is unclear whether there is an overall pattern to the drawings in Adair Glyph Cave because only two trips have been made into the passage to examine and photograph the glyphs and to gather charcoal for radiometric determinations. Plans are presently being made for complete photodocumentation of the floor and for the production of a cave map.

Zigzags appear to be one of the more common motifs present. Each zigzag is composed of parallel lines, which are usually spaced 2 or 3 cm apart. The zigzags occur in single and paired examples. The paired examples are very symmetrical, appearing as mirror images. Another form of zigzag appears as a series of single lines that overlap each other, forming a series of diamonds. Several of the zigzags are connected at the top, forming a pattern similar to a simple Christmas tree–like design. The sizes range from approximately 50 cm to well over 1 m in length and 20 to 30 cm in width. Frequently, the zigzags are found in rows paralleling one another.

The second most common motif is cross-hatching. Cross-hatching or grids are typically large and usually square, or nearly so, in the area they cover. The grids do not appear to be as carefully drawn as the zigzags. Spacing of individual lines is somewhat uniform, but lines terminate in a rather ragged fashion. Areas of cross-hatching range from about 50 cm to more than 1 m square.

Two chevrons were observed. These are in close association with one another and are approximately 1.5 m long and 50 to 70 cm wide. They taper abruptly from one end to the other.

All of the glyphs incised in the mud of the floor of Adair Glyph Cave are patinated. The modern traffic through the passage has broken the patination and can be readily differentiated from the drawings. A single charcoal sample from the passage has been dated. The sample was collected from a small area and is composed of charcoal from the cane torches used to illuminate the passage aboriginally. The extended count date obtained on 0.45 g of carbon was 3560 B.P. ± 110 years (Beta-16932) or 1610 B.C. ± 110 years. A second sample has been collected but has not been analyzed.

Several sets of glyphs have been identified in Salts Cave, Kentucky. The first is a series of cross-hatching situated near survey station P63, 485 m from the entrance. The second is 841 m from the entrance, situated approximately halfway between stations P50 and P53 (Watson et al. 1969:back map pocket, Figure 3).

In the area of P63 on the side of a ledge is a carbide sooted "f-s" or "x-s" with an arrow pointing downslope. To the left of the modern notation is an area of cross-hatching drawn with a cane torch. The cross-hatching covers an area 20 cm high and 70 cm wide. Because of the different styles and sizes of cross-hatching, it appears to represent three different events.

The glyphs halfway between P50 and P53 are drawn with charcoal from torches and are situated on the edge of a slab that is approximately 50 cm thick and 3 m wide (Figure 5.1). There are three central zoomorphic figures. In addition to the central figures, there are numerous charcoaled "random lines" and smudges present. There are also several incised random lines and cross-hatched areas.

The upper figure represents a turtle, approximately 10 × 10 cm. The carapace is round, and all four legs are extended, as are tail and head. The upper left portion of this figure is smudged. The upper extremities are poorly executed, irregular in size, and disproportionately large, especially the right side of the figure. The lower extremities are better executed and have better proportion, including the detail of digits or claws on the right foot (three) and left foot (four). The tail is represented by an elongated triangle.

The next figure is the most indistinct of the three. It is uncertain whether it is actually zoomorphic or possibly anthropomorphic. It is approximately 10 cm tall and 4 cm wide. The body is short and stocky with what appears to be a

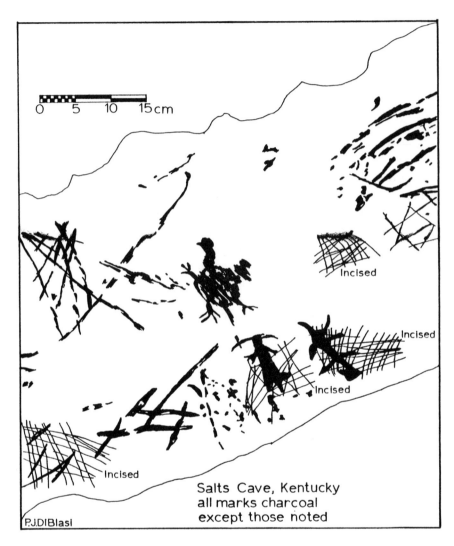

Incised

Incised

Incised

Incised

Incised

Salts Cave, Kentucky
all marks charcoal
except those noted

P.J.DIBlasI

5.1 Salts Cave Glyph

"head" near its top. Four short (less than 1.5 cm long), stocky (about 1 cm wide) appendages extend from the body. The upper left extremity has three digits or claws. A short (1 cm long), stocky (less than 1 cm wide) "tail" can be observed at the bottom of the body. Several incised, curved, randomly drawn lines transect the "torso" of this figure, and several incised straight lines transect the lower body, extremities, and tail. A curved charcoal line transects the head of this figure. It cannot be determined whether the random lines are part of the intended figure. If part of the figure, they might represent downward curved "horns."

To the lower right on the breakdown is a herpetomorphic drawing, possibly representing a salamander or lizard with a set of "horns." The body is long and thin (approximately 10 cm long, including the "tail," and 1 cm wide). The thoracic region appears broader than the abdominal area. The four extremities are proportionally drawn (about 1 cm long and 0.5 cm wide) with no detail such as digits or claws. The head is drawn as a round shape just above the upper extremities. From the head, in a crescent shape, are two disproportionately large "horns." An incised area of cross-hatching covers this figure and extends approximately 10 cm downward and to the right. This cross-hatching has removed the charcoal, indicating it was drawn after the salamander was created.

There are additional "drawings" found on the face of the breakdown slab. Approximately 25 to 30 cm left of the three central figures is an area of incised cross-hatching. This cross-hatching covers an area approximately 15 cm on a side. It is not horizontal in orientation; rather the lines are approximately at 45-degree angles to horizontal and vertical. As with the cross-hatching that occludes portions of the lower right figure, the margins of the cross-hatching appear frayed. In other words, the cross-hatching is not contained within a boundary; rather, the cross lines end at different distances past the last intersection. In addition, the lines making up the cross-hatching are not quite parallel; the surface contours of the rock or the angle of the "artist's" stroke may account for these irregularities. This incised cross-hatching has been drawn over several large, roughly horizontal charcoal lines.

Between the lower left figure and the incised cross-hatching is an area covered with broad, widely separated charcoal lines. There are four lines from upper left to lower right and three lines from upper right to lower left. These lines are approximately 20 cm long and irregularly spaced from about 1.5 to 2 cm apart.

Above and to the right of the lower right figure is a fourth cross-hatched area, which is incised. This cross-hatched area is 10 × 10 cm and is oriented more or less vertically.

Twenty centimeters to the right of the lower right figure is a fifth cross-hatched area. It is incised, and it is the most irregular of the cross-hatched areas (possibly a series of overlapping zigzags). It measures 15 cm tall × 15 to 20 cm wide.

To the left of the central figures is a cluster of "random lines." In this cluster are three oriented from upper left to lower right. Additionally, there are five or six lines that originate from upper right and extend to lower left.

Recently, several cross-hatched areas have been discovered in Salts Cave, and several others have been noted by cave surveyors in the past. All have been found in areas of extensive Late Archaic/Early Woodland traffic. These cross-hatched areas appear to be near intersections of cave passages.

Materials dated in Salts Cave demonstrate that the majority of prehistoric activity took place during the Late Archaic/Early Woodland periods (Benington, Melton, and Watson 1962; Watson 1971:25, 1972:50; Watson, ed., 1974; Watson et al. 1969; also Kennedy, this volume). A single date from 15Ad70 suggests a similar temporal association (DiBlasi 1986a, b).

Patty Jo Watson (personal communication) indicates that cross-hatching also has been found in Fisher Ridge Cave (located in Hart County, Kentucky). Radiocarbon determinations reveal that prehistoric peoples were in this cave between 1225 B.C. ± 80 and 800 B.C. ± 85 (Kennedy, Hensley-Martin, and Watson 1983:22).

In Mammoth Cave, again in areas known to have been visited during the Late Archaic/Early Woodland period, several charcoal drawings have been noted. Two charcoal drawings are known in Historic Mammoth Cave. One, known since the 1830s, is on an upright breakdown slab called "The Devil's Looking Glass" (Lee 1835). Unfortunately, none of the descriptions specifically describe the drawing, and it is extensively damaged by historic signatures. The only recognizable element at present appears to be a broad zigzag in the lower right corner of the slab. Because of extensive historic damage it is virtually impossible to discern any other detail, and it is unclear from the descriptions whether the feature known as the Devil's Looking Glass might refer to the charcoal drawings rather than to the unusual vertical slab of ceiling breakdown. Within 50 m of this feature is a drawing discovered by Carstens in 1978 during an examination of Historic Mammoth Cave (Watson and Carstens 1982:130).

The drawing is dissimilar from the other drawings described. It appears to consist of two principal elements. The first is a rectilinear form composed of three uprights that are transversely sectioned by lines. The other is spiral-like with several circles at the ends. It has been suggested that the spiral could be a cave map, the terminal circles representing deep pits. However, comparing modern maps with the area has yet to resolve this question.

Conclusions

Cave art is gradually becoming recognized as an important area of research. Until recent accidental discoveries, little was known of this specialized and highly symbolic underground activity.

Work at Mud Glyph Cave during the 1980s was used to help define a Mississippian tradition of cave art and symbolism, not unlike that found on artifacts from above ground Mississippian contexts (i.e., bone and shell engravings and various ceramic designs). Mississippian Cave art at Mud Glyph cave seems to have reached its peak between the thirteenth and fourteenth centuries and is composed of very natural and realistic figures, including recognizable human forms, herpetomorphic forms, horned serpents, anthropomorphic forms, geometric forms (circle, inverted "V," diamond or rhomboid, and ogee), arcs, crossed circles, Southern Cult motifs (weeping eye, bilobed arrow, and maces), and various animal motifs (owl, hawk, woodpecker, and opossum).

For the major caves in the Central Kentucky Karst, the majority of human caving activity dates to the Late Archaic/Early Woodland, not to the Mississippian period. Yet, here too, recent discoveries have demonstrated the presence of prehistoric drawings made by charred cane torches and incised on mud floors. At present, one radiocarbon assay supports a terminal Archaic date for this second millennium B.C. artwork, much earlier than the previously described Mississippian art. The Late Archaic/Early Woodland drawings include primarily geometric forms (zigzag, chevrons, and cross-hatching), zoomorphic figures, random lines, stroke marks, and herpetomorphic figures. Future cave surveys throughout the Central Kentucky Karst will undoubtedly locate additional sites with cave art that will further illuminate our understanding of ceremonial activity during the Late Archaic and Early Woodland periods.

6 | Radiocarbon Dates from Salts and Mammoth Caves

Mary C. Kennedy

THIS CHAPTER FOCUSES on the large, existing sample of radiocarbon dates from two caves in the Flint/Mammoth system, Salts Cave and Mammoth Cave. My purpose is to bring together in one location all the radiocarbon dates and the available information on those dates from these two sites in Mammoth Cave National Park (MCNP) and then to evaluate them. Although all of these dates have been published previously, the entire series has never been treated as a group. Because of ongoing archaeological investigation at these sites, such treatment seems warranted.

Background

Salts and Mammoth caves have been recognized as archaeological repositories for more than 150 years (Bullitt 1985). Some of the pioneers of North American archaeology have published descriptions of materials and excavations in both caves (Nelson 1917; Putnam 1875; Young 1910).

Over the course of the last 30 years, through the efforts of the Cave Research Foundation Archeological Project, a series of radiocarbon determinations (Table 6.1) have been reported for Mammoth and Salts caves (Benington, Melton, and Watson 1962; Gardner 1987; Munson et al. 1989; Watson 1966, 1985a; Watson, ed., 1974; Watson et al. 1969; Watson and Yarnell 1966). Through the radiocarbon technique the two sites have been shown to date to the same span of eastern North American prehistory, the first and second millennium B.C., the Early Woodland and Late Archaic periods. In fact, even though the cave entrances are believed to have been accessible throughout the entire span of human prehistory, and despite the fact that there are surface sites nearby that represent all periods of prehistory (Carstens 1980), there is as yet no unequivocal evidence that Salts or Mammoth caves were visited prior to the Late Archaic or after the Early Woodland.

Setting

Both caves are located in south central Kentucky, in Mammoth Cave National Park. The entrances are approximately 4.8 km apart in an area of heavily dissected karst upland terrain. Mammoth Cave and Salts Cave are part of a system of underground passages that constitute the world's longest cave. The fact that the historic entrance of Mammoth Cave, located in Mammoth Cave Ridge, and the entrance to Salts Cave, in Flint Ridge, are connected in one labyrinthine system was not proven by modern cave explorers until 1972 (Brucker and Watson 1976). It is assumed that prehistoric cavers were unaware of the connection and thought of these as separate caves.

The caves have been hollowed out of the massively bedded Mississippian limestones of the region by the action of surface water seeking Green River, the base level stream (Stein, Watson, and White 1981:532). The upper levels of the cave were formed between 10 million and 1 million years ago (Palmer 1981:133–35) and have been dry ever since water created lower levels in the limestone strata. This has resulted in an environment that is close to ideal for the preservation of uncharred organic material, material that does not commonly survive in open archaeological sites.

Mammoth and Salts caves were explored and exploited in prehistory. In both caves prehistoric cavers discarded a characteristic array of artifacts (Watson et al. 1969; Watson and Yarnell 1966): torch debris, campfire debris, human feces (Marquardt 1974; R. Stewart 1974; Yarnell 1969), fragments of cordage, twined vegetable fiber fabric, and twined slippers (King 1974; Watson 1974h; Watson et al. 1969). *Pepo* gourd (*Cucurbita pepo* var. *ovifera*) and bottle gourd (*Lagenaria siceraria*) containers, both whole and in fragments, have been recovered. Two desiccated human bodies, one from each cave, are documented as well (Meloy 1971; Meloy and Watson 1969; Neumann 1938; Pond 1937; Robbins 1974). There is considerable evidence of prehistoric mining in both caves (Munson et al. 1989; Watson 1974f; Watson et al. 1969). Wherever prehistoric materials are found, cave walls and sediments show signs of extensive battering and digging. An array of cave minerals including gypsum ($CaSo_4 \cdot 2H_2O$), both in powdered and crystalline forms; mirabilite ($Na_2SO_4 \cdot 10H_2O$); and epsomite ($MgSO_4 \cdot 7H_2O$) all appear to have been sought in a systematic way (Watson 1974b:69; White 1969).

The underground environment of the Mammoth and Salts cave interiors is one of nearly constant temperature and humidity. There is a complete absence of light; any human explorer must provide artificial illumination, which also explains the preponderance of torch and fire debris among the prehistoric remains. Processes that one expects on surface sites are negligible underground. Wind, water, and quantities of decaying organic matter are absent in dry passages of the cave; consequently there is no soil formation. Materials are not buried by wind or waterborne sediments. As a result, material carried into the cave and dropped in prehistoric times can lie next to material dropped yesterday, 30, 50, or 100 years ago. All of these objects can be in an excellent state of preservation.

Table 6.1. Radiocarbon Determinations from Caves in Mammoth Cave National Park, Kentucky (uncorrected, uncalibrated, Libby half-life)

Provenience	Material	^{14}C Age B.P. ± 1σ	2σ Range	Laboratory Number	Year Run
Salts Cave Vestibule					
1 Test H, F 2A	Charcoal	3490 ± 110	3270–3710	GaK 2767	1970
2 Test E, Level 5	Charcoal	3360 ± 220	2920–3800	GaK 2764	1970
3 Test G, Level 6*	Charcoal	3410 ± 100	3210–3610	GaK 2766	1970
4 Test E, Level 7b	Charcoal	2660 ± 100	2460–2860	GaK 2622	1970
5 Test E, Level 7b	Charcoal	2940 ± 120	2700–3180	GaK 2765	1970
6 Test JIV, Level 4	Charcoal	2470 ± 60	2350–2590	Beta 4649	1982
7 Test JIV, Level 6	Charcoal	2340 ± 50	2240–2440	Beta 4650	1982
8 Test JIV, Level 8	Charcoal	2430 ± 50	2330–2530	Beta 4651	1982
9 Test JIV, Level 11	Charcoal	2510 ± 60	2390–2630	Beta 4652	1982
10 Test KII, Level 4	Charcoal	2520 ± 70	2380–2660	Beta 4080	1982
11 Test KII, Level 6	Charcoal	2200 ± 60	2080–2320	Beta 4081	1982
12 Test KII, Level 11	Charcoal	2380 ± 60	2260–2500	Beta 4082	1982
13 Test KII, Level 14	Charcoal	2410 ± 60	2290–2530	Beta 4083	1982
Salts Cave Interior					
14 Upper Salts, P54	Paleofeces w/squash seeds	2240 ± 200	1840–2640	M 1573	1966
15 Upper Salts, P38	Paleofeces	2270 ± 140	1990–2550	M 1777	1966
16 Upper Salts, P63–64	Paleofeces w/gourd seeds	2570 ± 140	2290–2850	M 1574	1966

17	Upper Salts, P54	Soot	3075 ± 140	2795–3355	I 256	1966
18	Test A, 0–10 cm	Cane	2510 ± 140	2230–2790	M 1584	1966
19	Test A, 30–40 cm	Cane	2430 ± 130	2170–2690	M 1585	1966
20	Test A, 140 cm	Cane	2840 ± 150	2540–3140	M 1586	1966
21	Test A, 140 cm	Wood	2520 ± 140	2240–2800	M 1587	1966
22	Middle Salts, Blue Arrow, A60	Paleofeces w/squash pollen	2350 ± 140	2070–2630	M 1577	1966
23	Middle Salts, Blue Arrow, A42	Paleofeces w/sunflower achenes	2660 ± 140	2380–2940	M 1770	1966
24	Lower Salts, Indian Av. I76	Wood	2720 ± 140	2440–3000	M 1588	1966
25	Lower Salts, Indian Av. I67	Wood and bark	3140 ± 150	2840–3440	M 1589	1966
26	Salts Cave Mummy	Internal tissue	1920 ± 160	1600–2240	M 2259	1971
27	Salts Cave Mummy	Internal tissue	1960 ± 160	1640–2280	M 2258	1971

Mammoth Cave Interior

28	Upper Mammoth	Slipper	2230 ± 40	2150–2310	X[†] 8	1957
29	Upper Mammoth	Cane	2370 ± 60	2250–2490	X[†] 9	1957
30	Lower Mammoth, Ganter, B10	Wood	3000 ± 70	2860–3140	UCLA 1730B	1971
31	Lower Mammoth, Jessup, C7	Twigs	4120 ± 70	3980–4260	UCLA 1730A	1971
32	Lower Mammoth, W21-A	Cane charcoal	2920 ± 60	2800–3040	SI 6890A	1985
33	Lower Mammoth, W21-B	Cane charcoal	2495 ± 80	2335–2655	SI 6890B	1985
34	Mammoth Cave Mummy	Matting	2395 ± 75	2245–2545	SI 3007A	1976
35	Mammoth Cave Mummy	Internal tissue	1965 ± 65	1835–2095	SI 3007C	1976

Source: Data provided by the Cave Research Foundation Archeological Project.
*Tests E, G, and H are adjoining units. The south face of E is the north face of G, and the east fact of E is the west face of H.
†Dates run by Nuclear Science and Engineering, Pittsburgh, Pennsylvania.

Historic Use

Mammoth Cave has been a major tourist attraction since 1813 (Bridwell 1952; Bullitt 1985). In the course of its exploration and exploitation, it has been illuminated by cane torches, campfires, coal oil or kerosene lamps, candles, carbide lamps, and electric lights. In parts of Mammoth Cave, a layer of greasy soot covers everything. There have been major disturbances in portions of the cave that are shown to tourists; breakdown rock has been cleared away and trails have been built. In addition there was extensive mining of saltpeter during the War of 1812.

Salts Cave was commercialized and shown to the public early in this century (Watson 1974g; Watson et al. 1969:7–11), but the venture was never very successful, and alteration does not approach the level of disturbance in Mammoth Cave. Despite two centuries of disturbance, however, there is still a remarkable amount of prehistoric debris in both caves even in those passages that have been extensively disturbed (Watson 1985a:177).

Cave Interior

The Mammoth and Salts cave interior dates (Table 6.1) come from roughly similar contexts of dry-cave passage, deep underground, with stable environments that result in excellent preservation of organic material. The archaeological interpretation of material found in either cave's interior is complicated, however, by those same conditions because they result not only in excellent preservation but also in the contextual confusion described above. Everything found in the cave is a "surface" find in the sense that proximity of objects does not necessarily signify any temporal association.

Cave Vestibule

The environment in the Salts Cave Vestibule, the entry chamber from which one can see natural light entering the cave, is quite different from the cave interior and more what one expects from an archaeological site. There is moisture present, and preservation is limited to stone, bone, and charred organic material. There are also erosive and soil formation processes in play so that archaeological materials are buried. Entry to the Salts Cave Vestibule is at the bottom of Salts Sink, a large karst feature that acts as a drain for surface water. There is a spring at the entrance to the Vestibule. The breakdown slope that one descends from the entrance into the Vestibule is wet and slippery with water from the spring and surface runoff. At least once in the recent past (June 1984) during very heavy rains, mass wasting of the sinkhole blocked the Salts entrance completely. At that time water moved into the Vestibule with sufficient force to rearrange portions of the Vestibule floor. The Salts Vestibule served as a prehistoric habitation and/or mortuary site (Robbins 1974; Seeman 1986; Watson

1974d). The radiocarbon samples came from midden deposits interlain with waterborne strata.

Radiocarbon Determinations

The Salts Cave Vestibule dates are from samples of charcoal from the stratigraphic excavations in the Vestibule floor (Watson 1974a:71–82). In addition to charcoal, these excavations yielded quantities of bone, both human (Robbins 1974) and nonhuman (Duffield 1974), as well as chipped and ground stone tools (Watson 1974d).

Artifacts found in the interior of these caves are mainly of three different types: (1) torch and campfire debris, (2) human feces, and (3) rarer items such as squash, gourd, and fragments of cordage and textile (Watson et al. 1969; Watson and Yarnell 1966). Almost all artifacts found in the cave interiors are organic and can be dated directly. Radiocarbon determinations have been obtained on all three categories of material. In addition, there are dates on human tissue from two desiccated human bodies (Watson 1974e, 1985a). Material from the cave interiors, both Salts and Mammoth, was found either on the cave floor or amid the breakdown rocks that cover the floors of many passages. The exception to this is Test A in Salts Cave interior. Test A dates came from a 2 × 2-m excavation unit dug in arbitrary 10-cm levels to a depth of 1.5 m (Watson et al. 1969:20).

The various samples from each cave can be widely separated in space. There are more than 300 mapped miles of cave passage in the Flint/Mammoth system, several miles of which were explored prehistorically. The paleofecal sample from Upper Salts Cave found near survey station P54 is 1.3 km away from Indian Avenue in Lower Salts Cave where other samples were collected, and more than an hour of crawling and climbing is required to cover the distance. Similar spatial separation is the case in Mammoth Cave as well.

In addition to spatial separation, there is temporal variation in the dated material (Table 6.1). The oldest date from Salts Cave interior is the wood and bark from Lower Salts, Indian Avenue (3140 B.P. ± 150 [M1589]). The youngest is on tissue from the Salts Cave mummy (1920 B.P. ± 160 [M2259]). In Mammoth Cave the oldest date (4120 B.P. ± 70 [UCLA 1730A]) is on twigs from Jessup Avenue near survey station C7. The youngest Mammoth Cave date is on tissue from the Mammoth Cave mummy (1965 B.P. ± 65 [SI 3007C]). Again, these two locations are at a considerable distance from each other; it would take close to an hour to travel from Mummy Ledge, where the Mammoth Cave mummy was found, to survey station C7 in Jessup Avenue. The youngest Vestibule date (2200 B.P. ±60 [Beta 4081]) comes from unit KII, level 6; the oldest 3490 B.P. ± 110 [GaK 2767]) comes from unit H, level 2A.

I evaluate Mammoth Cave interior, Salts Cave interior, and Salts Cave Vestibule separately, although there is ambiguity in doing so. They could be treated as two sites—Salts Cave and Mammoth Cave—based on the fact that they are two caves, each of which probably had a single entrance during the period of prehistoric utilization. Conversely, it would be possible to treat each cave as several sites because of the number of passages involved and the great linear distances over which prehistoric debris is scattered. In practice, however, this would be difficult and arbitrary; artifact scatter is continuous throughout those portions of the cave that were explored prehistorically. A disparity between the initial radiocarbon determinations from Salts Cave Vestibule and those from Salts Cave interior coupled with the fact that the artifact assemblages from the vestibule and the interior are quite different established a precedent for evaluating the two areas of Salts Cave separately. I follow this precedent.

The MCNP determinations are predominantly (20 of 35 dates) first-millennium B.C. date ranges (Figure 6.1, Table 6.1). A few (4 of 35) straddle the first millennium A.D. and the first millennium B.C. A few more (8 of 35) have 2σ ranges that straddle the first and second millennia B.C. Two date ranges fall entirely within the second millennium B.C. A single range falls entirely within the third millennium B.C. Each of the three areas, the two cave interiors and Salts Vestibule, have first- and second-millennium date ranges. The third-millennium B.C. date is from lower Mammoth Cave.

In summary, then, the radiocarbon evidence is for heavy use of Salts and Mammoth caves during the first millennium B.C. and the first half of the second millennium B.C., the transition between the Archaic and Woodland periods of eastern North American prehistory.

Factors Affecting Accuracy and Precision

Before evaluating the dates in relation to each other or to broader issues in North American prehistory, the question of the accuracy and precision of the radiocarbon determinations themselves arises. These are dates on a variety of different materials discarded in an unusual underground environment. Samples were collected and laboratory determinations made over a period of almost 30 years by several different laboratories employing four variants of the gas-counting technique. The number of determinations is large and the results are consistent, but these same dates also raise a number of questions about the accuracy and precision of radiocarbon dating.

The radiocarbon process has been described and explained in various sources (Aitken 1974; Browman 1981; Currie 1982; Leute 1987; Libby 1952; Michels 1973; Renfrew 1973; Taylor 1987; Tite 1972). Interested readers are referred to these for an exhaustive treatment of ^{14}C and archaeology; I reiterate only the fundamental assumptions here.

When organic material is submitted to a laboratory for a radiocarbon determination, a number of basic assumptions about the radiocarbon dating pro-

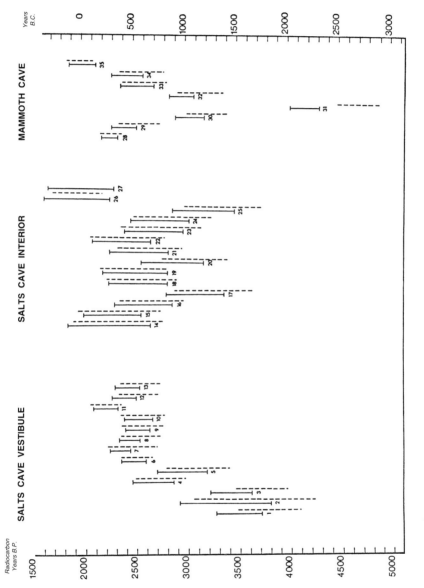

6.1 2 σ Range of Radiocarbon Determinations (*solid lines*) and Calibrations (*broken lines*) from Mammoth and Salts Caves

cess must be met for the determination to be valid and informative. Taylor (1987:3) presents five basic assumptions:

1. The concentration of ^{14}C in each carbon reservoir has remained essentially constant over the ^{14}C time scale.
2. There has been complete and rapid mixing throughout the various reservoirs.
3. Carbon isotope ratios in samples have not been altered except by ^{14}C decay since the death of the organism.
4. The half-life of ^{14}C is accurately known.
5. Natural levels of ^{14}C can be measured to appropriate levels of accuracy and precision.

Each of these assumptions can be violated, in some instances on a global or regional basis, in other instances on a sample-by-sample basis. The identification and subsequent correction of these violations have been essential to continued confidence in the radiocarbon method.

Interlaboratory Error

The MCNP dates were run at seven different laboratories (Table 6.2), all of which employed some variant of gas counting, including carbon dioxide, carbon dioxide–carbon disulfide, acetylene, and liquid scintillation (Kennedy 1990). In this situation one wonders to what extent the results from different laboratories are comparable. Would the same samples sent to different laboratories have yielded the same determinations? If all the samples had been run by one laboratory at one time, would our knowledge of the overall time span for prehistoric use of Mammoth and Salts caves be altered?

Radiocarbon laboratories have run comparisons to address these sorts of questions. They indicate that there is unexplained variation between laboratories and that the quoted error estimate alone on any radiocarbon date does not adequately reflect this (Clark 1975; Currie and Polach 1980; Polach 1972, 1979).

Counting error, represented by 1 standard deviation (σ), is only the statistical error (Leute 1987:44). Error resulting from failure or defects in machines and operators, systematic error, is much more difficult to estimate, although it undoubtedly exists (ibid.).

One interlaboratory comparison used portions of the same known-age, tree-ring samples sent to 20 different laboratories (International Study Group 1982). Results of that study indicate that the quoted error should be multiplied by a factor between 1.65 and 3, depending on the type of laboratory, to know what the "true" error is (ibid:622). The highest error multiplier is that for liquid scintillation facilities. The lowest, or the best estimates of true error, came from gas-counting laboratories that have a large (≥ 80 years) quoted error. Quoted error from high precision (≤ 20 years) and moderate precision (≤ 75–30 years) laboratories fall at an intermediate level of error underestimation.

These results suggest that in a case such as the MCNP series, run by different laboratories using different processes over a wide temporal span, the statistical uncertainty should probably be doubled. The 2σ standard error is probably an indicator of the 1σ "true" error. The International Study Group (1982:623) also urged "increased caution in attempting to resolve ^{14}C differences of less than 200 years."

Consequently, I present the MCNP dates as 2σ ranges (Figure 6.1, Table 6.1) and suggest, based on the above studies, that these should probably be regarded as the 1σ range for the series in question.

Half-life Correction

The original half-life of ^{14}C (5570 ± 30) as determined by Libby proved to be inaccurate. Several laboratories were responsible for determining that the more accurate half-life was 5730 ± 40, which came to be known as the Cambridge half-life. The Sixth International Radiocarbon Conference decided that radiocarbon laboratories would continue to employ the Libby half-life to avoid the confusion of having dates calculated by two different equations (Stuiver and Suess 1966:536). To correct a radiocarbon determination so that it reflects the Cambridge rather than the Libby half-life, the original determination should be multiplied by 1.029 (Browman 1981:244). This makes all dates slightly and uniformly older.

This correction was given relatively little attention because by the time it had been confirmed other factors had been recognized that had much more profound effects on the accuracy of ^{14}C dating (Stuiver and Suess 1966:536). Secular trend, reservoir effects, and fractionation effects, factors that affect dates differentially, proved more disquieting than a simple mathematical correction uniformly applied to all dates. Most important, by that time it was clear that the better fit to the sidereal calendar that the new half-life provided was less significant than calibration of the radiocarbon calendar to tree-ring chronology and ultimately to sidereal time.

Calibration

Radiocarbon concentration in the earth's atmosphere has not been constant through time (Damon 1982; Damon and Linick 1986; Suess 1986). Proof of this secular variation in atmospheric ^{14}C levels is provided when samples of known age—the age having been determined by dendrochronology—are radiocarbon dated. Over the last 20 years several radiocarbon laboratories have undertaken fine-grained studies of tree-ring samples. Both the ^{14}C age and the dendro date of samples are plotted on a master chart. This comparison of the two categories of data produces a sine wave with a peak-to-peak amplitude of about 10% and a period of about 10,000 years (Suess 1986:261). The master plot, once estab-

Table 6.2. Radiocarbon Determinations Arranged in Chronological Order by Year of Laboratory Determination

Laboratory Provenience	Material	^{14}C Age B.P. $\pm 1\sigma$	2σ Range	Number	Year Run
Nuclear Science and Engineering					
Upper Mammoth	Slipper	2230 ± 40	2150–2310	X 8	1957
Upper Mammoth	Cane	2370 ± 60	2250–2490	X 9	1957
Isotopes					
Upper Salts, P54	Soot	3075 ± 140	2795–3355	I 256	1961
University of Michigan					
Upper Salts, P54	Feces w/squash seeds	2240 ± 200	1840–2640	M 1573	1966
Upper Salts, P38	Feces	2270 ± 140	1990–2550	M 1777	1966
Middle Salts, Blue Arrow, A60	Feces w/squash pollen	2350 ± 140	2070–2630	M 1577	1966
Test A, 30–40 cm	Cane	2430 ± 130	2170–2690	M 1585	1966
Test A, 0–10 cm	Cane	2510 ± 140	2230–2790	M 1584	1966
Test A, 140 cm	Wood	2520 ± 140	2240–2800	M 1587	1966
Upper Salts, P63–64	Feces w/gourd seeds	2570 ± 140	2290–2850	M 1574	1966
Middle Salts, Blue Arrow, A42	Feces w/sunflower achenes	2660 ± 140	2380–2940	M 1770	1966
Lower Salts, Indian Av. I76	Wood	2720 ± 140	2440–3000	M 1588	1966
Test A, 70–80 cm	Cane	2840 ± 150	2540–3140	M 1586	1966
Lower Salts, Indian Av. I67	Wood and bark	3140 ± 150	2840–3340	M 1589	1966
Gakashuin					
Test E, Level 7b	Charcoal	2660 ± 100	2460–2860	GaK 2622	1970
Test E, Level 7b	Charcoal	2940 ± 120	2700–3180	GaK 2765	1970
Test E, Level 5	Charcoal	3360 ± 220	2920–3800	GaK 2764	1970
Test G, Level 6	Charcoal	3410 ± 100	3210–3610	GaK 2766	1970
Test H, F 2A	Charcoal	3490 ± 110	3270–3710	GaK 2767	1970

Sample	Material	Radiocarbon age	Calibrated range	Lab number	Year
University of Michigan					
Salts Cave Mummy	Internal tissue	1920 ± 70	1600–2240	M 2259	1971
Salts Cave Mummy	Internal tissue	1960 ± 70	1640–2280	M 2258	1971
UCLA					
Lower Mammoth, Ganter, B10	Wood	3000 ± 70	2860–3140	UCLA 1730B	1971
Lower Mammoth, Jessup, C7	Twigs	4120 ± 70	3980–4260	UCLA 1730A	1971
Smithsonian					
Mammoth Cave Mummy	Internal tissue	1965 ± 65	1835–2095	SI 3007C	1976
Mammoth Cave Mummy	Matting	2395 ± 75	2245–2545	SI 3007A	1976
Beta Analytic					
Test KII, Level 6	Charcoal	2200 ± 60	2080–2320	Beta 4081	1982
Test JIV, Level 6	Charcoal	2350 ± 50	2240–2440	Beta 4650	1982
Test KII, Level 11	Charcoal	2380 ± 60	2260–2500	Beta 4082	1982
Test KII, Level 14	Charcoal	2410 ± 60	2290–2530	Beta 4083	1982
Test JIV, Level 8	Charcoal	2430 ± 50	2330–2530	Beta 4651	1982
Test JIV, Level 4	Charcoal	2470 ± 60	2350–2590	Beta 4649	1982
Test JIV, Level 11	Charcoal	2510 ± 60	2390–2630	Beta 4652	1982
Test KII, Level 4	Charcoal	2520 ± 70	2380–2660	Beta 4080	1982
Smithsonian					
Lower Mammoth, W21-B	Cane charcoal	2495 ± 80	2335–2655	SI 6890B	1985
Lower Mammoth, W21-A	Cane charcoal	2920 ± 60	2800–3040	SI 6890A	1985

Source: Data provided by the Cave Research Foundation Archeological Project.

lished, also serves as a means of calibrating any ^{14}C date within that time period.

Calibrated dates are both a boon and a problem for archaeologists. In areas and time periods where independent chronologies already exist—the Old World civilizations of Egypt and the Fertile Crescent where records tie events to firm calendrical dates; the prehistoric American Southwest where dendrochronological sequences tie sites to the sidereal calendar; Mesoamerican sites that are tied to the Maya calendar—calibrated dates make it possible to relate ^{14}C determinations to independent chronologies (Taylor 1987:134). Calibration is widely employed in these areas and time periods.

But there is more than one calibration table. The first appeared more than 20 years ago (Suess 1967); many refinements have subsequently appeared (see Klein et al. 1982 for a list of 17 calibration tables appearing in a 13-year period); and although the decadal and bidecadal sample tables published in the proceedings of the Twelfth International Radiocarbon Conference (Pearson and Stuiver 1986; Stuiver and Pearson 1986) are by far the most fine-grained of these, they too will be superseded. To avoid confusion, the original ^{14}C determination must always be reported. If an archaeologist wishes to report a calibrated date, he or she must specify the calibration table that was used (Stuckenrath 1977).

There are areas of the world, such as the prehistoric eastern United States, where chronologies have been established solely on the basis of radiocarbon dates. Calibration is not widely employed in these areas because comparison is to other sites within the region, the dates of which are radiocarbon determinations rather than calendar dates. To report dates calibrated to sidereal time when the sequence has been established on radiocarbon time tends to confuse the issue. Presumably, as regional sequences are refined, calibration becomes more widespread and interregional chronologies are attempted, the use of calibration will become more widespread.

The Twelfth International Radiocarbon Conference adopted a bidecadal data set from A.D. 1950 to 2500 B.C. (Pearson and Stuiver 1986; Stuiver and Pearson 1986) as its recommended calibration curve. This internationally accepted data set was combined with others (Kromer et al. 1986; Linick, Suess, and Becker 1985; Pearson et al. 1986; Stuiver et al. 1986) for the period 2500 B.C. to 7210 B.C. to produce a radiocarbon age data set based on 20-year sample intervals back to 8200 B.P. (Stuiver and Reimer 1986). The University of Washington Quaternary Isotope Lab has made available interactive computer software that automatically calibrates dates against this bidecadal sample data set (ibid.). The MCNP dates have been calibrated using CALIB software, the 20-year sample, and no-error multiplier (Figure 6.1).

Calibrated MCNP dates (Figure 6.1) do not show a uniform relationship to the original ^{14}C determination. Most are slightly older, but some are slightly younger, one is significantly older, and all but two show an increase in the date range inherent in the calibration process. The two dates on the Salts Cave mummy have a decreased standard error because they have been averaged into a single calibrated date, a procedure that is warranted if there is more than one date on the same sample (ibid.). Calibration of the MCNP dates (Figure 6.1) does not significantly alter the time period for cave utilization. The dates still fall within the first and second millennia B.C., because this is a time when the radiocarbon and tree-ring curves are not widely divergent. The most striking effect of calibration is on the oldest date: it is made older still because it falls in a period when radiocarbon dates are younger than dendro dates, that is, a period when the atmospheric level of ^{14}C appears to have been greater.

This has a lengthening effect on the period of cave utilization. In radiocarbon years, the period of use extends from 1920 B.P. $\pm$ 160 to 4120 B.P. $\pm$ 70, or a 2,660-year span (2σ). Calibrating these dates produces a 2σ range from 1614 to 4849 B.P. (Kennedy 1990, Appendix B), or 3,235 years. If calibrated dates are used, then the duration of cave use is almost 600 years longer than when uncalibrated radiocarbon years are employed. In the case of Salts and Mammoth caves this effect is ameliorated to a certain extent because there is a single early date, and the other 34 dates remain clustered in a portion of the curve that is not greatly altered by calibration. It is, however, a strong argument for running the calibration program on any series of dates to determine and report the relative effects of calibration.

Contamination

Contamination is the presence of any carbon-containing compound not originally part of the sample and having a different ^{14}C activity—either younger or older—from that of the material in question. One of the most common contaminants of charcoal and wood deposited in soil is organic carbonate ($CaCO_3$) from percolating groundwater (Taylor 1987:41). The dissolved calcium carbonate in groundwater is composed of carbon whose ^{14}C activity can be very low. In the karst landscape of MCNP, water contains calcium carbonate dissolved from the 300-million-year-old limestones through which it has traveled. In view of the hydrologically active situation in Salts Cave Vestibule, charcoal from those excavations would be subject to carbonate contamination. Fortunately, the removal of $CaCO_3$ is the most widely used and effective pretreatment procedure for ^{14}C samples (ibid.). Pretreatment with a solution of hot hydrochloric acid (HCl) removes absorbed calcium carbonate from the sample so that only the original fixed carbon of the sample remains (Libby 1970; Olsson 1979:135).

Samples from the cave interior are not subject to groundwater contamination because the passages in question have been dry for hundreds of thousands of years before archaeological material was deposited there, but there are potential contaminants present in the dry cave interior. The use of various fuels for light has introduced fossil carbon contaminants. Today cave tours are lit by electricity, but in the commercial history of the cave, substances such as coal oil, kerosene, and calcium carbide have all been used. All of these substances are derivatives of coal, a fossil fuel, and all of them release a soot of dead carbon that, if present in sufficient quantity in a ^{14}C sample, could alter the date. The same procedure that removes calcium carbonate is effective in removing this soot. Treatment with a solution of hot hydrochloric acid eats away the outer layer of the sample on which the soot would have settled.

Even with careful pretreatment it is possible for samples to remain contaminated with either fossil or modern carbon. As a result, the level of alteration caused by various levels of contamination has been calculated (Olsson 1974, 1979). If the MCNP samples were contaminated to such a degree that pretreatment was ineffective in removing soot and 1% of the sample was actually composed of soot from the burning of kerosene or carbide, the date would be too old by 80 years. If contaminants comprised 10% of the sample the date would be too old by 800 years.

The likelihood of 10% contamination seems quite small because of the nature of the samples. These are whole, uncharred specimens of cane, wood, and human feces. In other words, there is little question as to the integrity of the samples. One exception to this is the date obtained on a sample of soot scraped from the cave wall at a single limited location in Salts Cave (3075 ± 140 [I-256], Benington, Melton, and Watson 1962). The date itself is consistent with the rest of the MCNP dates, although slightly older than most. This suggests that the soot being dated came predominantly from aboriginal torches, but if, for example, 12% is actually kerosene soot and 4% came from the burning of candles in the late nineteenth century, it would be not only quite difficult to determine this but also quite possible to get a "composite" date of 1190 B.C.

In addition to fossil carbon contamination, which would cause samples to date too old, modern organic material such as wood, candles, and lard oil also have been burned during the historic era of cave use. These could leave a film of modern carbon on prehistoric samples, which would result in dates that are too young. Modern contaminants can have a profound effect on ^{14}C dates if the samples are of Pleistocene age (Waterbolk 1971:18), but for material in the age range of the MCNP samples the effects are less dramatic: 1% modern contaminants would make the date 20 to 40 years too young, and 10% sample contamination would alter the date by 160 to 360 years (Browman 1981:251; Olsson 1974:313).

Although there is no substitute for informing a laboratory of all possible contaminants and for the rigorous pretreatment of samples, it is reassuring that with Holocene samples between 2,000 and 4,000 years old, contamination would have to occur on a very large scale to alter dates by more than a few decades (Taylor 1987:120). The period in question is, in many ways, the least problematic for the radiocarbon process.

An additional source of contamination is present in the form of radon gas. Radon levels in the Mammoth Cave system constitute sufficient health risk that Park Service personnel are allowed to spend only a limited number of hours underground within a given time period. Radon (^{222}Rn) is a naturally occurring, alpha particle–emitting product of the breakdown of the radioactive element ^{238}U (Nydal 1983:502). When present in a ^{14}C sample, radon causes the sample to return a date that is too young, because the decay of radon creates ^{214}Pb and ^{214}Bi, radioactive daughter elements that emit beta particles and add to the count rate in most gas-counting systems (ibid). The sample appears more radioactive than it actually is based on ^{14}C content alone. Because radon contamination is common, particularly in underground settings and in soils (Browman 1981:249; Olsson 1979), its potential as a contaminant in ^{14}C samples and laboratories was recognized quite early (Barker 1953; de Vries 1957; Suess 1954). Fortunately, the half-life of radon is only 3.824 days (Polach and Kaihola 1988:20). Once a sample is removed from a radon-contaminated environment, it need sit for only three to four weeks before radon decays to undetectable levels. Some laboratories routinely set samples aside for three to four weeks, once they have been converted to a gas, to alleviate the effects of radon contamination; others employ cold traps to separate radon from carbon dioxide (CO_2) (Browman 1981:249).

The MCNP samples have been subject to some of the most common contaminants. Laboratories have been apprised of the presence of groundwater and fossil fuels in the vicinity of the samples when samples were submitted and presumably have performed all necessary pretreatment procedures. Archaeologists were unaware of radon levels in the caves until after most of the MCNP dates were submitted. Materials submitted for radiocarbon dating in the future will include this information so that the laboratory is aware of the potential for contamination. In view of the short half-life of the isotope and of the fact that laboratories are routinely concerned with in-house radon levels, it seems unlikely that any of these potential sources of contamination have appreciably altered the dates from the Flint-Mammoth Cave System.

Carbon Isotope Ratios

In addition to contamination, another source of error in ^{14}C dates comes from differences in carbon isotope ratios in some types of samples. The atmospheric ratios of the carbon isotopes ^{12}C/^{13}C/^{14}C are 98.9:1.1:10^{-10} (Taylor 1987:76), but various circumstances can alter these natural or expected ratios.

Isotopic Fractionation

Isotopic fractionation can occur in chemical reactions involving carbon-containing compounds. Photosynthesis as well as other metabolic reactions present the opportunity for carbon to be taken up in something other than the expected ratios of stable (^{12}C) to unstable (^{14}C) isotopes. This sample-by-sample violation means that the ratio at the time of the sample's death was different from expected.

Fortunately, the $^{12}C/^{14}C$ ratio at the time of the sample's death is predictable from the ratio of the stable isotopes, ^{12}C to ^{13}C, regardless of the sample's age. The stable isotope ratio is measured with a mass spectrometer, a relatively simple and inexpensive procedure as long as the laboratory has access to such facilities. The $^{12}C/^{13}C$ measurement of a sample is referred to as its $\delta^{13}C$ value. Standards have been established for determining $\delta^{13}C$ values and for determining the true ages of samples with differing $\delta^{13}C$ values (Taylor 1987:100–101). The $\delta^{13}C$ value of a sample is determined in relation to the PDB standard. PDB stands for Peedee belemnite, a calcium carbonate fossil mollusc from the Cretaceous Peedee Formation of South Carolina (Browman 1981:249; Taylor 1987:100). The $\delta^{13}C$ of PDB is a "zero" standard; the $\delta^{13}C$ of a sample is expressed in relation to the standard in parts per mil. A wood sample usually has a $\delta^{13}C$ value of -25 per mil with respect to (wrt) PDB; it has 25 parts per mil or 2.5% less ^{13}C than the PDB standard (Taylor 1987:121). As a result, the wood sample appears 400 years older than a marine shell sample (with a $\delta^{13}C$ of 0) that is actually the same age as the wood.

If the $\delta^{13}C$ is known, the enrichment or depletion of ^{14}C can be determined from it. The $\delta^{13}C$ times two ($\times 2$) equals the difference in ^{14}C concentration of the sample (ibid.). By convention, the ^{13}C of wood (-25 per mil wrt PDB) is considered normal. When correcting ^{14}C determinations for isotopic fractionation, the sample is normalized to -25 wrt PDB.

Fractionation from Photosynthesis

One cause of isotopic fractionation is the photosynthetic reaction. When plants ingest CO_2 from the atmosphere, they discriminate against heavier carbon molecules (^{13}C and ^{14}C) (Browman 1981:270). But there are at least three different photosynthetic pathways, or three different levels of discrimination. Most plants native to temperate regions use the C_3, or Calvin-Benson, pathway; most grasses native to arid tropical environments use the C_4, or Slack-Hatch, pathway; a third group of plants native to desert environments employ the Crassulacean Acid Metabolism (CAM) pathway in the photosynthetic process (ibid.). What this means is that a temperate-region plant is taking in proportionately less ^{14}C than is the C_4 tropical plant. Consequently, a sample composed of pine (a C_3 plant) and a sample composed of corn cobs and kernels (a C_4 plant), even though the plants are the same age, would return disparate radiocarbon determinations. The corn would appear to be as much as 250 years younger than the wood because its C_4 pathway has caused it to have a higher proportion of ^{14}C than the C_3 plant (ibid.:271).

When the cave interior dates are arranged in chronological order (Table 6.3), one sees that dates on wood tend to be older than dates on nonwood materials such as cane (*Arundinaria*) and textiles. There are several possible explanations for this phenomenon:

1. The determinations are accurate. Of the MCNP material dated, the wood samples just happen to be older than the nonwood samples in most instances.

2. The nonwood samples are C_4 plants, and this causes them to return younger dates than the wood. Although *Arundinaria* is not listed among C_4 plants (Downton 1975; Rahavendra and Das 1978), these lists are not exhaustive. The fact that cane is believed to be native to Kentucky does, however, make it unlikely that it is a C_4 plant.

3. Another phenomenon may be responsible here. Nonwood material, particularly annual plants, tend to return dates that are too "young" by as much as 120 years (Baxter and Walton 1971). This phenomenon was originally explained as the result of heliomagnetic variation or short-term secular trend, which is visible in annual plants, but is averaged out in the composite dates of wood samples (Taylor 1987:47). Evidence for short-term perturbations in ^{14}C concentrations, although present, is still problematic (Browman 1981:263).

4. Estimates of fractionation effects do exist based on data from large numbers of $\delta^{13}C$ measurements (Burleigh, Mathews, and Leese 1984; Stuckenrath 1977; Stuiver and Polach 1977). These suggest that annual plants do tend to have a slightly higher $\delta^{13}C$ value (-20 to -22 per mil) than wood (-25 per mil), even when they are C_3 plants (Stuiver and Polach 1977:358). As a result, the nonwood dates would be made slightly (30–100 years) older by correction.

5. Finally, the older dates on wood samples could be the result of a bias toward greater age in wood samples inherent in the nature of the plant (Neustupný 1970:26). A mature tree can be anywhere from a few decades to hundreds of years old. Depending on what part of the ring structure comprised the material for dating, the ^{14}C determination might reflect the early years of growth rather than the date of death. In addition to this accident of sampling for any particular tree, wood presents other complications as a dating material. Any wood sample tends to be a composite of many years because of the ring structure of the tree, rather than a simple "year" in which it ceased to take in CO_2 (Dean 1986). Finally, trees can remain in a usable or combustible state for many years after the plant has died, a factor that can also contribute to "old" dates. All of these considerations muddy the meaning of a ^{14}C determination on wood. At most archaeological sites wood, in the form of wood charcoal, is the most commonly occurring and most reliable substance for dating. In rarer circumstances, such as those in the Mammoth and Salts cave interiors, where a wider variety of nonwood samples are available, these biases in wood dates may become more obvious.

To determine whether isotopic fractionation has occurred in a particular sample and whether the date should be corrected for fractionation, the $\delta^{13}C$ value would have to be determined (see above). No $\delta^{13}C$ values were run on any of the cave samples, and none of the dates have been corrected for fractionation. At the time when the majority of MCNP dates were run, it was not standard practice to request or run $\delta^{13}C$ values. Today, a conventional ^{14}C date, by agree-

Table 6.3. Cave Interior Dates Arranged in Chronological Order

Site Provenience	Material	^{14}C Years B.P. ± 1σ	2σ Range	Lab Number	Year Run
Salts Cave Vestibule					
Test KII, Level 6	Charcoal	2200 ± 60	2080–2320	Beta 4081	1982
Test JIV, Level 6	Charcoal	2340 ± 50	2240–2440	Beta 4650	1982
Test KII, Level 11	Charcoal	2380 ± 60	2260–2500	Beta 4082	1982
Test KII, Level 14	Charcoal	2410 ± 60	2290–2530	Beta 4083	1982
Test JIV, Level 8	Charcoal	2430 ± 50	2330–2530	Beta 4651	1982
Test JIV, Level 4	Charcoal	2470 ± 60	2350–2590	Beta 4649	1982
Test JIV, Level 11	Charcoal	2510 ± 60	2390–2630	Beta 4652	1982
Test KII, Level 4	Charcoal	2520 ± 70	2380–2660	Beta 4080	1982
Test E, Level 7b	Charcoal	2660 ± 100	2460–2860	GaK 2622	1970
Test E, Level 7b	Charcoal	2940 ± 120	2700–3180	GaK 2765	1970
Test E, Level 5	Charcoal	3360 ± 220	2920–3800	GaK 2764	1970
Test G, Level 6	Charcoal	3410 ± 100	3210–3610	GaK 2766	1970
Test H, F 2A	Charcoal	3490 ± 110	3270–3710	GaK 2767	1970
Salts Cave Interior					
Salts Cave Mummy	Internal tissue	1920 ± 160	1600–2240	M 2259	1971
Salts Cave Mummy	Internal tissue	1960 ± 160	1640–2280	M 2258	1971
Upper Salts, P54	Feces w/ squash seeds	2240 ± 200	1840–2640	M 1573	1966

	Material	Range	Lab No.	Year
Upper Salts, P38	Feces	2270 ± 140	1990–2550	M 1777	1966
Middle Salts, Blue Arrow, A60	Feces w/squash pollen	2350 ± 140	2070–2630	M 1577	1966
Test A, 30–40 cm	Cane	2430 ± 130	2170–2690	M 1585	1966
Test A, 0–10 cm	Cane	2510 ± 140	2230–2790	M 1584	1966
Test A, 140 cm	Wood	2520 ± 140	2240–2800	M 1587	1966
Upper Salts, P63–64	Feces w/gourd seeds	2570 ± 140	2290–2850	M 1574	1966
Middle Salts, Blue Arrow, A42	Feces w/sunflower achenes	2660 ± 140	2380–2940	M 1770	1966
Lower Salts, Indian Av. I76	Wood	2720 ± 140	2440–3000	M 1588	1966
Test A, 70–80 cm	Cane	2840 ± 150	2540–3140	M 1586	1966
Upper Salts, P54	Soot	3075 ± 140	2795–3355	I 256	1961
Lower Salts, Indian Av. I67	Wood and bark	3140 ± 150	2840–3440	M 1589	1966
Mammoth Cave Interior					
Mammoth Cave Mummy	Internal tissue	1965 ± 65	1835–2095	SI 3007C	1976
Upper Mammoth	Slipper	2230 ± 40	2150–2310	X 8	1957
Upper Mammoth	Cane	2370 ± 60	2250–2490	X 9	1957
Mammoth Cave Mummy	Matting	2395 ± 75	2245–2545	SI 3007A	1976
Lower Mammoth, W21-B	Cane charcoal	2495 ± 80	2335–2655	SI 6890B	1985
Lower Mammoth, W21-A	Cane charcoal	2920 ± 60	2800–3040	SI 6890A	1985
Lower Mammoth, Ganter, B10	Wood	3000 ± 70	2860–3140	UCLA 1730B	1971
Lower Mammoth, Jessup, C7	Twigs	4120 ± 70	3980–4260	UCLA 1730A	1971

Source: Data provided by the Cave Research Foundation Archeological Project.

ment of the scientists who run radiocarbon laboratories, is one that has been corrected for isotopic fractionation (Stuiver and Polach 1977). This is another case, however, where practice lags behind recommendation. Unless the laboratory has access to a mass spectrometer and the consumer requests a $\delta^{13}C$ determination, it will not necessarily be run.

The problem of fractionation was recognized very early in the life of the ^{14}C technique (Craig 1953, 1954), but the photosynthetic mechanism was not identified until much more recently (Bender 1968, 1971). Correction for isotopic fractionation did not become routine until this process was understood.

Fractionation in Animal Tissue

Three of the MCNP dates are from human tissue samples. Two (1920 B.P. ± 160 [M2259] and 1960 B.P. ± 160 [M2258]) are from the Salts Cave mummy (Robbins 1974) and were run by the University of Michigan lab. They show excellent agreement, as would be expected from two dates run on the same body. The third human tissue date is on the Mammoth Cave mummy (Neumann 1938; Pond 1937; Robbins 1974; Watson and Yarnell 1986). Several items believed to have been associated with the Mammoth Cave mummy were also dated (2230 B.P. ± 40 [X8]; 2370 B.P. ± 60 [X9]; and 2395 B.P. ± 75 [SI 3007A]). Internal tissue from the body itself returned a date of 1965 B.P. ± 65 (SI 3007C). The association between the body and either the torch (X8) or the slipper (X9) is somewhat tenuous; the material was believed to be in association with the body, but this is largely hearsay (see Kennedy 1990, Appendix A). The matting is attached to the body. Nonetheless, the 2σ ranges of the matting and the tissue dates do not overlap (Table 6.1). The body was on display in the cave for many years, and the matting may have been treated with a preservative (Watson and Yarnell 1986:245). In addition, isotopic fractionation is probably involved here. The laboratory indicates that the human tissue date may be too young by as much as 100 years "due to inherent metabolic isotopic fractionation in body tissues" (letter from Smithsonian Radiocarbon laboratory, Kennedy 1990, Appendix A). This is an estimated correction; no $\delta^{13}C$ measurement was made.

Few dates have been run on the soft tissues of mammalian species. The animal tissues that normally survive in archaeological contexts are bone and teeth. Consequently, there is a more extensive literature on the problems inherent in the dating of human and animal bone (Protsch 1986; Taylor 1982, 1987; Zimmerman and Angel 1986) and relatively little written about soft-tissue dates. The $\delta^{13}C$ values for 76 samples of healthy human tissue fell between -21 and -26 with a mean of -23 per mil (Lyon and Baxter 1978). Similar $\delta^{13}C$ values were obtained on nonhuman mammalian tissue. Sheepskins that had been made into parchment had a range from -18 to -24 (Berger et al. 1972). This expected enrichment in the carbon isotope ratios of animal tissue is consistent with the findings from MCNP, where the three human tissue dates are the three most recent dates for the entire series. If corrected for fractionation these dates would be older and more consistent with the other 32 dates.

An animal's stable isotope ratios are directly related to its diet (DeNiro and Epstein 1978). Testing of a variety of small animals, vertebrates and invertebrates, showed that the $\delta^{13}C$ value is slightly enriched (1 per mil ± 3 per mil) in comparison with the $\delta^{13}C$ of the diet (ibid.:495). Paleofecal specimens, being an amalgam of annual plants, animal tissue, and the secretions of the human digestive system, might also be expected to show evidence of isotopic fractionation. DeNiro and Epstein (1978:500) found that feces have a slightly different $\delta^{13}C$ value from that of the animal itself or the animal's diet.

Two things should be considered with regard to stable isotope ratios and the MCNP dates. First, isotope ratios can be estimated, but the only way to determine with any certainty whether corrections should be applied is to measure the stable isotope ratio for each sample (Stuiver and Polach 1977; Stuiver and Reimer 1986). Because $\delta^{13}C$ values were not determined for any of the samples, any attempt to predict whether corrections should be applied is informed speculation. Second, the estimated level of correction is small. Annual plants, human tissues, and paleofeces from a temperate environment would be expected to differ from the norm by only a few parts per mil, if at all. Correction would most likely make these dates older by a few decades or perhaps 100 years. The most extreme corrections for fractionation alter a date by 250 to 400 years, but these cases involve types of samples (C_4 plants, marine shell, bone apatite) not present in the MCNP series. Correction in this case would be expected to offer a form of "fine-tuning" rather than a major reordering of the dates.

Many violations of the basic assumptions of the radiocarbon dating process have been identified. But almost all of these—interlaboratory error, half-life correction, calibration, contamination, and isotopic fractionation—are predictable, understandable phenomena. Although these violations and discrepancies must be considered in evaluating the MCNP series, there is no convincing evidence that they significantly distort the determinations.

Interpretation of Dates

Regional Chronology

The periods of North American prehistory were formulated based on relative dating and cultural stages. In this original formulation, the Archaic was an aceramic period of diverse, highly adapted and adaptive hunting and gathering strategies. The succeeding Woodland period was characterized by the addition of pottery, agriculture, mortuary ceremonialism, and burial mounds to the cultural repertoire. This general schema was already in place when the radiocarbon dating process was introduced, making it possible to place prehistory on a more refined and absolute time line. The combination of ^{14}C dates and subsequent research has done a great deal to obscure the original elegance of the outline.

The presence of pottery is the most widely accepted diagnostic marker for the beginning of the Woodland period, but radiocarbon dates show that pottery was added to the material repertoire at different times in different regions. The earliest ceramics appear well before Early Woodland. Stallings Island pottery, a fiber-tempered ware from coastal Georgia and South Carolina, dates to 2500 B.C. (Jenkins, Dye, and Walthall 1986:546). In Mississippi and Alabama, Wheeler ceramics date to 1150 B.C. (ibid.:548). Vinette ware from southern Ontario and New York dates to 1000 B.C. (Emerson 1986:623). In east Tennessee the Watts Bar/Swannanoa pottery complex appears at 1000–700 B.C. (Butler and Jefferies 1986:531). In southern Illinois and extreme western Kentucky the earliest ceramics appear at 600 B.C. (ibid.:528). Along the Ohio River the earliest pottery appears at 600–500 B.C. (Emerson 1986:623). Consequently, even a single indicator such as the introduction of pottery does not provide a single answer to when Late Archaic ends and when Early Woodland begins.

Originally it was thought that the Early Woodland period saw the introduction not only of pottery but also of settled village life dependent on maize agriculture, which had come either from the southwestern United States or from Mexico (Griffin 1952b:358). Since the 1960s a wealth of subsistence data has been collected from a number of different projects throughout the Midwest and the Midsouth (see Fritz 1990; B. Smith 1989, 1992b; Watson 1989; Yarnell 1986 for summaries) that have radically altered this first interpretation. Present evidence indicates that maize does not appear until the Woodland period. Corn probably was not relied on as a major dietary complex of maize/beans/squash until the succeeding Mississippian period (Smith 1992a). More important, archaeobotanical evidence has shown that plants were intentionally grown and altered prior to the Woodland period. Depending on the species in question, the earliest evidence for domesticated forms in the eastern Woodlands has been pushed back to Late and even Middle Archaic (Fritz 1990; Smith 1992a, b; Watson 1989; Yarnell 1986). Among these are plants native to the area, which means that the domestication of plants not only preceded Early Woodland but also was, at least in part and perhaps in total, an indigenous development in eastern North America. These native crops are believed to have supplemented the array of gathered foods rather than replaced them.

These factors—the geographical and temporal variation in the introduction of pottery, the pushing back of the beginnings of plant cultivation into the Archaic, the pushing forward of the reliance on maize agriculture into the Mississippian, the limited geographical extent of certain mortuary manifestations such as burial mounds (Emerson 1986:621–22), an increasing awareness of the complexity of Archaic adaptations (Keegan, ed., 1987; Neusius 1986; Phillips and Brown, eds., 1983; Price and Brown, eds., 1985)—all serve to blur the original distinction between Archaic and Woodland.

This blurring has provoked a variety of responses. In some regions it has been suggested that there is no Early Woodland period (Gibbon 1986; Spence and Fox 1986). Some authors suggest that Early Woodland is an obsolete category (Lewis 1986:171). Recent discussions stress gradualism from Archaic through Woodland; they present the transition as accretional changes in a long-standing, successful adaptive strategy (Brown 1986:599; Watson 1989:557). Another response is to attempt to redraw the outline with new terms and special attention to new data (Stoltman 1978).

The terms with all their temporal/formal confusion are so firmly established, however, that whether or not it is the best scheme, there still seems to be need for terminology that includes a Late Archaic period, an Early Woodland period, and a date when the former ends and the latter begins. That has been placed at 1700 B.C. (Brown 1986:602), 1500 B.C. (Jennings 1977:24), 1000 B.C. (G. Willey 1966), and 700 B.C. (Stoltman 1978), and this is not an exhaustive list. I use 1000 B.C. as the dividing point between Late Archaic and Early Woodland for heuristic purposes.

Salts and Mammoth caves are more than two sites that date to the Archaic/Woodland transition. Both sites appear to have been utilized not only throughout the entire transition (by almost anyone's scheme) but also at no other periods. Both sites provide an extraordinary quantity and kind of evidence—hundreds of human paleofecal samples—for answering questions about what people actually ate. Add to this the fact that paleofeces can be dated by the radiocarbon method and that there is, in addition, an abundance of other datable prehistoric material present in either cave, and one begins to see why these sites (particularly Salts Cave, where the majority of archaeological work has been done) have figured in discussions of the Archaic/Woodland transition for the last 20 years and will continue to do so.

Salts Cave, Mammoth Cave, and the Origins of Horticulture

If the radiocarbon technique had never been discovered and the economic/ subsistence emphasis had not come to the fore in North American archaeology, Salts and Mammoth caves would still be noteworthy sites. They preserve quantities of perishable material, provide a unique record of prehistoric deep-cave exploration, and indicate the importance of certain cave minerals in prehistoric life. It is, however, as a source of detailed datable information on prehistoric diet that these two sites have been most informative. And it was in this context that the majority of radiocarbon dates were obtained. Any discussion of the Salts Cave and Mammoth Cave radiocarbon dates is difficult to extricate from a discussion of the origins of horticulture in the Eastern Woodlands of North America and from certain historical accidents of sampling.

The first series of dates obtained by the CRF archaeological project came exclusively from Salts Cave interior. These were dates on cane, wood, and paleofeces. The cane and wood came from both the upper and lower levels of Salts

Cave, the paleofeces from upper and middle Salts Cave. The dated paleofeces contained the same types of botanical material as the 100 analyzed specimens from Salts (Yarnell 1969, 1974b) and the 27 from Mammoth Cave (Marquardt 1974; R. Stewart 1974). They indicate that the complex of sunflower, sumpweed, and chenopod was a major element in the diet of the Salts cavers (Watson et al. 1969; Watson and Yarnell 1966). All five dated fecal specimens returned mid-first millennium B.C., or Early Woodland, dates (Table 6.1). There are two Salts Cave interior dates that span the Late Archaic/Early Woodland transition (based on 2σ range), but these are on a sample of soot scraped from the wall in upper Salts and from a sample of wood and bark from lower Salts. The evidence for prehistoric diet indicates that in the mid-first millennium B.C. people were making use of domesticated sunflower and sumpweed and of some form of chenopod as well as domesticated squash and gourd.

The second series of dates came from the Vestibule excavations. Flotation samples yielded the same types of plant material as the human feces, but the five radiocarbon determinations extended into the mid-second millennium B.C. and overlapped very little with the paleofecal dates from inside the cave. Squash was present in the Vestibule, but only in the uppermost habitation level. This led to speculation that it was the native cultigens, the indigenous weedy annuals and oily seed plants, that were first domesticated in eastern North America, followed later by the introduction of Mesoamerican domesticates (Watson 1974f:235; Yarnell 1974b:117).

This hypothesis was later shown to be in error, first at the Archaic shell mounds nearby on the Green River (Marquardt and Watson 1983b), and later at other sites throughout the Midwest and Midsouth where domesticated squash and gourd are present before any other cultigens. The most recent evidence indicates that squash and gourd may be domesticates of indigenous species rather than Mesoamerican imports (see Fritz 1990; B. Smith 1992a, for discussions and recapitulations of the evidence for early domesticates in eastern North America).

The initial dates from Salts Cave interior and Vestibule have been supplemented and corroborated by additional dates from Mammoth Cave and from Salts. Most notable of these are the dates on tissue from the two human bodies. In addition to dating the bodies, project personnel examined the intestinal contents of both mummies (Watson and Yarnell 1986; Yarnell 1974a): the two individuals were shown to have eaten the same types of food found in the paleofeces.

A third major series of dates has recently been obtained on material from the Vestibule excavations (Gardner 1987). These were run in hopes of resolving questions arising from the original archaeobotanical evidence. The initial series of Vestibule dates indicated that these are Late Archaic deposits, but the flotation samples contained a combination of plant material (sunflower, sumpweed, chenopod) not expected to be present in these proportions (estimated contribution to total food 42% [Yarnell 1974b:122]) until Early Woodland times (Gardner 1987:359). Gardner (1987:358–59) undertook this additional research for two reasons: (1) the radiocarbon dates had all come from Test E, whereas most of the archaeobotanical samples had come from unit JIV; and (2) the JIV flotation series was believed to be an inadequate sample, and therefore additional material from nearby unit KII was analyzed (ibid.:360, Figure 1). The new dates (Table 6.1) show that the JIV and KII deposits are Early Woodland rather than Late Archaic in age. The KII analysis indicates that cucurbits are present in the lower as well as the upper levels of Salts Cave Vestibule (ibid.:363).

Vestibule Dates

Although this new, larger sample alters the Vestibule chronology and brings it into agreement not only with the archaeobotanical evidence from inside the cave but also with archaeobotanical evidence for this region at this time, two problems remain unresolved. First, the Test E dates are significantly older than JIV and KII dates. Second, there is an inversion; the oldest date is on top in all three trenches (Table 6.4).

Various circumstances could explain the first anomaly. The most economical, and the preferred, explanation is that there is no anomaly, that all the determinations accurately and correctly (within the limitations of the technique) reflect the age of the sample that was submitted and, consequently, that the Test E deposit is older than the JIV or KII deposit. The depositional sequence in Salts Cave Vestibule is extremely complex (Watson 1974a). The Vestibule deposits are the result of two intermittently present factors: human activity and stream action (ibid.:77).

> The earliest events of which we have a record are breakdown and stream sands being laid down in front of the breakdown. Next a catastrophic fire occurred in and around the Sink, followed after an interval of uncertain duration by rainfall that resulted in much pulverized charcoal being transported into the Vestibule and eventually piled up by slowly moving water against and within the edge of the breakdown.
> Later rain storms resulted in faster moving water laying down sand and gravel that was subsequently eroded. More sand and gravel filled up the channel and was, for the first time, interleaved with midden debris. The stream dried and more midden accumulated in the C and E areas until a burst of stream activity occurred again and thick sands were deposited in C and E, but only sand lenses in JIV.
> The final event was once again breakdown and ponding in the C, E, and J areas, represented by the upper zone of breakdown debris and clay in all three trenches.

Given this level of hydrogeological activity, it seems possible that one portion of the Vestibule sediments might contain older deposits than another por-

Table 6.4. Salts Cave Vestibule Radiocarbon Determinations*

Level	Trench E,G	Level	Trench H	Horizon	Level	Trench JIV	Level	Trench KII†
5	3360 ± 220	2A	3490 ± 110	Stream sands Midden among breakdown	4	2470 ± 60	4	2520 ± 70
6	3410 ± 100			Midden-bearing brown clay alter-	6	2340 ± 50	6	2200 ± 60
7b	2660 ± 100			nating and interfingering with	8	2430 ± 50	11	2380 ± 60
7b	2940 ± 120			sand and gravel	11	2510 ± 60	14	2410 ± 60
				2σ Ranges				
	2920–3800		3270–3710			2350–2590		2380–2660
	3210–3610					2240–2440		2080–2320
	2460–2860					2330–2530		2260–2500
	2700–3180					2390–2630		2290–2530

Source: Data provided by the Cave Research Foundation Archeological Project. Adapted to Suggested Correlation of Levels (Watson 1974f:82, Table 11.7).

*Radiocarbon years before present (A.D. 1950), uncorrected, uncalibrated, Libby half-life.

†No stratigraphic correlations have been published for Trench K.

tion only 3 to 4 m away. There is a stratigraphic discontinuity between level 4 of JIV and level 5 in Trench E (Table 6.4) that supports this explanation. Although these levels are at roughly equivalent depths below surface, they are not the same stratum.

Alternative explanations for the age gap between the E,G,H, and JIV, KII deposits have to do with problems of sample composition. It is possible that the Test E samples were not adequately pretreated. Either carbonate or humic acid contamination can result in dates that are too old when the contaminating agent is a ^{14}C-depleted source of carbon. Groundwater in a karst landscape has the potential for such contamination, but the laboratory was informed in considerable detail of the situation in the Vestibule and presumably performed all necessary pretreatment procedures.

It is also possible that the laboratory process itself could have altered the first set of Vestibule dates. The first dates were run in an acetylene laboratory. A series of chemical reactions are required to produce acetylene from carbon dioxide. If the reaction is not carried to completion, isotopic fractionation can result. The discrimination is against heavier isotopes, the gas is depleted in ^{14}C in comparison with the sample, and the dates are too old. Although this would explain some discrepancy between the first and second sets of Vestibule dates, it would not explain a discrepancy of this magnitude. The largest error that is supposed to be introduced by an incomplete acetylene production reaction is on the order of 80 years (Suess 1954:6).

The only way to resolve the matter of the true age of the Trench E deposits is to run new dates on additional material from Trench E and see whether they agree or disagree with the original determinations.

Assuming that the former explanation is true, that each individual date is an accurate representation of the age of that particular sample, then the inversion still needs to be explained. How is it that older dates come from the upper levels of all three dated excavation units?

In trenches J and K, level 4, the uppermost dated stratum, appears older than the next dated level (level 6) below it (Table 6.4). This may be the case in appearances only. In reality the 2σ ranges of the two dates for unit JIV overlap by 90 years (Table 6.4). This is not the case in KII, however. In KII the 2σ range of level-4 date is not only older than the level-6 date but also shows no overlap at all (Table 6.4). The fact that older material appears above younger material in two adjacent squares suggests, although far from conclusively, that the inversion might be "real" after all.

Several independent lines of evidence indicate that the Salts Cave Vestibule strata are an intact temporal sequence reflecting change—environmental or cultural or both—through time (Watson 1974e:235–38). Some of the botanical evidence comes from unit JIV (Yarnell 1974b), as does the pollen (Schoenwetter 1974). Additional botanical samples came from KII (Gardner 1987). The faunal evidence (Duffield 1974) from Trenches C, C/N, E, F, G, H, and J I–IV was incorporated into site-wide horizons based on Watson's (1974f:82, Table 11.7) stratigraphic correlations. None of these analyses detected anything anomalous or discontinuous in the strata returning inverted dates.

The bulk of the environmental and botanical data comes from units J and K. The pronounced inversion is in Trench E and its adjoining extensions G and H. Level 2A in G and level 5 in E are stratigraphic equivalents (Table 6.4; Watson 1974f:82, Table 11.7). The dates are roughly equivalent as well, having a wide overlap in their 2σ ranges (Table 6.4). The third inverted date comes from level 6 in Trench G, which is the stratigraphic equivalent of level 6 in Trench E. Taken at face value, these three samples were from a deposit of mid-second–millennium B.C. material picked up elsewhere in the cave by stream action and then redeposited on top of the first–millennium B.C. midden deposits (level 7b) that can be found in most of the Vestibule excavation units (Table 6; Watson 1974a).

The hydrogeological regime in the Vestibule makes this plausible, but there is one independent line of evidence that appears to contradict it. Excavators recorded the angle of orientation for all the bones found in Trench E to test whether stream activity had affected the distribution of cultural materials. The assumption was that if the bones were carried by water, most of them would be uniformly oriented in the direction of stream flow (Watson 1974d:93). The actual orientation turned out to be random in all levels. In level 5 of Trench E there are a number of plotted bones randomly oriented (ibid.:92), which suggests in situ cultural deposition, yet the ^{14}C date is several centuries older than the levels below it. It is possible that charcoal could be redistributed by stream action insufficient to move larger or heavier materials such as bone fragments (ibid.:95) or by a form of stream activity that would result in a random orientation of bone fragments. It is also conceivable that the older charcoal was transported by human agency at the time that other cultural material was being deposited in levels 5 and 6. The inhabitants of the Vestibule could have moved sediments from one portion of the Vestibule to another, thus depositing older material on top of younger material and producing a random, rather than a stream-carried, orientation for the artifacts.

One more possibility deserves mention not because it is probable but because it appears to reconcile all the evidence for both Vestibule dating problems. If the Test E inversion is the result of carbonate contamination in the samples, if that contamination affected only the upper levels of Trench E, and if the level of contamination were on the order of 10% "dead" or ^{14}C-depleted carbon in the sample, then the dates would be 800 or perhaps 1000 years too old. If the same phenomenon were affecting the upper levels of Test J and/or K, but on a much reduced level of 1% (water standing for a much shorter time or much less often in J/K than in E), then the dates from the upper levels of J and K would be 80 or 100 years too old. The levels in all three trenches that returned inverted dates are at approximately the same depth below surface (40–60 cm [Watson 1974a:80–81]). Once again, the way to test this would be to run additional dates from E, paying special attention to pretreatment of the samples.

The much more likely explanation of the entire suite of Salts Cave Vestibule dates assumes that the ^{14}C determinations are accurate and that they reflect the complex sequence of cultural and natural deposition that occurs in the Vestibule.

Test A

There is one other set of MCNP ^{14}C determinations that comes from an excavation unit, Test A, located in the upper levels of Salts Cave interior. The dates for this unit appear problematic as well.

2510 ±140	0–10 cm
2430 ±130	30–40 cm
2840 ±150	70–80 cm
2520 ±140	140 cm

In fact, although there are approximately 1.5 m of deposit, the entire column is disturbed material resulting from aboriginal mining activity or perhaps from historic era disturbance. The cave wall, which served as the west wall of the excavation unit, is smoke-blackened 50 cm below the present surface, and the entire deposit had been moved about in search of cave minerals (Watson et al. 1969:20). It is not surprising, then, that samples of virtually the same age lay both at the bottom and the top of the column or that older material was found in the intervening levels. Test A is the result of human activity, but it probably includes the amalgamation of older artifacts discarded on the cave floor into the sediments being moved by aboriginal miners. For this reason I regard the Test A dates in the same poorly provenienced or surface category as the rest of the interior samples.

Salts and Mammoth Cave Interior

The interior dates are problematic for reasons already mentioned. This is material without good context. There is little or no deposition in dry areas of the cave, so material from one time period is found lying next to material from later or earlier time periods. The 14 Salts Cave interior and the 8 Mammoth Cave interior samples are sometimes widely separated by vertical and horizontal space. In addition, it is usually unclear whether any object is in its original discard location or whether it has been moved after its initial disposal. The interior dates are extreme examples of a principle that applies to any radiocarbon determination: a laboratory determination dates the sample itself, that sample's relation to particular levels, features, or artifacts within a site must be established (Taylor 1987:108). In reality, a piece of cane picked up from a particular spot on the cave floor is no different from charcoal excavated from a stratigraphic level. Either sample may have been moved from its original location of deposition; there is simply more likelihood of the cane's having been moved and more difficulty in showing that it has not.

Twenty-two dates from the cave interior may appear to be a fairly large sample. In reality, 8 dates from Mammoth Cave interior and 14 dates from Salts Cave interior make up a very small sample if one considers the area that these sites cover and the size of the sampling universe. There are literally thousands of datable prehistoric samples lying about in Mammoth Cave interior and Salts Cave interior. The addition of a few new dates to any of the subsamples can cause major interpretive changes.

The Vestibule is one example of this. Originally there were five dates ranging from 3490 B.P. ± 110 to 2660 B.P. ± 100. There was a tendency to ignore the early interior dates (3140 B.P. ± 150 to 2720 B.P. ± 140) and to concentrate on the paleofecal evidence (2660 B.P. ± 140 to 2240 B.P. ± 200 (Gardner 1987:359; Seeman 1986:567). This suggested that there was a marked discontinuity in the temporal span of the interior and the Vestibule. Eight new dates from two excavation units that had not previously been dated showed that the Vestibule contained material in good temporal agreement with the paleofeces (Gardner 1987). The same sort of clarification might be forthcoming from additional interior dates, albeit clarification in the other direction, interior dates that match the mid-second-millennium dates from the Vestibule.

What the 22 interior dates have already established is that Mammoth and Salts caves were extensively exploited in a relatively limited time span of about 1,000 years. Cave minerals were systematically sought in many parts of Salts and Mammoth caves during the first millennium B.C. (Munson et al. 1989). Some of this exploitation may have been for spiritual/ceremonial uses rather than for utilitarian purposes (ibid.:129–31), or the Salts/Mammoth cavers may have pursued a ceremonially valuable item, satinspar and selenite crystals, for its trade value. This resource exploitation seems to have been the major reason for human presence in the caves, the dietary evidence being a fortuitous consequence of resource procurement.

In addition to extensive first-millennium B.C. use there is an Archaic component to cave use that has not been well defined. The cave passages of the Flint/Mammoth system have been divided into six levels (Palmer 1981:129–48). The large trunk passages of Salts Cave and Mammoth Cave lie at elevations between 175 and 190 m above sea level. Indian Avenue in Salts Cave as well as Ganter Avenue and Flint Alley in Mammoth Cave are smaller passages lying at lower elevations (168–150 m) and are consequently referred to as lower Salts and lower Mammoth (Table 6.1). Sixteen of the 22 interior dates come from upper-trunk passages. Of the six dates that do come from the lower levels, four are quite early in the series (4120 B.P. ± 70 to 2920 B.P. ± 60). With the single exception of the soot date from upper Salts, these are the four oldest interior dates. Although the sample is small it is a tantalizing prospect for future research that the Archaic dates seem to be concentrated in the lower-level passages. This at least suggests three things: (1) that the limits of deep-cave exploration were probably accomplished early on, (2) that extensive first-millennium use of the upper-level passages may have obscured earlier, less intensive exploration trips, and (3) that the lower levels of the cave may be the best place to seek evidence for Archaic mining and/or diet.

Summary

In summarizing these dates and these sites, I emphasize several aspects: (1) the somewhat unusual nature of the sites; (2) the fact that the dates are consistent but not as precise as we would like them to be; (3) that the method is reliable and informative in a way that surpasses almost any other technique available to archaeologists; and (4) that the period and sites in question are important and that their research potential has not been exhausted.

Salts Cave and Mammoth Cave are unusual archaeological sites for several reasons: (1) the number of dates already obtained, (2) the quantities of archaeological material that are retrievable without excavation, (3) the fact that almost all artifacts within the cave interior are organic and therefore directly datable, (4) the necessity for strict adherence to the primary caveat of all archaeological radiocarbon dating that the determination dates the sample itself and that the sample's relation to any other objects or features remains to be established, (5) the temporal limitation of these two sites to the Archaic/Woodland transition despite their apparent accessibility throughout prehistory.

The accuracy and precision of these ^{14}C determinations could have been altered in various ways. Contaminants are present. Isotopic fractionation can modify stable isotope ratios in some of the materials that have been dated. Calibration of radiocarbon years to calendar years can alter the time period. The potential for interlaboratory error requires a larger statistical uncertainty.

It is difficult to say with certainty that contamination has or has not affected a series of dates, but once there are 35 dates from two closely related sites—and all 35 dates are clustered within the same time span—albeit a fairly lengthy one of about 1,500 years, contamination or fractionation causing significant interpretative error seems less and less likely. The period in question, the first two millennia B.C., presents only minor discrepancies in calibration. Similarly, contaminants must constitute a relatively high proportion of Holocene samples to alter the determinations by more than a few decades. Any differences in stable isotope ratios are also expected to change determinations by a few decades or perhaps 100 years. In fact, the major problem with the MCNP series is one of precision. The statistical uncertainties are larger than we would like them to be.

Because of the inherent limitations of radiocarbon dating and of the increased potential for interlaboratory error in this series of dates that came from many different laboratories over a period of many years, it seems prudent to regard these dates at the very least at their 2σ uncertainty. In that form they are not precise enough to resolve whether a particular sample is older or younger than the other samples that cluster around it in time. This is not a problem unique to these sites or this series of dates, but one that limits interpretation of any set of radiocarbon dates from any combination of laboratories.

Limitations notwithstanding, the MCNP series is an excellent illustration of the general utility, reliability, and information value of the radiocarbon method. Considered as date ranges of two standard deviations (Figure 6.1), these determinations present overwhelming evidence for exploitation of the mineral resources of Salts and Mammoth caves during the first two millennia B.C. The greatest use of the cave undoubtedly occurred during the first millennium B.C. Thirty-two of the 35 date ranges at least touch on this 1,000-year period. Twenty of the ranges fall entirely within the first millennium B.C. The emphasis does center on the Early Woodland time period, but too many (9 of 35) of these determinations fall either partly or wholly within the second millennium B.C. to dismiss the Late Archaic component to cave exploration and exploitation. Forty years after the introduction of radiocarbon dating, we take its utility and information value for granted. We tend to call its reliability into question whenever the results are something other than expected.

At one time Salts Cave Vestibule presented the earliest evidence for native cultigens in Eastern North America. Vestibule dates indicated that sunflower, sumpweed, chenopod, knotweed, and others were being grown or harvested in significant proportions by 1500 B.C. As more and more sites throughout the region were subjected to similar investigation, it became clear that these were not the earliest examples of these plants. It also became clear that squash and gourd were cultivated prior to sunflower, sumpweed, chenopod, and so on. Eventually a sufficient body of archaeobotanical data was collected according to which the association between the Vestibule dates and the Vestibule plant remains became suspect: the association of those species in that complex in those proportions does not occur at any other site in the Late Archaic. Enough evidence had accumulated to make the native North American complex "diagnostic" for Early Woodland, that is for mid-first–millennium rather than mid-second–millennium B.C. sites. This in turn prompted the running of new dates on material more closely associated with the botanical remains. The new dates pull the botanical evidence into line with the region at large.

Presently Salts and Mammoth caves hold the largest and most complete body of evidence available for Early Woodland–period subsistence, a body of evidence that appears to be as diagnostic for the period in these latitudes as a grit-tempered cord-marked sherd. Perhaps the most intriguing possibility suggested here is that, in the future, a corresponding body of evidence about Late Archaic diet could be recovered from these same sites.

Before the radiocarbon method, Salts and Mammoth caves were well-known but enigmatic sites, containing no temporally diagnostic material. Pottery was absent, suggesting that the sites might be quite old, but whether they were a few hundred years or several thousand years old was simply conjecture in the absence of diagnostic material. Only with the introduction of the radiocarbon technique was it possible to say at what time during prehistory these sites were visited. Although it is always possible that additional material will return dates from other time periods, many such dates would have to be obtained before these sites appeared representative of anything other than the Late Archaic/Early Woodland transition.

7 | Managing Kentucky's Caves

Jan Marie Hemberger

Caves have long been an object of human curiosity, drawing people inexplicably into their dark recesses. There human beings have found shelter (for both the living and the dead), important natural resources, satisfaction for an innate need to explore, secluded and mystical places for ritual, and literary settings. In the first four pursuits, human beings have left behind numerous and varied evidence of their presence, and through the last they have fostered fascination with caves.

Evidence left in caves by human beings provides information about their adaptation to their surroundings. The constant temperature and humidity found within caves preserves bodies, woven materials and paleofeces, and other cultural items not usually found at open sites. Caves also preserve evidence of caving activities, such as mining, that once took place within the subterranean passages.

Caves, although capable of preserving fragile resources, are themselves fragile resources, and irreparable damage can easily be caused to caves and the cultural resources they contain. In this chapter, I discuss the importance of caves as cultural resource repositories and suggest ideas for their conservation.

Three prehistoric cave sites, representing three different cave types and management problems, are presented, and management approaches are proposed and discussed. The three sites are: Adair Glyph Cave, 15Ad70, a rather typical multilevel cave containing unique mud glyphs drawn on the floor of one passage; Pit of the Skulls, 15Bn51, a pit cave containing human remains; and Sinking Creek Cave, 15Si9, a section of trunk passage containing stratified cultural deposits.

Adair Glyph Cave

Adair Glyph Cave, a multilevel cave, situated in Adair County, Kentucky, has been noted in caving literature since 1965 (DiBlasi 1989, this volume; George 1986:14; Nantz 1972:53–54; Wainscott 1965:7–8). The first mapping survey of this cave was completed in 1975, resulting in 1,623 m of mapped passage and an additional 914 m of explored passage. No evidence of prehistoric activity was noted during the mapping and exploration.

In 1986 prehistoric mud drawings were discovered on the floor of an upper-level passage that had not been previously surveyed or mapped. Realizing the importance of the find, the discovers retraced their steps to avoid further damage to the glyphs and to report the find.

Fortunately, two of the cave party members had been involved in an archaeological survey of small caves and were able to provide valuable preliminary information. The drawings were described as being incised in mud and covered with manganese deposits and fungi. Motifs described included chevrons, zigzags, cross-hatching, snakes, sun bursts, and trailed lines.

A trip was made to assess the drawings, photograph them, collect radiocarbon samples, and look for other evidence of aboriginal activity. Reaching the glyph passage on the third level of the cave required traversing several areas that presented logistical problems. The entrance level includes a 30-m-long stoop, a plunge pool, and 1,000 m of stream passage. Reaching the second level requires climbing a steep muddy bank. Then, a crawl averaging 60 by 60 cm must be negotiated, and a pit with rapidly flowing water in the bottom must be traversed. Reaching the third level requires scaling a 2.5- to 3-m wall. Once there, the researchers traversed a soft mud floor, where they found and flagged two aboriginal footprints. They also had to negotiate a 30-cm high crawl before reaching the glyphs.

Once in the glyph passage, the party immediately determined that almost the entire floor was covered with drawings and that already some had been destroyed by "modern traffic." An observable "path" made by recent cavers was followed to the end of the passage, which measured 100 m long and 4 m wide.

A technique for recording the drawings was established. Two people recorded descriptions of the glyphs as the party moved forward. Two photographers worked on the task of photodocumentation. All of this work had to be accomplished without stepping off the narrow path. On completion of the examination, and while carefully exiting the passage, the investigators collected charcoal from the cave floor for radiometric determinations.

It was tentatively decided that the drawings were aboriginal based on the motifs and the prints of bare and/or moccasined feet as well as charcoal smudges or stoke marks found throughout the passage. Because the cave was known to be heavily traveled and the landowner was known to allow anyone into it, we discussed the situation with the cave owner, stressing the extremely fragile nature of the new find. The owner agreed to limit access to the cave, but to allow continued archaeological investigations. The site was determined eligible for inclusion in the National Register of Historic Places (DiBlasi 1986b), thus affording it protection under Section 106. During the nomination process, however, it was determined that the entire cave was not legally owned by the person who owned the entrance. Rather, two other individuals owned portions of the cave, because a 1920s decision of the Kentucky Supreme Court considers cave rights similar to mineral rights, that is, those owning surface property also own what is beneath it (*Edwards v. Sims*, December 3, 1929).

Since the discovery and preliminary description of Adair Glyph Cave, a new Kentucky Cave Protection Act (KCPA) (K.R.S. 433.871–885) has been passed. In effect the new law makes it a class A misdemeanor to "knowingly or willfully deface" archaeological materials. However, just walking in this passage could "deface" the drawings. The only legal way to protect Adair Glyph Cave is to have the owner of the entrance post the cave as per the cave law and have the owner of the passage post the interior of the cave. This would meet all legal requirements of the law, but in actual practice would be virtually impossible to enforce.

At present, the most feasible option for the preservation of the mud glyphs is to accomplish state-of-the-art photodocumentation and videotaping of the drawings. Casts also might be considered, but a small area should be tested first to ensure that damage to the glyphs will not occur. Then enforcement of the cave protection law should be pursued as rigorously as possible. In addition, use of various cave-gating techniques, both at the entrance and at the glyph passage, may be desirable protection.

Pit of the Skulls

Pit of the Skulls is situated in Barren County, Kentucky. As its name implies, it is a pit cave containing human remains (Haskins 1988; Hemberger 1982, 1985). It was first discovered and explored in June 1981 by members of the Cave Research Foundation. Survey disclosed the pit to have four distinct levels, a depth of 30 m, and a surveyed length of 82 m. Scattered human remains, representing a minimum of five individuals, were recovered including two exhibiting occipital deformation and one showing evidence of dismemberment or butchering. None of the individuals was complete due to the method of collection, rodent gnawing, and mode of disposal. Also present in the collection were the remains of seventeen nonhuman animal species.

A thorough examination of material from the Pit of the Skulls resulted in two conclusions. First, the animal bones recovered occurred in the pit naturally. No butchering marks were noted nor was there any evidence of burning; it appears that live animals accidentally fell into the pit and died there. The depth of the pit (30 m) perhaps prohibited its use as an animal trap by prehistoric hunters, but it clearly served as a specialized disposal area for human remains. It is highly unlikely that so many people fell accidentally into the pit. Evidence for the dismemberment of one individual indicates that some form of processing took place prior to final deposition in the pit.

Technical abilities required to gain access to this cave make the site "self-protecting" but at the same time pose a data-recovery dilemma. To enter the cave safely takes vertical ropework. "Surface" collections of easily recognizable items from the pit floor were made by the cavers mapping the cave.

Sinking Creek Cave

The Sinking Creek Cave System, located in Simpson County, Kentucky, has a section of trunk passage containing stratified cultural deposits. The cave was being explored and mapped as part of a master's thesis about karst hydrology by a Western Kentucky University student, who received assistance from the Green River Grotto. Survey members found a projectile point in a stream within the cave, but they became aware of more significant cultural deposits when vandals started looting a portion of the cave known as the "loft."

The cave system's amphitheater-like entrance was examined by archaeologists and by a vertebrate paleontologist called by members of the Green River Grotto. The investigators determined that significant cultural deposits, both prehistoric and historic, were confined to the main trunk passage (Wilson 1984:27–28). Human remains, collected by the landowners after the looting activity, included elements of two adults and one infant. In addition, the remains of white-tailed deer were identified (ibid.:30).

In 1984 Sinking Creek Cave became the focus of a court case. While archaeologists from the University of Louisville and Washington University were trying to gather scientific information from already disturbed cultural deposits, further extensive damage was done by looters. Criminal charges were eventually pressed against one of the looters.

The Coroners Law (K.R.S. 525.110—desecration of a venerated object) and the State Antiquities Act (K.R.S. 164.730—failure to report an archaeological site or object of antiquity) were the only two laws the landowners could use to protect the site. Donation of an archaeological easement had been discussed, but it could not be pursued because the land was in receivership with a federal land bank association in Elkton, Kentucky. Had this been an *actual* federal land bank, vandals might have been charged with violation of the Archaeological Resources Protection Act (ARPA) of 1979 because the site would have been temporarily owned by the federal government and thereby afforded protection under ARPA.

Philip J. DiBlasi, staff archaeologist, University of Louisville, convinced the Simpson County prosecutor to prosecute the vandal for violating the Kentucky Antiquities Act and for "desecrating a sacred burial place" (K.R.S. 72:525.110). The county prosecutor would not press charges until a complaint had been signed (Simpson County District Court Case Number 84-M-126).

The outcome of the trial was less than encouraging. The charge of desecration was dropped because the judge thought the looting of prehistoric burials had not caused a "public outcry" (as defined by Kentucky Revised Statutes

K.R.S. 72:525.110). The defendant was found guilty only of not reporting a site in accordance with the Kentucky Antiquities Act (K.R.S. 164); however, this carried no penalty. The defendant did sign a bond indicating he would not dig or promote digging for prehistoric materials in caves within Simpson County, Kentucky, for a period of *one* year.

Prompted by the wholesale looting of prehistoric burials at 15Un28, the Slack Farm site, penalties for both charges (KRS 164; 72:525.110) have since been upgraded by an emergency act of the Kentucky legislature to felonies. It is possible that if the Sinking Creek Cave case were tried today, the defendant might be convicted of two felony counts and the class A misdemeanor charge for cave looting (K.R.S. 433.873). Sinking Creek Cave has been irreparably damaged, but upgrading the Coroner's Law and the State Antiquities Act to felonies should serve to protect other such sites.

Conclusion

As demonstrated by the diverse nature of the cultural material and the cave environments described in the three examples, it is clear that there should be careful consideration of data-recovery, documentation, and protection methods when dealing with cave sites. Methods presented range from low-impact recording methods to means for site protection using recently passed legislation.

Photodocumentation of archaeological sites and materials is important. In a cave, photography can prove to be extremely difficult. Cave photography is very specialized because of the complete lack of light. Assistance for lay photographers can be found in such publications as the National Speleological Society's *News*. It is important also to be aware of the extreme conditions photographic equipment can be exposed to in a cave. Special consideration should be given to equipment being totally submerged in water or dragged through passages containing extremely abrasive gypsum sand. Successful cave photography requires that equipment (particularly the flash system) be in working order when it is needed.

It is also important to consider recovery and curation of materials from caves. Location controls are mandatory, as they are in open-air sites. Working survey station to survey station or dividing a large passage into units can be most helpful. Artifactual materials should be well documented before being moved, and all materials should be packed well before transport. It is always important to remember that transportation even a short distance through a cave system can quickly destroy very fragile remains.

Determining the size of the sample to be removed must be decided on a case-by-case basis. Should a cave be relatively well protected, either physically or legally, removing only a small sample of materials would be adequate. If materials are not in imminent danger of vandalism, the best preservation option is to leave them in the cave environment. Often, caves are brought to the attention of archaeologists only because of active looting. Stringent protection measures should be sought and implemented in such cases. Materials, if removed from a cave, should be curated in a facility that is capable of replicating the constant temperature and humidity of cave environments.

Protecting the archaeological, biological, and geological resources of caves is important. Legal and physical means of protecting caves must be actively implemented and enforced.

The KCPA, enacted in 1988, provides caves, including those privately owned, with legal protection. Also, the landowner lease/easement agreement, an important piece of interim legislation, allows for privately held properties to be leased or easements to be donated to the state to provide legal protection. The penalties for the State Antiquities Act (K.R.S. 164) and the Coroner's Act in Kentucky have been upgraded from misdemeanors to felonies.

Clearly even the best legislation will not protect all archaeological sites. Physical means are also needed to protect sensitive cave resources. Currently, the most commonly protected cave resource is bats, protected most frequently by cave entrance gates. Gates allow bats and authorized individuals to pass. Several cave-gating methods are described in a publication provided by the National Speleological Society titled *Cave Gating* (Hunt and Stitt 1981). The construction of a cave gate must also take into account environmental impacts prior to construction. The area of gate placement should be checked for archaeological deposits. Also consideration should be given to how the gate type will change water flow, air flow, temperature, and humidity (ibid.:32, 24). To change these factors significantly could damage or destroy the resources to be protected.

Caves that are extremely complex or that require specialized equipment or knowledge to enter are reasonably "self-protecting." However, pressures from uninformed or untrained individuals increase as the recreational nature of caving grows. Even the most untrained picnickers can "accidentally" find their way into an archaeologically sensitive passage and cause damage.

Public education has great potential in the long-term preservation of archaeological materials in caves. If the public is made aware of the nature and scientific value of these materials, then the chances of inadvertent damage will be reduced. But this is not the only answer. The ultimate solution to the cave-protection problem is in the effective use of both public education and the legal and physical means of protection for caves. Thoughtful and well-planned management will ensure that caves are preserved as valuable resources for the future.

8 | Botanizing along Green River

Gail E. Wagner

ONE OF THE hallmarks of Patty Jo Watson and her colleagues' research along Green River has been an interdisciplinary focus on subsistence, particularly the recovery and study of plant remains. Through the years our Green River projects have played a critical role in eastern North American archaeology in three main respects: (1) demonstrating the feasibility and effectiveness of interdisciplinary research projects; (2) contributing substantially to formulations of the sequencing of plant cultigens and domesticates in the midcontinent; and (3) pioneering and publicizing botanical recovery techniques.

In 1979 I presented a paper at the Southeastern Archaeological Conference on the plant remains from the 1978–79 excavations at the Carlston Annis shell-mound (1979). I would like to reintroduce some of that material in this chapter, directing my remarks toward two of the three main points just made. I will concentrate on and begin with contribution three, recovery techniques.

Watson (1976) published a description of a mechanized flotation system—the SMAP machine—designed to process dirt samples from Green River projects. Six years later I used the Carlston Annis data to help illustrate the use of carbonized poppy seeds to test the effectiveness and consistency of different flotation techniques (Wagner 1982).

More recently I have been concerned with recognizing bias and comparability among data (Wagner 1988), partially as a result of realizing how much bias is introduced in how we conduct our recovery. I am now prepared to report on a new facet of those flotation recovery and analytical bias studies. During analysis of the Carlston Annis 1978–79 samples, I tabulated light flotation fractions separately from the heavy fractions in each individual sample. This analytical approach probably resulted in sacrificing accuracy in quantification because only small quantities of remains were present in any one sample, and it certainly took longer to complete than would fewer weighings of much larger combined samples.

Nevertheless, I thought it was important because I was faced with estimating bias and comparability between the earlier analysis of the 1972–74 material by Crawford (1982, in prep.) and my own analysis (Wagner in prep.). As is true of many multiyear projects, our work along Green River encompassed changes through the years in our field, recovery, and analytical techniques, as our understanding of the techniques and our questions about the region evolved (Wagner 1988). Because of time and money constraints, all earlier botanical analyses of samples from Green River's Big Bend sites were limited to tabulation of plant remains captured in the flotation light fraction, that is, those that were light enough to float (Crawford 1982). The heavy fractions had been saved but were not completely sorted or analyzed.

Comparison between the types and amounts of plant remains recovered in each fraction indicates the nature of the bias that may occur when only light flotation fractions are analyzed, as opposed to both light and heavy fractions combined. Table 8.1 illustrates the raw data used in this study.

For all samples from the four excavation units combined, 89% by weight of the overall carbonized wood and nut remains greater than 2 mm in size was recovered in the heavy flotation fractions, whereas only 11% by weight was recovered in light fractions. This is hardly surprising because heavy remains (which, of course, may contribute more to the overall weight of the analyzed sample) tend to sink or suspend deeply under water. However, the bias is not consistent across all categories of plant remains (Table 8.2).

Anywhere from 95% to 100% of the hickory nutshell was recovered in the heavy fractions, as was 93% to 100% of the hazel nutshell and 100% of the black walnut shell. In one of the units, 64% of the acorn nutmeats and shells was recovered in the light fraction, but in the other three units 71% to 100% of the acorn was recovered in the heavy fractions. The distribution of woods was variable, with anywhere from 2% to 66% recovered in the light fraction.

Most seeds were recovered from the light fraction with the exception of plum and hackberry. These two species were recovered only from the heavy fractions in these samples. Persimmon, redbud, and grape seeds were found in both heavy and light fractions.

To address the implications for comparison between the two analyses, I turn to a discussion of the second main contribution outlined at the beginning of this paper: the sequencing of plant remains. On the basis of the analysis of three stratigraphic series of flotation light fractions from Carlston Annis (units A4, C1, and C13) and one series (unit A3) from the nearby Bowles site, Crawford (1982, in prep.) distinguished three vertical zones within the shell midden (Table 8.3).

The two upper shell midden zones appear also in the 1978–79 units, along with an overlying shell-free midden that was not recognized or sampled in the earlier excavations. Zone III, the deepest levels of the shell midden, was identified botanically in two of the 1972–74 excavation units (C1 and C13). This zone has few plant food remains, mostly hickory nut shell, and little variety in seeds. Just over half the identified seeds are those of fleshy fruits.

Shell midden Zone II appears to have accumulated between the mid- and early fourth millennium B.C. (corrected dates based on Pearson and Stuiver

Table 8.1. Recovery of Light versus Heavy Fractions[*]

Plant Remains	Weight (g)							
	D14–2		J		E12		E16	
	Light	Heavy	Light	Heavy	Light	Heavy	Light	Heavy
Wood	40.03	33.91	0.03	1.84	0.06	0.10	1.23	0.62
Hickory nutshell	10.23	350.89	0.08	47.07	0.19	4.01	1.03	21.31
Walnut nutshell	0.0	4.57	0.0	2.28	0.0	0.33	0.0	0.42
Acorn meat & shell	4.22	2.36	0.0	0.09	0.0	0.10	0.05	0.12
Hazel shell	0.08	1.06	0.0	0.12	0.0	0.0	0.0	0.0
Total	54.56	392.79	0.11	51.40	0.25	4.54	2.31	22.47

[*]D14-2 midden, levels 1–20, 69 liters of dirt. Excluding possible features 8/1, 11/2–3, 15/1–2. Operation J, all samples, 152.5 liters of dirt. Unit E12, levels 2–7, 59 liters of dirt. Unit E16, levels 2–7, 95 liters of dirt.

1986). Analysis of the light fractions (Crawford 1982, in prep.) reveals a high overall density of plant remains, mostly hickory, along with a high number and variety of seeds. Analysis of light *and* heavy fractions from the 1978–79 excavations lends support to Crawford's earlier work, in great part because of Crawford's careful selection of those analytical categories that now, in retrospect, seem least affected by the lack of a heavy fraction component. One way to underscore the density of plant remains from this zone is to note that, although it comprised only 25% of all dirt floated in 1978–79, it returned 43% by weight of all plant food remains, 73% of the wood, and 55% of the seeds.

Crawford's (1982, in prep.) model of the shell midden plant remains shows an increase in the amount of acorn in the uppermost Zone I, in conjunction with a relatively low density of plant remains. This zone contains all but one of the identified squash rind fragments. The light plus heavy fraction samples corroborate an increase of acorn remains. Table 8.4 illustrates this by two different measures. In the acorn column, 82% of all acorn remains by weight were recovered in shell midden Zone I. However, keep in mind that 50% of the dirt by volume also came from this zone.

A better measure, one suggested by Crawford (in prep.), is the ratio of acorn to hickory. I see hickory as a good baseline because it comprises 84% to 99% by

Table 8.2. Recovery of Light versus Heavy Fractions (%)

Plant Remains	D14-2		J		E12		E16	
	Light	Heavy	Light	Heavy	Light	Heavy	Light	Heavy
Wood	54	46	2	98	37.5	62.5	66	33
Hickory nutshell	3	97	*	100	5	95	5	95
Walnut shell	0	100	0	100	0	100	0	100
Acorn meat & shell	64	36	0	100	0	100	29	71
Hazel shell	7	93	0	100	0	0	0	0
Total	12	88	*	100	5	95	9	91

* Less than 1%.

weight of all the plant food remains level by level, regardless of the quantity of matrix examined. Under the acorn-to-hickory ratio column, the highest ratio occurs in shell midden Zone I.

The shell-free midden may be divided into two zones based on the density and composition of the plant remains (Table 8.4). Shell-free Zone II, identified in only one excavation unit, contains a high density of 0.58 g of plant food per liter of sediment, of which hickory averages 95%, walnut averages 2%, and in which seeds are rare. There is a sharp drop in acorn frequency from the preceding shell midden Zone I.

The uppermost shell-free midden Zone I, identified in four excavation units, contains a low density of 0.17 g of plant food per liter of sediment, of which hickory averages only 88%, walnut 9%, acorn and hazel together 2%, and seeds are rare. When the four units are examined separately, two show elevated frequencies of black walnut to hickory (J, E12), one has an elevated ratio of hazel to hickory (D14–2), and one has an elevated ratio of acorn to hickory (E12).

Differentiation of the shell-free midden would have been difficult using only the flotation light fractions. Two of the critical ratios, those of hazel and black walnut to hickory, are unlikely to have been accurately portrayed without the heavy fraction counts and weights. Small fragments of both types of nut did occur in the light fractions, but because they were smaller than 2 mm in size, they were neither individually counted nor weighed.

Because most seeds, both numerically and by taxa, occur in the light fractions, there should be relatively little bias in seed associations between the two

Table 8.3. Carlston Annis Midden—Changes through Time

Stratum	Plant Food Density	Nut Remains	Seeds/Other
Shell-free midden			
Zone I	Low	Increase in walnut and hazel	Rare
Zone II	High	Mostly hickory	Rare
Shell midden			
Zone I	Low	Increase in acorn	Squash present
Zone II	High	Mostly hickory	High no./variety
Zone III	Low	Mostly hickory	Little variety (>50% fruits)

analyses. The few exceptions are those seeds that are larger than 2 mm in size; being larger and heavier, they are more likely to sink.

Given these problems, in which ways can two such disparate sets of data be compared? Obviously, raw numbers—or even percentages and ratios—are not directly comparable, except perhaps for the small seeds. What does seem to be comparable are the *sequences*. Last, I would like to provide a little more detail about seeds and sequencing at the Carlston Annis site. Crawford (in prep.) notes the difficulty in arguing for or against a trend toward increasing ecological disruption at the shell mound based on the 1972–74 excavation results. The question boils down to how great a role plant husbandry played in the Big Bend Late Archaic. Although no additional squash rinds have been identified from the 1978–79 units, various other potential cultigens and weeds have been noted. Two positive and four possible erect knotweed achenes, one positive and one probable maygrass, one possible little barley, and five purslane seeds have been recovered from Zone I of the shell midden. Erect knotweed and purslane were found also in Zone II, along with seeds from a variety of fleshy fruits.

Although this additional sequence has yet to be fully worked out, it does seem to indicate an increase in disturbed and open habitats during the time that squash remains are found. A later, different sort of change seems indicated by the elevated amounts of black walnut and hazel in the uppermost portion of the shell-free midden (Zone I). Without an accompanying sequence of pollen or wood charcoal identifications, we are not able to distinguish whether this is a change in the local vegetation, a change in subsistence strategy, or an indication that the dirt in the small areas tested accumulated in a "patchwork" manner rather than following a strict "homogenization model" (Asch and Sidell 1988).

Table 8.4. Comparison of Shell-free and Shell Zones

Zone	Percent[*]					Ratio[+]		
	Hickory	Acorn	Walnut	Hazel	Liters	Acorn to Hickory	Hazel to Hickory	Walnut to Hickory
Shell-free Zone I	4	3	27	11	14	0.11	0.07	1.04
Shell-free Zone II	10	1	10	7	8	0.02	0.02	0.17
Shell Zone I	41	82	39	51	50	0.32	0.035	0.16
Shell Zone II	44	14	24	31	27	0.05	0.02	0.09
Total[++]						0.16	0.03	0.17

[*]Weight or count of category in each stratum compared to total weight or count in all four strata are combined for that category.
[+]Ratio x 10.
[++]Mean ratio given below the ratio column.

For example, elevated amounts of hazel could result from increased disturbance and opening of the forest canopy, yet seeds of weedy plants are uncommon. Also possible is that the increase in hazel, acorn, and black walnut relative to hickory indicates a broadening of subsistence choices. Disturbed bankside and colluvium deposits on top of the shell-free midden returned two small maize cupules. There has also been one tobacco seed recovered at the site, from Unit D15–4, level 2, the first excavated level beneath the plow zone and at the top of the shell midden. Both the corn and tobacco from the Carlston Annis site presumably date to Woodland or more recent periods and likely are associated with the scattered ceramics from this site.

Patty Jo Watson and her colleagues' research along Green River has served as a model for the effectiveness of interdisciplinary research projects (Chapman and Watson 1993; Ford 1988). The Green River projects have figured prominently in formulations of plant domestication and cultivation in the midcontinent (for recent summaries of the sequences and the history of the discovery see Chapman and Watson 1993; Fritz 1990; Smith 1987; and Watson 1985b, 1989). Archaeological projects along Kentucky's Green River will yet contribute to the development and honing of recovery techniques, to formulations of the sequence of plant domestication in eastern North America, and to demonstrations of the effectiveness of integrated interdisciplinary projects.

9 | Lithic Materials from the Read Shell Mound

A Reanalysis of a Works Progress Administration Collection

Christine K. Hensley

THE STUDY OF Green River shell middens has been prominent historically in American archaeology. William S. Webb and his associates located 36 shell mounds along Green River in west-central Kentucky and directed the Works Progress Administration (WPA) to excavate 10 of those mounds. The Read Shell Mound, 15Bt10 (hereafter Bt10), was among those excavated (Figure 9.1). Because the Bt10 artifacts were recovered using late-1930 methods, inherent biases in field recovery methods and interests are present in the artifactual collection. In this chapter I explore the nature of bias in the lithic assemblage and describe it in terms that make the data more amenable for current research questions. I have used a bifacial reductive trajectory typology to aid in understanding the lithic industry at Bt10.

Read Shell Mound

In 1937 approximately 30 unemployed men were hired under the auspices of the WPA to excavate a prehistoric shell midden in the Little Bend of Green River, Butler County, Kentucky (Figure 9.2). Their efforts resulted in the total excavation of Bt10, the Read Shell midden. Thousands of artifacts were recovered, as well as more than 200 human burials (Haskins and Herrmann, this volume). William S. Webb, director of the WPA archaeology program in Kentucky, published a 44-page report describing the excavation, the artifacts, and his interpretations of the material (Webb 1950b).

The WPA began work on Bt10 on December 28, 1937, with Albert C. Spaulding as project supervisor. Spaulding established both the field methods and the recording system for the site excavation. He left Bt10 on September 8, 1938, to be replaced by his assistant supervisor, Ralph D. Brown. Brown directed fieldwork until the project closed on March 2, 1939. Excavation of the site was almost continuous except for a three-week layoff in October 1938 and another during February 1939, when high water prevented access to the site. Bt10 was backfilled in early March 1939.

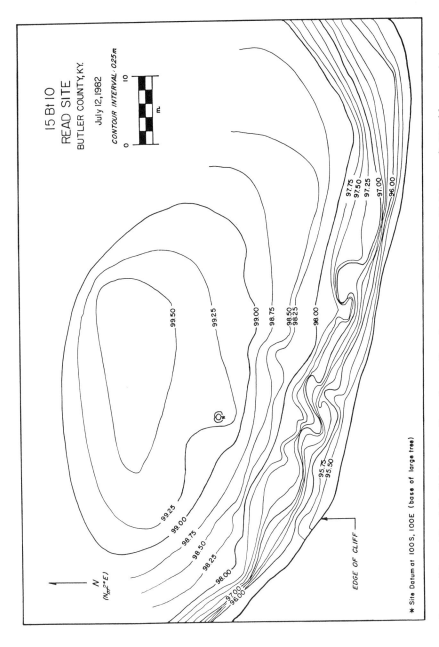

9.1 Contour Map of Read Shell Mound, 15Bt10. *Source:* Based on a map by William H. Marquardt. Used by permission.

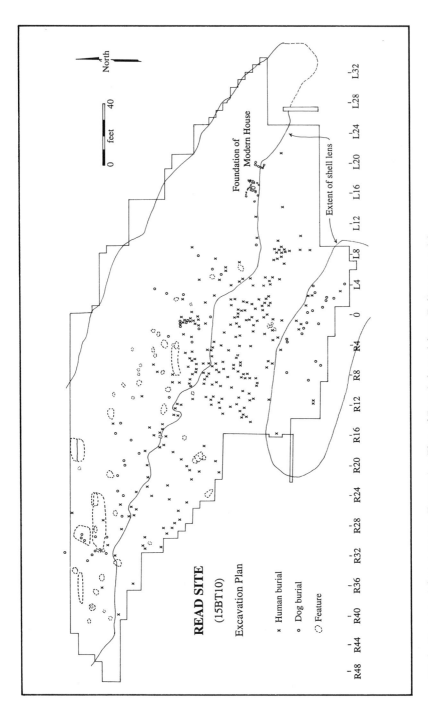

9.2 Works Progress Administration Excavation Plan of Bt10 (adapted from Rolingson 1967)

The excavation procedure at Bt10 was comparable to that at other sites dug throughout the WPA era: shovels were the primary tools, and dirt was not screened. This is not to say that the excavation was not systematic, for it was, but by today's standards the quality of recovery is questionable. A total of 41,400 square feet (3939.1 m^2) was excavated at Read, almost the entire deposit. A baseline was laid out along the northern extent of the midden. The baseline was divided into 5-foot (1.52-m) intervals, and at each interval an east-west stake line was established at right angles. During the early days of the excavation, a 10-foot-wide (3.05-m) trench was placed between R14 and R16. This trench ran on a north-south line and extended the entire width of the site. It enabled the supervisors to define a northern and southern shell lens and a clay ridge that separated them.

Digging proceeded in a southerly direction, upslope, which made backfilling easier. Both Brown's summary and photographs of the excavation indicate that a uniform trench (as long as 200 feet [60.96 m] at times) was maintained; as the work moved southward, dirt from the trench under excavation was tossed in the finished unit to the north. Dirt was removed in arbitrary 9-inch (23.08-cm) levels. The top level, defined by the supervisors as plowzone, was "more rapidly handled than the underlying soil" (R. Brown 1939). Each succeeding level was "double-shoveled" if the level proved to have sufficient archaeological material.

All burials were carefully uncovered with a trowel, knife, and brush. Once revealed, each burial was cleaned, photographed, and recorded on a burial form. A number was assigned to each human skeleton recovered, for a total of 247 burials. At the time, much emphasis was placed on human burials and/or burial traits. Yet, the human remains were in very poor condition. Webb, therefore, decided not to pursue a detailed analysis of the burials (Webb 1950b:365). Age and sex determinations were made in the field by the site supervisors. Of the 247 recovered burials, 172 had no accompanying burial goods; 229 had articles that were thought to be the remains of clothing or personal adornment (nonburial goods); in a few cases, projectile points were imbedded in the skeleton. Six burials contained caches of artifacts. Webb concluded that grave goods were rarely placed with the dead and that many of the recovered articles were related to what the person was wearing at the time of interment. Webb also believed that the bodies were placed near hearths and for the most part were flexed or partially flexed in shallow circular pits. This association could be fortuitous, however, considering that the shell middens contained numerous burials and hearths.

Sixty-three dogs were buried throughout the mound. Although the majority were interred in a manner similar to human beings (small circular pits large enough to hold the body), no dog burial had associated artifacts with it, nor were any dogs found in association with human beings.

Features were also given consecutive numbers as they were uncovered and recorded on feature forms; photographs were often taken, too. Post molds and small empty pits were halved to expose profiles. Features identified by WPA workers include human material thought to be unintentional burials, or in some cases isolated finds of human or dog bone, caches of implements, rock beds, hearth loci, areas of burned dirt or burned shell, and pits with and without refuse. In two cases workshop areas were defined on the basis of large quantities of lithic debris, rejects, hammerstones, and antler billets. Only the largest and/ or most typical rock beds were recorded because of the abundance of small rock concentrations throughout the site. Features were concentrated in the northwestern third of the mound. The most curious of these were two circular pits 2.5 feet (76.2 cm) in circumference dug into subsoil clay. Neither pit contained any material that would indicate its purpose. A second problematical feature was a lens of burned and calcined shell (10 × 15 × 6 feet [3.05 × 4.57 × 1.83m]), which Webb interpreted to be ceremonial. "It was clearly too large and too hot a fire to have served for domestic purposes of either heating or cooking" (Webb 1950b:262–63). Webb gives no information in his published account about where the features are located or at what level they were first encountered. The site map in Rolingson (1967) exhibits what I believe to be these features; yet the map key does not identify the shaded areas as such.

Material defined as occupational debris (refuse bone, flint, other stone chips, and bone and stone implements both broken and complete) were bagged in the field according to excavation unit and level. So-called field specimens were recorded on either burial or feature forms as well as numbered and recorded on a field specimen form. Once in the laboratory, field specimen forms were amended to include catalog numbers. Only those artifacts deemed to be tools or diagnostic items were curated; all other material, such as debitage, was weighed and then discarded. No records of the weighed debitage were available at the time of my study.

Aside from burial, feature, and specimen forms, there is little in the way of field notes. Brown mentions a field notebook where "minor disturbances of the earth" were described, but no such notebook has been found.

At the start of excavation, profiles were drawn every 5 feet (1.52 m) on the north faces of the east-west walls. Profiles were less enlightening than expected; hence they were subsequently recorded every 10 feet (3.05 m). Although Brown reports that all horizons were even throughout the mound with little or no stratification, the northern shell deposit was twice the volume of the southern one. The depth of the deposit also varied. At the north bluff it was 4 feet (1.22 m) deep. Near the top of the mound it was approximately 5 feet (1.52 m), but for the most part it was reported to be 45 inches (1.14 m) (Webb 1950b:384). The final report about the WPA excavations at Read was published in February 1950 in one of Webb's last reports from the New Deal program. Howard Winters

(1974:vi) states: "It is to be regretted that he deferred these projects to his waning years, when he could no longer bring to his writing the clarity of insight and acuity in analysis that marked the years of his peak productivity."

The Read site report reflects this lack of clarity but does contain many valuable tables summarizing artifact assemblages and the human burials. The bulk of the report is divided between description of the many burials and description of the "atlatl complex." Schwartz (1967), summarizing Kentucky archaeology, noted that archaeological reports in the Commonwealth, including those of Webb's during the post–World War II era, were oriented toward trait lists, which paid little heed to cultural reconstruction or cultural dynamics (see also Taylor 1971:73–78).

The Read site can be characterized, according to Webb, as a single-component site of the Archaic tradition, probably late in the Archaic to judge from the presence of winged and geniculate atlatl weights made from slate. Most human activity was apparently carried out on a clay ridge between the north and south shell lenses. Burials are fairly evenly divided between the clay ridge and the northern shell lens. Because the burials are located in both the residual clay and the shell deposit, Brown (1939:3–4) conjectured (and Webb reiterates in the 1950b report) that the primary concern with respect to burial placement was the availability of high ground, not the ease of digging a grave.

Lithic Analysis

The first objective of my study was to provide a more complete description of the Bt10 lithic assemblage. A typology based upon reductive stages of biface production trajectory was chosen. Such typologies, although varying in detail, have been widely employed near the Green River geographical region (Collins, ed., 1979; Johnson 1981; Morrow 1982). Instead of categorizing lithic material in a traditional manner using only functional designations (e.g., projectile point, endscraper, and so on), this typology follows the reductive sequence used in making bifacial tools. The classification also notes what type of edge modification has been made.

The typological key used for the Bt10 material was modeled on one developed by Carol Morrow (1982) for a Middle Archaic assemblage from Illinois.

Typology

A biface production trajectory typology organizes the assemblage so that information about the production of tools and about the roles of informal versus formal tools is accessible. The key is organized around a series of questions listed in a specific order. This order is crucial to the classification scheme. The key divides the assemblage into two main branches: those artifacts that are bifacially symmetrical and those that are not. If the artifact in question is symmetrical in cross section, then it is considered to be a bifacial tool; hence, the analysis proceeds vertically in the typological key. The definition of a bifacial tool rests on the concept of symmetry in lieu of the more traditional definition based on whether two opposing surfaces have been flaked (Crabtree 1972). According to Morrow, "Bifacial symmetry may be conceptualized as an imaginary line encircling the lateral edge of an artifact so that if the artifact is split transversely along this plan, the two resulting halves are mirror images of each other. If flakes are removed to produce a biface and are therefore oriented along this bifacial plane, each removal is within the symmetrical shape being developed and contributes to the overall symmetry" (Morrow 1982:1292).

Those artifacts that do not meet the definition of bifacial symmetry are considered to be by-products of the manufacturing process, and, therefore, the analysis follows a horizontal branch of the typological key. This does not imply that those artifacts classified as by-products are excluded from the universe of "tools"; by-products that show evidence of modified edges are considered to be "informal tools."

After making the initial distinction between products and by-products of the lithic industry, one asks further questions as one proceeds through the key. Morrow provides a more detailed explanation of this process than need be repeated here. In my research, I have defined each stage of the reduction sequence and how the by-products are categorized.

The typological key used for the Bt10 material departs in one way from that used by Morrow (1982). I have added two additional categories to the "flake" branch of the key. Instead of limiting the distinction between types of informal tools for a branch to those with either unifacially or bifacially worked edges, I noted whether the edge in question was the transverse margin (in traditional terms, an endscraper). After the initial examination of the collection, I noted that a large number of finished bifaces (i.e., projectile points) had been reworked into finished bifaces with either a transverse unifacial or bifacial edge (see Hensley-Martin 1986:82–124 for further discussion). Therefore, I expanded the typological key to distinguish such artifacts from other flake tools with either unifacial or bifacial edges. The remainder of the key and the definitions of the various classes (stages) are much the same as Morrow's (1982).

In addition to classifying each specimen by Morrow's typological key, I recorded several attributes for the artifacts. Basic measurements were made such as length, width, and thickness, as well as the weights of all unbroken specimens. Length was measured along the longest axis of the artifact if it had no clear orientation. For artifacts with recognizable proximal and distal ends, length is that measure from midpoint of the proximal end to the distal portions. Width refers to the widest portion of the artifact perpendicular to the length. Thickness is the thickest point of the artifact. If the artifact was broken, only those measurements that were complete were recorded. Additional measurements were taken on some artifact classes with special morphological features. For instance, the widths of hafting elements on artifacts were measured. The edge angles of hafted endscrapers, finished bifaces with transverse unifacial or bifacial edges, and flakes with transverse unifacial or bifacial edges were also recorded (see Hensley-Martin 1986).

Thermal alteration was noted if present in the form of spalling or crazing. Other possible characteristics such as gloss (Purdy 1974) were not used as indicators of heat treating because no experimental studies were carried out or are available for the specific chert types found at Bt10. No attempt was made to determine whether the thermal alteration occurred prior to reductive activities to aid in knapping or whether the spalling or crazing resulted from postdepositional processes.

Initially, chert types were described in terms of grain size, color, texture, and whether they were fossiliferous or not, in the hopes that such description would allow identification of at least the most distinctive geological sources. A portion of the Bt10 sample was examined by Thomas Gatus, an expert on chert sources from Kentucky (Gatus 1979, 1980, 1983a, b, 1984a, b).

The Sample

To report the number and kind of tool designations without first considering the limitations of the sample would be misleading. A widespread conception concerning WPA sites is that recovery procedures were heavily biased toward what is known in the vernacular as "the goodies." That is, the excavators or supervisors kept only recognizable tool types (e.g., projectile points, scrapers, drills) and discarded debitage as well as crude nondescript tools. By classifying the artifacts in a reductive trajectory scheme, one may gain further insight into the range of items considered worth keeping by the WPA supervisors. In addition to delineating the biases in WPA collecting procedures, I also wanted to know simply what quantity of the original archaeological sample was recovered by the WPA excavation strategy.

In an attempt to answer these questions, I plotted the original WPA artifact classification by the density of lithic artifacts per square for each of the six arbitrary levels. The greatest number of lithic artifacts recovered from any one square per level is six, with one artifact being the mode. Considering that a square is 5 feet (1.52 m) on a side and a level is 9 inches (22.86 cm) deep, the number of artifacts collected is extremely low for a habitation site believed to represent annual seasonal occupation for at least a millennium.

Despite this unexpected and very disappointing recovery rate, I tried to identify spatial patterns that might reflect the two workshop areas Webb mentions in his report (1950b:362–63). The site map included in Rolingson's (1967) dissertation shows the location of both human and dog burials as well as shaded areas believed to be features, but the features are not identified in the map key. I plotted the frequency of each artifact class (finished biface, preform, blank, and so on) by square. The small sample size with respect to the surface area involved made attempts to plot the distribution by level and by square useless. The resulting plots showed no clear patterns. It was hoped that blanks and preforms would have overlapping distributions, possibly indicating workshop areas. This was true to a small degree, but there certainly is no distinct clustering. The two classes, blanks and preforms, overlap no more than any other two classes. If the artifact plots are taken at face value, one could conclude that the site had no specific lithic workshops or work areas that demanded specific tools, such as drills. Given the recovery rate, however, this is a dubious conclusion.

Nevertheless, the suggestion that the WPA workmen kept only finished artifacts does not hold true for Bt10. All stages of the bifacial reduction sequence are represented, but with one qualification: the flakes all have some secondary retouch and were presumably utilized. Hence, it appears that the WPA did not save all the debitage per se, but neither did they collect only the "goodies."

Finally, the sample that was available for my study differs in number from that used by Webb when writing his monograph and by Rolingson at the time of her dissertation research. A total of 1,679 artifacts was catalogued by the WPA as coming from Bt10. I classified 1,513, a difference of 166 artifacts. There are two immediate explanations for the discrepancy. First, at the time I borrowed the assemblage from the University of Kentucky's Museum of Anthropology, not all the artifacts from Bt10 were in the appropriate location and thus were not included in the loan agreement. It is also possible that the missing artifacts have been lost or are on loan to other institutions.

Rolingson (1967:275) reports 426 projectile points from Bt10; I received only 362 from the University of Kentucky's Museum of Anthropology. Sixty-four artifacts are missing. There are also 29 artifacts within my sample that do not have corresponding WPA records. The most likely explanation for this latter discrepancy is clerical error. Several of the artifact catalogue numbers are difficult to read, but all are clearly marked as being from Bt10.

Manufacturing System

It is difficult to interpret the raw numbers resulting from the bifacial reduction scheme in Table 9.1 given the strong biases in the sample. Nevertheless, it is possible to make a few observations about the overall assemblage.

My purpose in applying this reductive typology was to identify the characteristics of the production system used at Bt10. The nature of the sample makes this difficult, but not impossible. The presence of at least one core and 23 angular fragments indicates that some initial reduction activities took place

Table 9.1. Bifacial Reductive Classification of Works Progress
Administration Artifacts from 15Bt10

Class	Frequency	Cumulative Frequency	Percent	Cumulative Percent
Angular fragment	1	1	0.07	0.07
Angular fragment w/bifacial edge	11	12	0.73	0.79
Angular fragment w/unifacial edge	11	23	0.73	1.52
Blank	69	92	4.56	6.08
Core	1	93	0.07	6.15
Drill	189	282	12.49	18.64
Finished biface	432	714	28.55	47.19
Finished biface w/transverse bifacial edge	4	718	0.26	47.46
Finished biface w/transverse unifacial edge	379	1097	25.05	72.50
Flake w/bifacial edge	22	1119	1.45	73.96
Flake w/unifacial edge	11	1130	0.73	74.69
Flake w/both unifacial and bifacial edge	127	1257	8.39	83.08
Flake w/transverse bifacial edge	7	1264	0.46	83.54
Flake w/transverse unifacial edge	69	1333	4.56	88.10
Preform	179	1512	11.83	99.93
Unidentified	1	1513	0.07	100.0

at the site. Middle-stage manufacturing activities are evidenced by the number of blanks and preforms (unfinished tools) found. A total of 248 unfinished tools was recovered compared with 1,005 finished tools (finished means finished bifaces, finished bifaces with transverse unifacial or bifacial edges, and drills). There is a ratio of one unfinished tool for every 4.05 finished. The absence of final-stage, thinning flakes is undoubtedly a result of recovery bias; therefore, there is no conclusive evidence that the final stage of bifacial production occurred at Bt10. However, the presence of 1,005 finished artifacts suggests that it did. At this point, it is difficult to say beyond presence or absence what the character of the lithic industry was and what percentage of the reduction process is represented.

Approximately 16% of the artifacts are flake tools or what are considered here to be informal tool types. If angular fragments with secondary retouch are included in the informal tool group, then the total is raised to more than 17%. Formal tools account for approximately 82% of the assemblage. Formal tools include finished bifaces, finished bifaces with either unifacial or bifacial transverse edges, drills, blanks, and preforms. Blanks and preforms, as the words themselves indicate, are not tools. But, in fact, the definitions I used necessitate considering for each tool the stage of the manufacturing process it represents. Nor do my definitions exclude the possibility of such items being used for various purposes without further modification. I consider blanks and preforms to be formal tools—not so much on the basis of use as on the basis that they were intended to be transformed into finished bifaces—but for one reason or another were instead discarded.

Another characteristic of the assemblage is the predominance of recycled tools, especially finished bifaces with transverse unifacial edges (379, 25% of the total sample analyzed). Recycling or rejuvenation of tools could reflect scarcity of raw material, but an alternative explanation in this case is that the practice of recycling is an inherent feature of Middle to Late Archaic industries (Jefferies 1982:350). As Jefferies points out, the "projectile points" from the Woodland period are not suitable for recycling as heavy-duty scrapers because they were designed to tip arrows as opposed to spears and atlatl darts (ibid.). Jefferies (ibid.) also concludes for Carrier Mills areas A and B "that the percentage of hafted endscrapers decreases through time [that is, from the Middle/Late-Archaic to the Woodland period] while the percentage of other types of endscrapers increases."

This trend is also present in the Bt10 data, but not in a very dramatic way. The percentage of hafted endscrapers (finished bifaces with transverse unifacial edge) steadily increases from level 6 to 2 (presumably these levels represent the early to middle portions of that part of the Archaic tradition represented at Bt10) (see Haskins in prep. for a discussion of Bt10 radiocarbon dates) but drops off from level 2 (8.81%) to 1 (7.99%) (the termination of the Archaic?). Other endscrapers (flake with transverse unifacial edge) decrease from level 6 to 5 but continue to increase from level 5 to 1. It should be noted that almost every class of lithic artifacts decreases from level 2 to 1, so that although it may be true that the trend reported by Jefferies is repeated at Bt10, it may simply be characteristic of the entire Bt10 assemblage.

Gatus (1984a) has conducted a survey of available chert sources within a 50-square-mile area of the Big Bend of Green River. According to him, most cherts mapped within the area are not suitable for making chipped stone tools. Eleven chert types found within his study area are considered to be minimally suited for stone tool production. Of these eleven, the two best chert-bearing units are Vienna and St. Louis. Both of these cherts are highly siliceous, and both occur in sufficient quantity to be dependable sources. Although Gatus's study provides only a general overview of where chert sources are located along the Middle Green River drainage, it is clear that many good-quality cherts are locally available.

The Bt10 lithic artifacts appear to have been made from locally available chert sources. Gatus made a preliminary macroscopic examination of a small sample (less than 75 specimens) of Bt10 projectile points. The majority were made from either St. Louis or Ste. Genevieve chert. These two sources cannot be distinguished from each other macroscopically. The remaining chert formations represented include Fort Payne, Girken, Menard, Vienna, Kinkaid, Salem/Harrisburg, and Warsaw (Gatus, personal communication). Gatus also has briefly examined Rolingson's type collection and states: "I would suspect that many of the items observed in Rolingson's collection originated near the western border of the coal fields and to a lesser degree, from the southern and eastern borders, in that order" (Gatus 1984a).

Summary

Webb (1950b) concludes that the Read site was a single-component site. The occupation lasted late into the Archaic, but because the site is located on a bluff top away from the immediate riverbank, it was not used during either the Woodland or Mississippian periods. Rolingson (1967) disputes the interpretation that the site is single component. However, Webb's assessment that the site was occupied late into the Archaic period is substantiated (Haskins and Herrmann, this volume; Hensley-Martin 1986:125–56; Rolingson 1967).

It is difficult to interpret the artifactual material given the almost total lack of context. To add to Webb's interpretation of the site, we need a much more ambitious study, one that incorporates all of the materials recovered as well as a more detailed study of the excavation records. At the time I received the lithic collection from the University of Kentucky's Museum of Anthropology, accessibility to the WPA records was hampered because of a lack of organization of the archival material. That situation has since been remedied, and now archival material is available and easy to retrieve (see Milner and Smith 1986b for detailed explanation of the museum's holdings).

This study provides insights into the WPA collection bias at the Read site specifically (and probably at the other Green River sites as well) and into aspects of Archaic technology. Furthermore, it allows for a comparison of the Read site with other Archaic sites (Hensley 1994). My analytical use of a bifacial reductive trajectory made it possible for me to discern what types of stone tools were kept by WPA-era personnel at the Read site. Although the frequency of formal tools (bifaces) is greater than the informal (flake tools) by a 5:1 ratio, it was encouraging to discover that at least some flake tools were kept. It was also observed that there was some initial reductive activity at Bt10 as well as intermediate stage reduction of lithic material. However, no direct evidence of final-stage production or maintenance activities (i.e., no bifacial thinning flakes) is present, and it must be inferred based on the presence of complete bifaces. Recycled tools (specifically, hafted endscrapers) are a major feature of the chipped-stone assemblage. The majority of chert types used for tool production are believed to be local.

The most disappointing data elicited by my research was the recovery rate of lithic artifacts by WPA excavators. Only one chipped stone artifact per 9-inch (22.85-cm) level within a 5-feet-square (1.52-m) excavation unit was the norm, and the greatest number of lithic artifacts from one unit per level was only six. These low numbers make it difficult to discern spatial patterns.

The majority of tools came from the second level, 9 to 18 inches (22.85 to 46.15 cm) below ground level. Hence, the description given by Webb (1950b:362–63) of the features and associated materials appears to be the most detailed information currently available about intrasite patterning at Bt10. This could be remedied if all the site's artifacts, not just the lithics, are plotted.

One of the objectives of my study was to evaluate the feasibility of analyzing material from the WPA era to add to the growing body of knowledge of the Archaic tradition. Given our current understanding of the Archaic, can WPA collections contribute to today's archaeology? I believe they can. In fact, WPA materials must be studied today. It is very difficult to compare Green River Archaic site data from older accounts with Green River Archaic site data acquired in the past few years (Hensley 1994). For instance, in the case of projectile point types, WPA reports give tables of descriptive types (e.g., long-stemmed point or short-stemmed point) that could be construed as equivalent to today's Late Archaic straight-stemmed point types. But the lack of definitive measurements and of illustrations depicting these points leaves considerable doubt as to whether or not the points are indeed similar. Quantified descriptions of points in WPA collections could yield solid and useful data (see, for example, Hensley-Martin 1986:125–56).

Given that sites excavated by the WPA either no longer exist or contain few or no undisturbed deposits, I believe it essential to continue examining older collections in light of present-day information.

10 | Shell Mound Bioarchaeology

Valerie A. Haskins and
Nicholas P. Herrmann

THE RICH ARCHAEOLOGICAL resources of the Green River drainage in Kentucky have yielded some of the most important collections of human skeletal remains in the southeastern United States. It has been widely acknowledged that excavation of these sites, particularly the large shell middens, was critical in developing our conception of the Archaic tradition in Kentucky (e.g., Chapman and Watson 1993). Analyses of the skeletal remains recovered from these sites have similarly shaped the field of bioarchaeology. In this chapter we examine the impact of such analyses and demonstrate that skeletal research in this region may be viewed as a microcosm of trends and techniques in North American archaeology and in physical anthropology during the past century. The role of the best known of the Green River shell mound sites, Indian Knoll (15Oh2), is examined in detail. A summary of paleodemography at the Read site (15Bt10) is offered as an example of current research.

The three orientations that characterized the history of North American archaeology—the speculative, empirical, and explanatory approaches outlined by Schwartz and others—may be seen in the history of Kentucky archaeology as well (Schwartz 1967). The evolution of skeletal research in the Green River drainage mirrors that of archaeology through the past few decades. These trends are demonstrated in the first descriptive reports of isolated exotic phenomena and in the most recent multidisciplinary synthetic approaches.

Speculation, Description, and Racial Typology (1700s–1930s)

The earliest human remains described from the Green River drainage include the desiccated bodies found in the large, dry caves of south-central Kentucky. Many antiquarians believed that there was a connection between Egypt and the New World. These "mummies," as the preserved bodies were called, initially provided substantiation for the common misconception that Egyptians, rather than prehistoric American Indians, built the large earthworks that dotted the landscape. Others, such as Squier and Davis (quoted in Putnam 1875:314–22), Jones (1876:1–5), Bushnell (1920:66), and Nelson (1917:27) were confident that the preserved bodies were indeed those of prehistoric Indians. In addition to the descriptions of mummies, other early reports include accounts of isolated skeletons in caves and tales of huge, cavernous charnel structures filled with bodies beneath the city of Lexington. (See George, ed., 1990; Haskins 1988; Meloy 1971; Meloy and Watson 1969 for comprehensive assessments of historical cave burial documentation in Kentucky and elsewhere in the southeastern United States.) These finds (and fantasies) were recorded in the early histories of the settlement of Kentucky as curiosities, but little or no explanation was offered.

Following these early speculations, a more empirical approach was taken by the turn of the century. "Modern" excavations were undertaken by Nels C. Nelson in the Vestibule of Mammoth Cave and by Clarence B. Moore at large shell middens along Green River (Table 10.1). Moore spent nine weeks during the fall and winter of 1915–16 investigating sites along Green River before he devoted, as he says, "nearly five months . . . to rather profitless work on Ohio and Mississippi Rivers" (C. Moore 1916:431). Few human remains were recovered from Nelson's endeavors at Mammoth Cave, but Moore's excavations at Indian Knoll alone yielded 298 burials in addition to a number of scattered bones. An idea of the methods employed by Moore's workmen may be inferred when one realizes that eight men spent only 179 hours excavating the site (C. Moore 1916:445). Although clearly not recovered under ideal conditions, these collections were the first of the large skeletal series to be obtained from this region.

Consistent with conventions current at the time, most of the burials were not completely removed, and much post-cranial material was reburied at the sites. Only 66 crania from Indian Knoll were saved. Moore (1916:438) notes, "As usual, we have forwarded to the Army Medical Museum, Washington, D.C., all pathological specimens obtained during our season's work, otherwise all skulls and skeletons saved have been sent to the United States National Museum" (now known as the National Museum of Natural History at the Smithsonian Institution). There the remains were analyzed by Aleš Hrdlička, curator of the Division of Physical Anthropology, and his young assistant, T. Dale Stewart. Hrdlička's preliminary observation was that the crania were "typical, unde-formed, Algonquin skulls" unrelated to the Shawnee (Moore 1916:448). Of particular interest was a human lumbar vertebra transfixed by an antler spear point.

A series of standard metric measurements were performed on the crania, the results of which were published in the 1927 Proceedings of the United States National Museum (Hrdlička 1927; see also Von Bonin and Morant 1938). The hallmark of research in skeletal biology during this period was to attempt to determine racial affinity (through anthropomorphic techniques) to establish the history of a population. A sense of time depth was lacking; many sites were known to be old, but sites such as Indian Knoll were thought to be inhabited a

Table 10.1 Pre-1930 Human Skeleton Collections from the Green River
Drainage Basin

Site	Number of Individuals	County	Culture	Investigator
Indian Knoll	298	Ohio	Archaic	Moore (1916)
Bluff City	17	Henderson	Archaic	Moore (1916)
Calhoun	16	McLean	Archaic	Moore (1916)
Smallhous	5	Ohio	Archaic	Moore (1916)
Martin	15	Butler	Mississippian	Moore (1916)
Cherry	4	Butler	Mississippian	Moore (1916)
Little Reedy Point	1	Butler	Mississippian ?	Moore (1916)
Mammoth Cave	3	Edmonson	Multicultural	Nelson (1917)
Rockshelter	1	Edmonson	Archaic ?	Nelson (1917)

mere thousand years ago. Many physical anthropologists, including Hrdlička, thought that typologies based on cranial indices could help indicate racial affinity, and it was not uncommon to compare materials from sites separated diachronically by thousands of years. Although criticisms of the racial typology approach had been offered by Virchow and Boas at the turn of this century, their comments were directed toward the methods used rather than the theoretical or conceptual principles (Armelagos, Carlson, and van Gerven 1982). Hrdlička and others believed that standardization and yet more measurements would provide the answers to these problems.

The typological approach to racial affinity continued to be used for many decades. Earnest A. Hooton was one of the strongest proponents of this approach, and skeletal biology research was dominated by Hooton and his students until the late 1950s. Trained at Harvard by Hooton, Charles E. Snow became a crucial figure in the skeletal research conducted on sites along Green River. He supervised physical anthropology at the University of Kentucky for many years. Best known for his 1948 analyses of the Indian Knoll skeletons, Snow (along with two fellow Hooton students, Ivar Skarland and H. T. E. Hertzberg) wrote many of the skeletal reports included in the monographs published by Webb and others about sites excavated along Green River during the 1930s and 1940s. It is during this time that the large-scale Works Progress Administration (WPA) excavations yielded the large skeletal collections that are the primary focus of this chapter.

The New Deal Era: More Descriptions (1930s–1950s)

Spurred by Moore's earlier accounts of the Indian Knoll excavations, his survey and testing in the area during the 1920s (Funkhouser and Webb 1928, 1932), and his work on large-scale projects in Tennessee, northern Alabama, and Mississippi (Webb 1938, 1939; Webb and DeJarnette 1942), William S. Webb thought that the massive shell middens along Green River would be ideal sites to investigate using the large WPA work forces available to him. Unemployment was high in western Kentucky, and the laborers provided the labor pool necessary to excavate such large sites. Milner and Smith (1986a, b, 1988), among others, have summarized the details and implications of the New Deal–era excavations; for more information regarding these projects in Kentucky, see Cotter (1938), Griffin (1985), Guthe (1952), Haag (1961, 1985), Hensley-Martin (1986), Jefferies (1988, 1990), Lyon (1982), Rolingson (1967), and Schwartz (1967).

Webb's excavations in the Green River drainage during the 1930s and 1940s resulted in a minimum of 2,991 burials being excavated. Of these, 2,720, or nearly 91%, were attributed to the Archaic (Table 10.2). Augmenting the 298 burials previously noted by Moore, WPA excavations resulted in the recovery of an additional 880 burials at Indian Knoll alone. Although few burials were recovered at some of the sites, and adjustments have since been made to the vast numbers recovered from others, the percentage of Archaic burials remains overwhelmingly high. Green River skeletal series are, therefore, the most significant single source of data regarding bioarchaeology for the Archaic in Kentucky and are crucial for the southeastern United States as a whole.

It is clear that the research potential of Green River skeletal collections has not been fully realized. With the exception of data from Indian Knoll and Chiggerville (15Oh1), descriptions of skeletal remains were relegated to tables or appendices in site reports. Few of the assemblages were systematically analyzed, and many of the age and sex classifications in the reports are based only on the supervisors' observations in the field. Often, only the burials that included significant artifacts (such as atlatl components) were carefully studied by Snow. As a result, our information about the mortuary characteristics of Green River sites and the physical anthropology of these populations is heavily biased—and often erroneous.

Recent Research: Bioarchaeological Approach (1960s–Present)

Until the 1960s research in skeletal biology tended to be particularistic in nature. Cranial metric and nonmetric studies oriented toward establishing racial affinity dominated. Paleopathologies were often merely noted, although there are a few exceptions such as Hooton's (1930) epidemiological perspective for Pecos Pueblo. Biases were prevalent in the collection and analysis of skeletal

Table 10.2. Human Skeleton Collections from the Green River Drainage Basin (New Deal and Post–World War II Era: 1930–1950)

Site	Number of Individuals	County	Culture	Investigator(s)
Page	271+	Logan	Mississippian	Webb & Funkhouser (1930)
Chiggerville	114	Ohio	Archaic	Webb & Haag (1940)
Ward	433	McLean	Archaic	Webb & Haag (1940)
Kirkland	70	McLean	Archaic	Webb & Haag (1940)
Indian Knoll	880	Ohio	Archaic	Webb (1946)
Barrett	412	McLean	Archaic	Webb & Haag (1947)
Butterfield	153	McLean	Archaic	Webb & Haag (1947)
Read Shell Midden	247	Butler	Archaic	Webb (1950b)
Carlston Annis	390	Butler	Archaic	Webb (1950a)
Bowles	21	Ohio	Archaic	(unreported)

remains; crania and well-preserved elements were saved, but cremated and fragmented materials were often reburied. Special attention was given to those burials that contained associated grave goods; in other cases, the initial field observations may be the only recorded documentation. With the exception of Indian Knoll (Snow 1948), most sites received little formal analysis on the skeletal materials (Skarland 1939).

Concurrent with trends in physical anthropology and archaeology during the 1950s and 1960s, skeletal researchers turned toward a more populational orientation (Armelagos et al. 1982). This culminated during the 1970s in the establishment of the field of *bioarchaeology*, in which osteological data are examined within an archaeological, environmental, and cultural framework. This has been the dominant explanatory approach for the last 20 years. Descriptive analyses such as aging and sexing are still prevalent, but multivariate morphometric techniques are employed to establish firmer conceptions about the paleodemographic profiles of skeletal series, which can then be compared on a regional scale. Mortuary customs are investigated in terms of differences in socioeconomic status as reflected in skeletal stature estimates and dietary practices, as well as inclusion of associated burial goods. Paleopathological analyses incorporate assessments of nutritional status, dietary stress, and infectious diseases, using an epidemiological approach first utilized by Hooton. Data regarding prehistoric faunal and botanical exploitation are incorporated, as well as geophysical, chemical, and environmental factors. In short, all available data are utilized to present a complete picture of individuals within a populational structure.

Currently, scholars are discovering the value of curated materials in archaeological research (see, for example, Cantwell et al. 1981; Hensley, this volume). This includes human skeletal material. Today, many new techniques are available to go beyond estimating age and sex, and the skeletal collections from the Green River drainage have been the source of some of the most important bioarchaeological data compiled during the last 30 years. Indian Knoll, because of its vast number of well-preserved individuals, is the best documented of these sites, but various others, including Chiggerville, Carlston Annis (15Bt5), and now Read and Kirkland (15McL12), have been reanalyzed and interpreted within a broader biocultural context. Although skeletal research conducted on collections from Green River drainage sites has been dominated by those dating from the Archaic, analyses on materials from more recent sites has also been undertaken in the 1990s. Few burials were recovered from most of these sites; these are not discussed here.

Our aim is not to present a detailed assessment of all the bioarchaeological analyses that have been conducted with Green River sites but, rather, to offer a brief review of the research conducted on Archaic shell mound series to illustrate the richness and importance of this research. Many aspects are explored, including biodistance, paleodemography, mortuary behavior and social organization, paleopathology and paleonutrition, and growth and development. In addition, research conducted on these skeletal materials has been integral for developing and testing some of the most useful and important new methods for osteological analysis. A summary of these studies and their importance follows.

Biodistance

Biodistance studies, aimed toward distinguishing genetic differences within and among skeletal series, is primarily based on the presence or absence of discrete, phenotypic, metrical, and nonmetrical traits (including craniometrics); these studies are a natural outgrowth of the racial typology investigations discussed earlier in this chapter. Using multivariate techniques on various skeletal series from the Green River drainage, a number of researchers tested their hypotheses about biological relationships within and between groups. Because of the large sample size and remarkable preservation, as well as the availability of thousands of metric and morphometric observations recorded by Snow and others, the Indian Knoll collection has been the major focus of research.

Studies of biodistance in the Indian Knoll series were primarily designed to determine how this population compared with other series (Long 1964, 1966). Snow (1948:Table 1) recorded 69 metrical variables on Indian Knoll crania, an average of eight measurements for each major long bone, and also recorded non-metrical traits. Snow's observations were analyzed qualitatively rather than quantitatively because he was interested in establishing predefined racial types within the series. Similarly, Long analyzed 10 metrical traits in a sample of 131 crania and used multiple-discriminant analysis to assign these to racial (e.g., Iswanid) types (see also Neumann 1952). Original measurements from both studies are available at the University of Kentucky Museum of Anthropology.

Other studies of biodistance in the Indian Knoll series used smaller samples. Higel (1965) reports the results of an analysis of 91 skeletons, and Prewett and Wolf (1979) examined a smaller sample in a comparative study of biodistance. Hardy's study (1974) reports the effect of variation in size on the metrical study of biodistance between skeletal series (see also Droessler 1981).

Paleodemography

Paleodemographic studies have dramatically increased since the 1970s. The large skeletal collections recovered from the shell middens along Green River are characterized by excellent preservation of fetal and infant remains as well as those of adults; these series have provided data sets from which mortality rates, male-to-female ratios, differential mortuary treatments, and other population parameters could be investigated. Indian Knoll has figured prominently in many studies of prehistoric demography (Blakely 1971; Howells 1960; Johnston and Snow 1961; Kelley 1980; Sundick 1972a, b). The most recent paleodemographic analyses from the Green River region include those of Mensforth (1986, 1990, in press) for the Carlston Annis population and currently our work on the Read site materials (Haskins in prep.; Herrmann 1990). Both sets of researchers found that all three populations share relatively similar survivorship profiles; all three series exhibit a Type II (Weiss 1973) survivorship profile with high infant mortality and a relatively early onset of increased mortality in adults. Our preliminary results are discussed under *Current Perspectives* later.

Mortuary Behavior and Social Organization

Some of the most useful data regarding mortuary behavior and social organization have been compiled from the Indian Knoll site. Nan Rothschild's work (1975, 1979), in particular, has been instrumental in establishing our current understanding of the social dimensions of mortuary practices during the Archaic period. She demonstrates that the Indian Knoll population exhibits little variation in social status among members and none that appears to be ascribed. Analysis of exchange in artifacts has also failed to demonstrate evidence of strong social boundaries (Winters 1968, 1974). It must be cautioned, however, that there is some variation in the distribution of grave goods between biological males and females, prompting Boisvert (1979:11) to suggest there was a "certain degree of social inequality present." It is possible that this difference in grave good associations may simply reflect the role of the individual in the society. Finally, the large numbers of infants and children at Indian Knoll buried with grave goods (e.g., shell beads and tortoise-shell rattles) present some interesting patterns of differential burial associations that appear to be age rather than status related (Thiel 1972).

These data from Indian Knoll, taken together with mortuary studies among Archaic populations in Illinois (e.g., Charles and Buikstra 1983; Phillips and Brown, eds., 1983) and biodistance studies, such as those conducted by Long (1964, 1966), indicate that Late Archaic societies had relatively fluid boundaries, little variation in social status, and wide-ranging social and exchange networks. This lack of marked social boundaries within and between populations during the Late Archaic supports the inference that intrapopulational variation may be attributed to temporal factors rather than to social distinctions. Finally, the uses of the shell middens as formal mortuary facilities is being explored by Claassen (1992 and this volume).

Paleopathology and Paleonutrition

The role of health and disease in populations is fast becoming a major focus of bioarchaeological research, although it has long been of interest. Some of the earliest research focused on the role of diet, health, and disease in Green River shell mound collections. Leigh (1925:179–96), for instance, was far ahead of his time in his investigations of the relationship between diet and dental attrition. Wakefield and Dellinger (1940:453–62) reviewed some of the paleopathologies noted from the Indian Knoll series in their description of diseases evident in prehistoric remains from the southeastern United States. In 1939 Skarland (1939:28–49) conducted a thorough analysis of the Chiggerville skeletal remains, incorporating many of the biocultural dimensions used today (1939:28–49). Rabkin (1943:355–66) was also concerned with the patterns of dental attrition and disease observed in the Indian Knoll series. In general, however, although pathological specimens were noted, little problem-oriented research was conducted.

Many aspects of diet and disease on Green River skeletal series have been investigated since the 1970s, including work by Adkins (1988), Belovich (1993), Brothwell (1970), Cassidy (1972, 1980, 1984), Haskins (in prep.), Kelley (1980, 1982), Knutson (1982), Mensforth (in press), Perzigian (1971, 1977a), Pierce (1987), Robbins (1974, 1977), Sullivan (1977), and Ward (in prep.). Avenues of inquiry include the incidence of degenerative joint disease (such as osteoarthritis and intervertebral osteochondrosis), trauma, osteoporosis, fluctuating dental asymmetry, dental pathology, infectious disease, and metabolic disorders at Indian Knoll, Chiggerville, and Carlston Annis, in particular. Many of these studies are ongoing. A more detailed discussion of studies concerning the health and disease of Green River Archaic populations is presented by Powell (this volume).

Growth and Development

Studies relating to skeletal growth and development have provided some of the most useful data from U.S. sites. The works of Johnston (1961, 1962, 1968, 1969), Johnston and Snow (1961), Snow (1948), and Sundick (1971, 1972a, b) include observations for skeletal growth and development at Indian Knoll. Other studies of this series interpret smaller samples: Sarnas (1957, 1964) reports variation in cranial development as well as dental decay in a small sample of teeth; Ruff (1980) also reports on age-related craniofacial changes in individuals from Indian Knoll. Mensforth (1986) examines patterns of relative tibia long bone growth at Carlston Annis and compares the results with Libben, a Late Woodland site in Ohio. Wyckoff (1977) investigates biological relationships and growth at Chiggerville. These studies incorporate macroscopic and radiographic observations for age-related sequences of dental eruption, diaphyseal growth, and epiphyseal union. The work of these researchers has been extremely influential within physical anthropology and is a primary source for those interested in determining Amerindian subadult age (see, for example, Ubelaker 1985).

Hamilton (1975) and Allaway (1980) report findings of significant sexual dimorphism in the Indian Knoll populations. Hamilton focused not only on absolute size differences but also on differences in shape between the sexes because these appear to vary significantly between men and women in many societies. Similarly, Fenton (1993) has noted intrapopulational variation in age- and sex-related bilateral asymmetry of the upper and lower limbs in the male and female sample as a whole and between young men and young women. Like Bridges (1989a), he attributes these differences to a reflection of the division of labor in hunting and gathering societies, such as the use of the atlatl at a young age in males. In other studies using skeletal age- and sex-related factors, Finkenstaedt (1984) examined morphological differences in pelves to estimate age at first pregnancy among females at Indian Knoll; Tague (1986, 1988, 1989) also examined pelves from Indian Knoll in his studies related to obstetric changes in hominids. Other specific skeletal features, such as the development of the vermiculate pattern in brow ridges (Tappen 1983), have also been investigated.

Methodology

In addition to the studies noted, a great deal of research relating to testing existing osteological techniques and developing new strategies has been conducted on Green River skeletal series. Once again, the Indian Knoll materials have provided one of the most useful and important data sets for this work. In particular, this series has been utilized for many studies assessing forensic approaches for estimating skeletal and dental growth and development, including criticisms of some of these techniques and/or interpretations of the data (e.g., T. Stewart 1957, 1962). Other diverse types of analyses have included investigations of trace elements in teeth (Steadman et al. 1959), dental attrition scoring techniques (Scott 1979), and the use of the weights of elements from Indian Knoll to interpret bone survival rates in postdepositional mortuary contexts (Fenton 1991, 1993).

Current Perspectives

Although we have attempted to demonstrate, through this brief summary, the importance and vast richness of skeletal research conducted on collections from the Green River drainage, many sites remain to be examined in light of new techniques and perspectives. We chose one of these collections, the Read site, for our paleodemographic and paleopathologic studies. The site dates from the mid–Late Archaic period, with uncorrected radiocarbon dates ranging from 3350 ± 70 to 3470 ± 200 B.P. (Haskins, in prep.), contains no intrusive Mississippian components, and is located near Carlston Annis, allowing us to make some comparisons with the bioarchaeological results recently obtained by Adkins (1988), Belovich (1993), Kelley (1980, 1982), Mensforth (1986, 1990, in press), and Ward (in prep.), and eventually with other studies in progress, such as Haskins's work (in prep.) on the Kirkland (15McL12) and Butterfield (15McL7) collections. The Read materials had not previously been systematically analyzed. A brief summary of a portion of this work, the paleodemography of the Read site, is presented in the following section. More detailed information regarding the methods and results of this analysis are presented in Herrmann (1990, 1993); results of the Carlston Annis and Indian Knoll analyses are summarized by Powell (this volume).

Demographic Parameters for the Read Site, 15Bt10

Specific methods were employed in the demographic analysis of the Read site human skeletal series so that the results could be compared with the Carlston Annis data. Mensforth (1986, 1990, in press) approached the Carlston Annis assemblage from a populational perspective. In his study, he seriated each age indicator (such as auricular surface, pubic symphysis, dental attrition, and radiographs of the proximal femora and clavicles) from what appeared to be the youngest to oldest and then divided the series into various age classifications according to age-specific criteria. Finally, he assigned differential weightings to various age indicators for the generation of his composite age estimates. In the Read study we employed both a case-by-case and a populational approach. Each skeleton was aged on an individual basis according to set standards. The available auricular surfaces and pubic symphyses were then seriated according to Mensforth's standards.

A total of 247 burials was identified during the excavation of the Read site, but only 152 were removed because of poor preservation. Our analyses demonstrated that the 152 burials actually represented a minimum of 173 individuals, of whom 24 could not be placed into specific age ranges. Herrmann conducted a series of statistical tests to show that the analyzed sample was representative of the total burial population and that all age indicators were similarly represented throughout all age ranges. Comparisons of the age distributions derived from the WPA field supervisors' estimates (Webb 1950a) to the analyzed sample resulted mainly in differences between the two distributions in the general age classifications of infants and young adults. These differences could reflect the identification of some infants and young adults as child or adult, respectively, in the WPA study. Additional infants were also found mixed with adult burials during our inventory. A Kolomogorov-Smirnov test of the two distributions showed that they did not differ significantly at the $p > 0.01$ level. Similarly, a chi-square value was insignificant (3.07; $p > 0.05$), illustrating that the high percentage of adults (23.1%) who do not fit into a specific age range should not influence the Read age distributions.

Human archetypal fertility data were incorporated into the life table analysis in accordance with the assumptions of stable and stationary population theory. A life table was derived for the Read series using the methods defined in Weiss (1973).

The population parameter data from the Read site match well with Mensforth's Carlston Annis results; the two sites are almost identical. The mean and median ages for Read are 22.3 and 22.5 years, respectively. For Carlston Annis the mean age was 21.9 years, and the median age was 22 years. The mean ages for adults (+15) for Read and Carlston Annis were 32.9 and 34.7 years, respectively.

The paleodemographic results from the Read site were compared to both Carlston Annis and Indian Knoll (Johnston and Snow 1961). The adult sex ratio (1.10) more closely resembled that from Indian Knoll. The life expectancy profiles of Read, however, compared well with Mensforth's Carlston Annis results. The life expectancy at birth, e_0, for Read, Carlston Annis, and Indian Knoll was 22.2, 22.4, and 19 years, respectively. Life expectancy at the beginning of adulthood, e_{15}, for Carlston Annis and Read were 19.4 and 18.9 years, respectively; however, e_{15} at Indian Knoll was only 14.6 years.

The survivorship curves for Read, Carlston Annis, and Indian Knoll were also compared. Read demonstrates a moderately high infant mortality with a fairly regular mortality rate until the mid-forties. The survivorship rate for individuals from birth to 10 years at Read is greater than for the other two sites. During the early teens, however, the survivorship rate drops rapidly and falls in line with the rates for Carlston Annis and Indian Knoll. The Indian Knoll population's survival rate declines steadily from age 25 to 40 years, whereas the Carlston Annis and Read populations experience a sharp decline in age range of 40 to 45 years. These differences in the survival rate may be the result of differential preservation and poor recovery of infants, high age estimations for individuals over 50 years in the Carlston Annis sample, or low age estimations for individuals over 50 years in the Read series.

The death probability for Carlston Annis's population displays a smooth, gradual increase after one year, with no substantial peaks in mortality. Indian Knoll and Read mortality, however, peaks at ages 35 to 40 years. These differences may be attributed to the age criteria employed for each study. For instance, Mensforth (1986, 1990, in press) used trabecular and cortical bone involution of the clavicle and proximal femur for which age estimates could be over 60 years. For the dental age, he extended estimates into the eighth decade; these dental estimates differ greatly from the age estimates for other indicators.

The Read research shows that differing methods applied to related populations can produce similar results. The major differences in findings between Carlston Annis and Read occur in the data on survival in the age categories below one year and over 55 years. Several explanations of these differences are possible. First, the numbers of infants at Read may be underrepresented because of poor preservation. Second, the adult age indicators employed for each study varied. For example, age estimations for Carlston Annis adults could extend to 70 years. Third, dental age criteria for Carlston Annis could result in overestimates compared to other age indicators. In sum, the mortality patterns from Read are similar to those from Carlston Annis and Indian Knoll, and the few differences shown in the samples probably result from methodological variations and taphonomic processes.

Summary

It is clear that the human skeletal series from the Green River drainage provide some of the most important research foci in the southeastern United States. Indeed, they are the premier source of Archaic bioarchaeological data. Significant strides are being made in the manner in which we interpret human remains. Skeletal materials are unique because they provide a picture of past individuals as well as of populations. Ongoing research is very promising and very exciting. As we enter the late 1990s, we hope to continue our investigation of these collections, most of which have not been systematically analyzed, to establish a synthesis of the bioarchaeology of these ancient peoples.

11 | Health and Disease in the Green River Archaic

Mary Lucas Powell

H<small>ASKINS</small> AND HERRMANN (this volume) reviewed major theoretical and methodological developments over the last century in bioarchaeological analyses of skeletal series representing Archaic period populations from the Green River region in western Kentucky as a prelude to the presentation of their own recent analysis of the Archaic skeletal sample from the Read Shell Mound (15Bt10). As a complement to their historical overview, I present here a brief synthesis of available data on selected aspects of health and disease patterns in Green River Archaic Native Americans. I have drawn on the multifeature studies of Cassidy (1972, 1980, 1984) and Kelley (1980), as well as on more particularistic studies of demography (Johnston and Snow 1961; Mensforth 1986, 1990; T. Stewart 1962; N. Sullivan 1977), biological relationships and growth (Cook 1971; Perzigian 1972; Snow 1948; Wyckoff 1977), osteoporotic bone loss (Perzigian 1971, 1973), dental pathology (Adkins 1988; Leigh 1925; Perzigian 1977b; Rabkin 1943; Ward, in prep.), and infectious disease (Brothwell 1970; Brothwell and Burleigh 1975; Mensforth, in press; Snow 1948; N. Sullivan 1977).

Sites

Indian Knoll

Cassidy (1972, 1984) compared Archaic hunter-gatherers from Indian Knoll (15Oh2) on Green River with Fort Ancient maize farmers of the late prehistoric/ protohistoric period from the Hardin Village site (15Gp22) in northeastern Kentucky. Kelley (1980) drew similar comparisons between the Indian Knoll Archaic people and two later populations: prehistoric maize farmers at Grasshopper Pueblo (P:14:1) in Arizona and historic Arikara hunter-farmers at Mobridge Village (39WW1) in South Dakota. Both authors carefully consider the influences of environmental settings, settlement strategies (seasonal mobility versus year-round sedentism), and diet (relative reliance on cultivated versus gathered plant foods and the importance of hunting, fishing, and shellfish collecting) of these diverse cultures in shaping the observed patterns of health and disease (mortality, traumatic injuries, nutritional deficiencies, dental pathology, osteoarthritis, and specific and nonspecific infectious disease experience).

Chiggerville

Skarland (1939) wrote a brief overview of the skeletal population sample recovered by Webb and Haag (1939) from the Chiggerville site (15Oh1) located 3 miles downriver from Indian Knoll. Norman Sullivan (1977) analyzed in greater depth the mortality patterns and skeletal pathology at that site. Wyckoff (1977) examined patterns of skeletal growth in this same series and also evaluated its biological relationships to Indian Knoll and other Archaic and Woodland period populations from the adjacent Eastern Woodlands.

Carlston Annis

Adkins (1988), Belovich (n.d.), Mensforth (1986, 1990), and Ward (in prep.) collected comparable data in many of these categories from the Archaic skeletal sample from Carlston Annis Shell Mound (15Bt5), located several miles upstream from Indian Knoll and across the river from Read Shell Mound (15Bt10).

I will first present the reported data for these skeletal series, categorized by topic, and then discuss the comparisons drawn by these researchers between Green River Archaic and other Native American population samples.

Demography

Frequent subadult mortality was a sad reality of Green River Archaic life (Table 11.1). At Indian Knoll, Carlston Annis, and Chiggerville, approximately one out of five infants died before the age of one year. Skarland (1939:30) called the "large number of infants, constituting more than one-fourth of the Chiggerville population" a "striking fact." Children who survived their first year had a somewhat better outlook, at least until puberty: the decade between 5 and 15 years showed the lowest mortality experience in all of the samples reported here. The slight rise in mortality around puberty probably reflects adolescent participation in life-threatening "adult" activities: pregnancy and childbirth for girls, hunting and warfare or raiding for boys.

At Indian Knoll Kelley (1980) noted that 57% (463 of 813) survived to age 15. He calculated life expectancy as 19 years at birth; a 15-year-old could reasonably expect to live an additional 15.4 years (Table 11.2). At Carlston Annis, 54% (191 of 354) survived to age 15; Mensforth (1990, Table 4) calculated life expectancy at birth at 22.4 years, with an additional 19.4 years for those surviving to age 15. Mensforth (1990:81) interprets the demographic patterns in his sample as "indicating a healthy population with a substantial capability to replace preceding generations." Archaic adult mortality generally peaked during the fourth decade of life, and few people survived into their sixth or seventh decades (Table 11.3). At Indian Knoll, female mortality exceeded male mortality for ages 15 through 25, but this pattern was strongly reversed in the following

Table 11.1 Mortality to Age 20 in the Green River Archaic

Deaths (%)	Birth–1 Year	1–5 Years	6–10 Years	11–15 Years	16–20 Years
20–30	Indian Knoll K = 20.3 C = 22.8 Carlston Annis M = 24.6 Chiggerville W = 22.0 S = 25.0				
10–20	Indian Knoll J&S = 19.5 Sn = 15.1	Indian Knoll K = 10.6 C = 11.6 S = 14.9 Chiggerville W = 11.4			
0–10		Indian Knoll J&S = 9.6 Carlston Annis M = 9.9	Carlston Annis M = 4.0 Indian Knoll K = 5.4 C = 4.6 S = 8.5 J&S = 6.2 Chiggerville W = 4.8	Carlston Annis M = 7.6 Indian Knoll K = 6.2 C = 5.6 S = 8.5 J&S = 6.1 Chiggerville W = 3.8	Carlston Annis M = 9.9 Indian Knoll K = 6.9 C = 7.4 S = 8.5 J&S = 7.1 Chiggerville W = 1.9

C, Cassidy 1972, Table 10; J&S, Johnston and Snow 1961, Table 1; K, Kelley 1980, Table 5; M, Mensforth 1990, Table 5; S, Skarland, 1939; Sn, Snow 1941, in Johnston and Snow 1961, Table 1; W, Wyckoff 1977, Table 3.

decade and almost equalized in the next (Cassidy 1972:57; Kelley 1980:54–59). Norman Sullivan (1977:50, Figure 7) reports a similar pattern at Chiggerville. At Carlston Annis male mortality exceeded female until age 45 (Mensforth 1990:88). All three of these researchers report far more adults older than 40 years than did Johnston and Snow (1961) in their reassessment of Snow's (1948) original demography. This change is undoubtedly due to the development of new techniques for age estimation that are more sensitive to distinctions among older adult skeletons.

Cassidy (1972, 1984) compared demographic profiles from Indian Knoll with those of the late prehistoric/protohistoric Fort Ancient farmers from Hardin Village in northeast Kentucky. She found a striking reversal of the Late Archaic pattern of high first-year mortality followed by improved survivorship for older infants and weanlings: whereas 70% of Archaic deaths in the birth to four-year age category occurred during the first year, 60% of the deaths at

Table 11.2. Life Expectancy at Birth and at Age 15 in the Green River Archaic

Sample	At Birth	At Age 15
Indian Knoll	C = 17.9 years (F) 21.8 years (M)	C = 18.1 (F) (total = 36) 20.2 (M) (total = 42)
	K = 19 years	15.4 (total = 34.4)
Carlston Annis	M = 22.4 years	19.4 (total = 34.4)

C, Cassidy 1972, Table 13; K, Kelley 1980, Table 7; M, Mensforth 1990, Table 4.

Hardin Village in that age category occurred during years three and four. Mortality was generally higher for all ages at the later site, with 54% of all Hardin Village deaths aged 17 years or younger compared with 45% at Indian Knoll. Life expectancies at birth also differed considerably: 16 years for males and 17 years for females at Hardin Village, compared with 22 years and 18 years, respectively, at Indian Knoll.

When Kelley (1980) compared the Indian Knoll hunter-gatherers with sedentary agriculturalists from Grasshopper Pueblo in Arizona and semisedentary early historic Arikara from Mobridge in South Dakota, he found similar contrasts: 23% mortality by age 2 versus 31% at Grasshopper and 46% at Mobridge. Indian Knoll life expectancy at birth was higher (19 years) than at either of the other two sites (16.5 years and 13 years, respectively), but subsequent life expectancy was lower (15.4 years versus 24.6 and 18.5 years). Indian Knoll survivorship to age 15 (52%) was higher than at Grasshopper (36%) or Mobridge (33%), as was survivorship to age 40 (5.9% versus 13.2% and 9.6%, respectively). Adult mortality by sex was similar at all three sites, with female deaths outnumbering male deaths until age 35 and equality approached only in old age.

Reported Archaic adult sex ratios (males/females × 100) (Table 11.4) are all skewed in favor of males: for Indian Knoll, 124 (283/228) by Johnston and Snow (1961), 132 (90/68) by Cassidy (1972), and 115 (248/215) by Kelley (1980). Other researchers, however, reported more balanced adult sex ratios. Sullivan's (1977) Chiggerville sex ratio (107, 32/30) closely approaches equality, as does the ratio reported by Mensforth (1986, 1990) for Carlston Annis (98, 108/110). Both Stewart (1962) and Mensforth question the accuracy of Snow's original sex estimates. Other recent reanalyses of skeletal series originally examined by Snow (Milner and Jefferies 1986; Powell 1988) have also noted his strong bias toward estimates of male sex, perhaps confirming Weiss's (1972) cautionary admonition.

Skarland (1939:30) reports 40 males, 22 females, and 12 "intermediates" in a sample of 74 Chiggerville "juveniles and adults," noting, "In general, the

Table 11.3 Mortality over Age 20 in the Green River Archaic

Deaths (%)	20–30 Years	31–40 Years	41–50 Years	50+ Years
20–40	Indian Knoll K = 20.4 C = 21.1 S = 35.8 J&S = 23.3	Indian Knoll K = 23.7 J&S = 25.3		
10–20	Carlston Annis M = 18.4 Chiggerville Su = 16.2	Indian Knoll C = 10.9 Carlston Annis M = 12.4 Chiggerville Su = 15.2	Indian Knoll C = 11.6 Chiggerville Su = 18.1	
0–10		Indian Knoll S = 6.4	Indian Knoll K = 5.8 J&S = 2.3 S = 1.3 Carlston Annis M = 8.8	Indian Knoll K = 0.1 C = 4.6 S = 0.8 J&S = 0.1 Carlston Annis M = 5.1 Chiggerville Su = 6.7

C, Cassidy 1972, Table 10; *J&S*, Johnston and Snow 1961, Table 1; *S*, Snow 1941, in Johnston and Snow 1961, Table 1; *K*, Kelley 1980, Table 5; *M*, Mensforth 1990, Table 4; *Su*, Sullivan 1977, Table 5.

Chiggerville females show more masculine traits than white skeletal series." Surprised by the preponderance of males, he concludes, "The large number of infant skeletons found and the small number of females might suggest that female infanticide was practiced." However, his earlier comment on the moderate degree of skeletal sexual dimorphism suggests that some older females may have been misidentified as males.

Skeletal and Dental Pathology

Arthritis

Patterns of osteoarthritis and skeletal trauma at Indian Knoll reflect a physically strenuous way of life. Snow (1948:498) noted that "approximately 60% of the adult population of Indian Knoll was afflicted with lumbar arthritis," and that several very young adults already displayed signs of "arthritic formations." He hypothesized a possible infectious etiology for this condition, noting that 44% of adult males and 31% of adult females (aged 20 to 55+ years) displayed both arthritis and dental abscesses.

Cassidy (1972:75, Table 16) reported an overall prevalence of 58% for spinal

Table 11.4 Adult Sex Ratios in the Green River Archaic
(males/females × 100)

Calculated Sample Ratios

Indian Knoll	C = 132 (90/86)
	J&S = 124 (283/228)
	K = 115 (248/215)
	S = 120 (48.8%/40.5%)
Chiggerville	Su = 107 (32/30)
Carlston Annis	M = 98 (108/110)

C, Cassidy 1972; J&S, Johnston and Snow 1961; K, Kelley 1980; M, Mensforth 1990; S, Snow 1948; Su, Sullivan 1977.

arthritis in her sample from Indian Knoll, with more males (57 of 91, 63%) than females (36 of 68, 53%) affected. This difference decreased with age to near equality in adults older than 40 years. Females displayed more arthritis of major joints only among older adults. By contrast, Hardin Villagers showed a lower overall frequency (44.3%), with females (39 of 73, 53%) more affected than males (23 of 67, 34%) and no difference by sex for extravertebral arthritis.

Kelley (1980) reports separately prevalence rates for vertebral osteoarthritis (39%) affecting the actual vertebral articular joints and for intervertebral osteochondrosis (14%) affecting the intervertebral disc and adjacent vertebral plates. Males were somewhat more frequently affected than females by both conditions, 42% versus 39% and 16% versus 12%, respectively. Indian Knoll adults show higher rates of both conditions than do age- and sex-matched adults at Grasshopper Pueblo (23% for vertebral arthritis and 2% for intervertebral osteochondrosis) or Mobridge (35% and 1%, respectively). This pattern parallels the results of Cassidy's comparison with Hardin Village. Kelley also notes a high prevalence of wrist and elbow joints affected at Indian Knoll, as contrasted with higher rates of elbow and shoulder arthritis at the other two sites. These patterns perhaps resulted in part from the Archaic reliance on the spearthrower (atlatl), contrasted with the use of the bow and arrow by the later populations. Bridges (1989b) has reported greater upper-limb asymmetry in Archaic than in Mississippian population samples from north Alabama, also perhaps reflecting this differential use pattern.

Sullivan (1977) reports almost equal prevalence of osteoarthritis in adult males and females at Chiggerville, with only a few differences: 32% of males showed arthritic involvement versus only 5% of females, but this sex ratio was reversed for sacroiliac surface arthritis, evident in only 5% of males but 27% of left female innominates and 47% of right female innominates. Females suffered higher rates of spinal arthritis from the thoracic region (38% versus 24% in males) downward through the lumbar (38% eroded vertebral centra in females versus 7% in males) and the first segment of the sacrum (60% arthritic in females versus 23% in males). The mechanical strains of pregnancy and childbirth might have contributed significantly to the marked sex differential in this particularly vulnerable weight-bearing region.

These analyses address forms of degenerative joint disease that reflect repetitive patterns of mechanical stress. B. M. Rothschild and Woods (1990) reported a different kind of arthropathy at Carlston Annis: erosive joint lesions suggestive of rheumatoid arthritis, a disease whose etiology they believe may involve an infectious agent. They examined all articular and periarticular surfaces in 65 female and 64 adult males, with follow-up radiographic examination of five female and two male pathological cases identified. The lesions are concentrated most strongly in the wrist, ankle, and digit joints, with several shoulder and hip joints also affected.

B. M. Rothschild and coworkers (Rothschild, Turner, and DeLucca 1988; Rothschild et al. 1992) reported similar pathology in Archaic samples from northwestern Tennessee (Eva) and Alabama (Seven Mile Island) located along the western valley of the Tennessee River. The pattern also appeared in late prehistoric samples (i.e., Thompson Village and Averbuch, and Koger's Island) but was absent in skeletal samples outside this focal area except at two Late Woodland sites in Ohio, Libben and Fort Ancient. Their discovery challenges the longheld view that rheumatoid arthritis originated in western Europe where it was first clinically distinguished from ordinary osteoarthritis in 1785.

Trauma

Snow (1948) describes numerous fractured bones in the Indian Knoll skeletal series. Cassidy (1972) reports 12 adult males and three females with fractures, 9% of her sample, a somewhat higher prevalence than at Hardin Village (6%, five males and three females). Kelley (1980) notes that his Archaic population displayed more long-bone fractures (27% in males, 15% in females) than his samples from Grasshopper (11% and 13%) or Mobridge (7% for each sex). The Archaic series also showed a strong age effect: more than 50% of adults aged 45+ years showed at least one fracture, more than double the rates in the two other samples. Vertebral compression fractures were more common at Indian Knoll (8.6%) than at Grasshopper (4.4%) or Mobridge (1.8%).

Fractures suggesting interpersonal violence were observed in 3.5% of the Archaic adults versus 1.8% at Mobridge and 0.5% at Grasshopper. At Indian Knoll 1.3% (6 of 463) of the adults bore projectile points lodged in their bones, contrasted with 1.2% (2 of 164) at Mobridge and none at Grasshopper. However, three adults at the latter site bore cranial cutmarks indicative of scalping, a form of mutilation not observed at Indian Knoll.

Fractured long bones were uncommon in the Chiggerville series: four males (two aged 30–39 and two aged 40–49) and two females (aged 40–49) exhibit a total of nine fractured limb bones. This sex ratio is drastically reversed in regard to compression fractures of the vertebrae, with eight females but only one male affected.

Dental Pathology

The general picture of nutrition in Archaic peoples of the Green River region suggests a well-balanced array of food resources hunted and gathered from forests and freshwater streams. Researchers who examined patterns of dental pathology have all commented on the very heavy dental wear and minimal evidence of caries in these Archaic populations (Adkins 1988; Cassidy 1972; Kelley 1980; Leigh 1925; Rabkin 1943; Skarland 1939; Snow 1948; Ward, in prep.). Snow (1948:501) remarked, on the danger of penetration of the dental pulp cavity from rapidly progressive attrition of the enamel: "Occasionally, Mother Nature came to the rescue of some of these Indian Knoll people in supplying quickly secondary dentine which was deposited in the pulp chamber to preserve the tooth. Sometimes in deeply worn teeth, cross-sections have revealed the complete filling of the chamber . . . and there are numerous examples where the teeth have been worn to the gum line without injury or infection."

Kelley (1980:128) noted heavy wear and high prevalence of apical abscesses in Indian Knoll dentitions (54.3% versus 20.7% at Mobridge and 9.1% at Grasshopper), and also the abundance of "completely or near-edentulous jaws" (15.5% versus 3.3% at Mobridge and 11.3% at Grasshopper). Skarland (1939:34) noted that for the Chiggerville dentitions, "abscesses are present whenever the teeth are worn, even with the alveolar border. Many of the abscesses lead into the maxillary sinus." The gritty nature of the diet has been blamed for this pattern of wear, particularly the freshwater molluscs whose shells gave the Shell Mound culture its archaeological name.

Kelley (1980) reports that only 10.2% of the Indian Knoll adult dentitions he examined showed dental caries, compared with 35.6% of the Mobridge farmer-hunters and 60.8% of the Grasshopper maize agriculturalists. This pattern parallels Leigh's earlier (1925) comparison of Indian Knoll with Arikara and Zuni samples. Dental wear and prevalence of dental caries show an inverse relationship in human dentitions (Powell 1985) because abrasive substances such as grit in the oral environment scrub away traces of food trapped on dental surfaces, thereby ameliorating to some extent the optimal environment created for cariogenous bacteria by the decay of carbohydrates. Cassidy (1972) notes this inverse relationship in dental wear and caries at Indian Knoll and Hardin Village: in the heavily worn Archaic dentitions the most lightly worn (latest erupting) tooth type (maxillary 3rd molars) is also the most frequently carious: 19.7% in males, 16% in females. In Hardin Village farmers the maxillary 2nd molars are the most carious (52% in males, 81% in females) because, since they erupt at approximately 12 years, they are only lightly worn during the highly caries-susceptible period of childhood exposure. Antemortem tooth loss at Indian Knoll was age (and wear) progressive, related primarily to pulp cavity penetration. At Hardin Village, antemortem tooth loss began much earlier in adult life and was related primarily to carious destruction of tooth crowns with subsequent abscessing.

Ward (in prep.) reports a similar pattern of heavy dental wear at Carlston Annis, noting that "molar attrition in the Bt5 sample is remarkable for its rapidity." Scanning electron microscopy of selected Bt5 deciduous and permanent molars reveals a pattern of microwear striations produced by abundant angular particles in the oral environment, probably representing grit contained within the freshwater shellfish that comprised a major dietary component at this and other Late Archaic Green River sites (see Claassen this volume for a different perspective). Ward (ibid.) comments, "The oral health of the Bt5 population is best summarized as a persistent confrontation with pyogenic and septic disease from early adulthood until death. . . . When all modes of antemortem tooth loss are considered, caries and trauma are the least important factors." He discovered carious lesions only on interproximal or cervical dental surfaces, affecting fewer than 5% of all teeth observed. Adkins (1988:103, Table 2) reports a carious rate of 11% in another small sample from Carlston Annis, compared with 48% in a sample of Fort Ancient maize farmers from the Buckner site in northeastern Kentucky. Sullivan (1977:77) stated, "The people from the Chiggerville site suffered from very poor dental health," with higher-than-expected rates of antemortem tooth loss probably promoted by the very abrasive diet.

Perzigian (1977b) examined fluctuating dental asymmetry, the nonpatterned unequal dimensions of antimeres (paired left and right teeth within an individual dentition) as a measure of disturbed dental development caused by systemic physiological stress during early childhood. He compared the prevalence and degree of asymmetry in permanent dentitions from Indian Knoll with data from two Native American agricultural groups (the late Mississippian Campbell site population in southeastern Missouri and the protohistoric Arikara from the Larson site in South Dakota) and a modern black-and-white medical school cadaver sample from Cleveland (the Hamann-Todd collection). The greater degree of dental asymmetry in the Archaic sample supports his earlier arguments (1971, 1972, 1973) that the Indian Knoll diet was nutritionally inadequate.

Metabolic Disorders

Skeletal evidence of metabolic disorders are rare in Archaic population samples. No cases of scurvy (vitamin C deficiency) have been identified to date. Snow (1948) reports rickets (vitamin D deficiency) in an Indian Knoll infant, and Kelley (1980) observed seven cases, aged four months to two years at death, suggesting that "inadequate calcium in infants' diet or other cultural practices (e.g., wrapping the infants in skins)" were responsible. Kelley (1980:169–70) also notes three cases of urinary calculi (two cases of kidney stones, one case of bladder stone) identified by Smith (in Snow 1948:510–13), pointing out that western Kentucky lies within the "stone belt" of the southeastern United States, whose regional incidence of 2 persons per 1,000 is double the national incidence, perhaps partially because of its moderately "hard" water.

Severe chronic iron deficiency anemia was also evidently rare in Archaic populations, judging from the low reported prevalence of cribra orbitalia and porotic hyperostosis, the diagnostic resorptive lesions of the eye orbits and cranial vault, respectively. Cassidy (1972:72) notes that resorptive lesions in Indian Knoll crania were so minor in nature that she doubted whether they truly represented pathology. By contrast, she reports a prevalence of 8.2% of the distinctive lesions representing anemia in her Hardin Village sample. Kelley (1980) reported 13 cases of skeletal lesions denoting anemia in 345 Indian Knoll subadults, more than three-quarters occurring in children aged three years or younger at death. This prevalence rate of 3.8% slightly exceeds that (2.1%) of his Mobridge hunter-farmers, but both samples are dwarfed by the 22.2% prevalence in the maize agriculturalists from Grasshopper Pueblo (a pattern similar to Cassidy's findings). Sullivan (1977:77) reports "no evidence . . . of gross nutritional deficiency" at Chiggerville.

Perzigian (1971, 1973) reports faster rates and greater overall osteoporotic bone loss (demineralization) in radii of age-matched adults from an Illinois Middle Woodland Hopewell site (Pete Klunk) than those from Archaic Indian Knoll. Bone loss was faster and greater in both sets of prehistoric females than in males, as in modern clinical samples. Although the Hopewell diet was judged to be more similar to a modern clinical population from the United States (and therefore more nutritionally adequate) than was the Indian Knoll diet, Hopewell bone loss was relatively greater. This pattern suggested to Perzigian (1973:93) that the Hopewell and modern diets abundant in protein and calories "did not contribute significantly to their adult skeletal maintenance. And, conversely, the relatively poor diet of Indian Knoll did not increase bone loss over what is normally expected in a well-nourished population."

Infectious Reaction

Kelley (1980) notes that the Grasshopper subadults show a higher prevalence of cranial (9.6% versus 4.1% at Indian Knoll and 4.8% at Mobridge) and postcranial (5.1% versus 3.0% and 1.2%, respectively), nonspecific periosteal lesions. He believes that this pattern indicates generally poor resistance to infectious disease in the Pueblo community. Nonspecific osteomyelitis was more common at Indian Knoll (2.4% versus 1.9% at Grasshopper and 1.8% at Mobridge), but most Archaic cases appeared in adults with evidence of skeletal trauma, to which it was probably consequent. Cassidy (1972:86, Table 21) notes a higher prevalence of nonspecific infectious skeletal reaction in subadults from her Hardin Village sample (16 of 152, 10.5%) than at Indian Knoll (3 of 125, 2.4%) and observes that the age-associated prevalence parallels the higher subadult mortality profile at the later site. Adults in her samples show no significant difference in prevalence of this condition at the two sites. Sullivan (1977:77) reports "little evidence of bone infection" in the Chiggerville series.

Mensforth (in press) compares the nature and prevalence of periosteal inflammatory reactions in subadults from Carlston Annis and from Libben, a Woodland period site in Ohio. He observed a higher proportion of very young subadults with unhealed lesions in the Libben series than at Carlston Annis, where many infants show no signs of infection but failed to survive the first year of life. This epidemiological distribution suggested to him that the Archaic infants were dying predominantly from bacterial infections that killed them so quickly that skeletal reaction to infection was forestalled, whereas the typical course of disease in the Woodland period infants was long enough for them to develop the characteristic periosteal lesions before they died. Drawing on the extensive clinical literature of early childhood infectious diseases, Mensforth states:

> [T]he elevated infant mortality rate combined with the low frequency of periosteal reactions . . . suggest that acute diarrheal infections may have been the predominant force of infant mortality in the Archaic group [noting that] severe acute attacks can be fatal in 24 hours or less due to rapid dehydration and critical electrolyte imbalance. In contrast, the relatively low infant death rate combined with the high frequency of periosteal reactions which were observed in the Libben infants suggest that respiratory tract infections and otitis media may have been the more important force of mortality for the Late Woodland population infants. (Mensforth in press:75)

He does not, however, hypothesize why this differential disease pattern might have occurred in the two populations.

Both Cassidy (1972) and Kelley (1980) expressed interest in the possibility of diagnosing specific infectious diseases. Neither researcher reports the presence of skeletal lesions suggestive in form or patterning of tuberculosis, although Kelley (1980) does identify this deadly disease at the protohistoric Mobridge site. However, both report evidence of another infectious disease, apparently an endemic form of treponematosis similar to modern endemic (nonvenereal) syphilis or yaws. This disease has been identified in numerous late prehistoric populations throughout the Southeast and Midwest (Powell 1992a, b) but rarely from Archaic contexts. Brothwell (1970; Brothwell and Burleigh 1975) had earlier reported cases of endemic treponematosis from Indian Knoll (citing Snow 1948 descriptions) and at an Archaic site (May's Lick) in eastern

Kentucky. This disease produced widespread morbidity, including moderate skeletal involvement in many individuals, but unlike venereal syphilis, it exerted a negligible impact on mortality and fecundity.

Summary

Cassidy's and Kelley's comparisons between Indian Knoll hunter-gatherers and later Native American groups reveal striking differences in patterns of mortality, morbidity, and mechanical stress. Kelley explains the differences in mortality and morbidity among his three samples in terms of *region-specific* cultural and ecological contexts, noting that each population had its own particular pathological burdens not shared equally by others. He concluded that the Indian Knoll people were better off in some respects, worse off in others, compared with the people of Grasshopper Pueblo and Mobridge. Cassidy's findings support her initial hypothesis that increasing reliance on plant domestication and the consequent shift toward sedentism resulted in increased patterns of biological stresses for sedentary agricultural populations relative to their nomadic predecessors.

Perzigian (1977b:107), however, reached a different conclusion vis-à-vis the quality of life at Indian Knoll. He argued that "several lines of evidence suggest that population pressure and environmental stresses were severe" at Indian Knoll, particularly during the terminal Late Archaic. He reports shorter adult stature, smaller permanent tooth size, more severe dental asymmetry, and decreased skeletal robusticity (measured by radius metrics) in a sample from Indian Knoll compared with an Illinois Woodland (Hopewell) sample and concludes that "the Indian Knoll population was seemingly disadvantaged socioeconomically and nutritionally" (1977b:109). He places primary blame on overreliance on a restricted range of food resources, noting that a major dietary item, shellfish, was a poor source of fat, protein, and calories, citing Parmalee and Klippel (1974), and that hickory and walnuts, intensively collected for centuries at the site, suffered "an overall decline in abundance during the closing centuries of the Late Archaic." Cook's (1971) observations of slower rates of subadult long-bone growth at Indian Knoll than in Illinois River Valley Woodland population samples lend sport to Perzigian's assessment.

So what may we conclude about patterns of growth, health, and disease during the Green River Archaic, based upon these studies? Were their lives indeed "nasty, brutish, and short," as the popular imagination often visualizes human existence before the development of agriculture and sedentary civilization? On the contrary, their lives were less nasty (because less contaminated by their own refuse), certainly not brutish (to judge from their skillfully made tools, weapons, and ornaments), and longer than the average late prehistoric lifespan. It was their successors who lived in crowded, contaminated hives of contagion, veritable havens for a plethora of infectious pathogens and parasitic organisms preying on populations weakened by dietary limitations and held captive by their domesticated plants.

The patterns of health and disease observed in the Archaic peoples of Indian Knoll, Carlston Annis, Read Shell Mound, Chiggerville, and other Green River sites recall the epidemiological descriptions of temperate-climate, historic, and recent hunter-gatherer peoples by Dunn (1968) in the well-known symposium volume, *Man the Hunter*. These early Kentuckians fed widely and well on the natural bounty of prehistoric Kentucky and adapted themselves to the constraints of their environment without exhausting its resources. They are deserving of our admiration, and we would do well to match their skills at living well.

12 | Research Problems with Shells from Green River Shell Matrix Sites

Cheryl Claassen

Shell debris found in archaeological sites is typically treated as food debris attracting the attention of faunal analysts eager to engage in dietary and environmental reconstruction. In some cases shell is also present in archaeological context as ornaments or tools. Ornaments, ecofacts, and shell objects of unknown role are present in large numbers in the Archaic shell mounds of Kentucky's middle Green River area. Instead of serving only to provide answers for standard archaeological questions, however, the nature of the shell debris of these sites actually stimulates many research questions not typically raised for shell-bearing sites. Problematizing the presence of both the freshwater and marine shell contained in these sites erodes the very foundation of their interpretation as either village sites or processing stations and of the shell as simply food debris and costume jewelry.

Research Problems with Shell Ecofacts

Many of the typical problems archaeologists address with freshwater shells in prehistoric sites have been performed with small shell samples from the DeWeese and Carlston Annis mounds in the Big Bend of Green River (Claassen, in prep.; Patch 1976, respectively). Bivalve shell density varies from top to bottom in these middens as does gastropod density. At DeWeese aquatic gastropods grossly outnumber land gastropods in the lower 40 cm of the midden, but the opposite situation prevails in the upper 2 m of shell midden. A seasonality study (Claassen 1986) indicates that shells examined from one column in each site died in summer and fall. The suggestion that the shells were harvested seasonally, rather than year round, is one of many pieces of evidence now being cited to support an interpretation of these sites as seasonal aggregation points, rather than year-round settlements (Hofman 1985).

Habitat Reconstruction

One curious problem that was raised by the Shell Mound Archeological Project (SMAP) concerns the habitat from which the 60 species of Carlston Annis shells were harvested. Using modern habitat records, Patch (1976) concluded that these shells came from a quite shallow riffle-run habitat. Julie Stein (1982), however, concluded that Green River had been deep in the vicinity of the mound, with a silt-mud bottom.

Suspecting that a broader sweep of modern habitat studies for freshwater bivalves would resolve the conflict, I enlarged on the number of sources used by Patch when I was analyzing the DeWeese bivalves (Claassen, in prep.). Fifty-six percent of the 32 species contained in a single DeWeese column were present in Green River in 1965 (Stansbery 1965), 53% of which could be found on mud or silt bottoms, and 88% could be found in deep water. Although these figures would seem to mean that far more of the Carlston Annis shells could have lived in a deep and muddy Green River than Patch recognized, the resolution of the problem is not so easy. Two of the four species that have not been recorded in deep water represent 47% and 48% of the valves found in the columns at Carlston Annis and DeWeese. Four possibilities are suggested: (1) that these two species do live in deep water in spite of our inability to document such a habitat, (2) that the river reconstruction is incorrect, (3) that these animals have developed a shallow-water habitat preference in historic times, or (4) that both reconstructions are correct, meaning that the shells were not harvested from Green River.

That people would transport shells over any significant distance may seem the least likely of the four explanations, but just such an interpretation has been offered in several other archaeological situations. Pacific coastal shells in large numbers have been recovered at mountain sites in California, over 10 miles from the sea, and in Peru, some 200 miles inland. More than 10,000 valves of the Gulf Coast bivalve *Rangia cuneata* have been recovered from the Arrowhead Farm site in Kentucky. Revised sea level charts still leave Archaic peoples of the Hudson River valley to carry tons of oyster shells 200 m or more then up bluff faces or by longer gradual routes to bluff tops. Likewise, the inhabitants of Globe Hill in West Virginia and of the Carlston Annis and DeWeese mounds in Kentucky had to haul shells up an incline. If one is willing to discard shells on top of an incline rather than at the creek, one might also be willing to walk over generally flat land to transport shellfish or shells from shallower tributary streams to the shell mound loci.

Paired Valves

Several excavators have commented on the high frequency of paired valves in these sites and similar sites elsewhere in the Midsouth. What is most significant about the reported pairing is that shells do not stay paired in areas being disturbed, yet these shell mounds always have been interpreted as village sites. Villages are scenes of many surface and subsurface cultural formation processes that would quickly and easily disturb paired valves—digging, walking, running—as well as would natural processes such as rodent burrowing. Apparently a high proportion of valve pairs can survive 5,000 or more years of earthworm processing (Stein 1983).

The extent of the pairing needs to be quantified during excavation. Julie Stein (personal communication, 1985) recalls pairing to be greatest on the river side of the Carlston Annis mound. The column removed from the DeWeese mound, in which many paired valves were encountered, was also on the river side of that mound. In some of the 5-cm-thick levels removed from the 25- × 25-cm² column at DeWeese, the percentage of paired valves was as high as 100%. Is pairing most frequent on the river side or is it ubiquitous? Do paired valves represent unutilized meats?

Research Problems with Ornamental Shell

Origin of Busycon

The presence of marine gastropods at interior riverine sites has received some attention since the Works Progress Administration (WPA)–era excavations of these sites (Claassen, 1991a; Goad 1980; Griffin 1952a; Ottesen 1979; Winters 1974). The movement of exotic lithics around the landscape of the Eastern Woodlands appeared prior to 7000 B.C., a cycling that was gradually expanded to include, among other substances, copper, and marine shell. The marine shell distribution is more extensive geographically than that of copper, and the major concentration of each substance is complementary rather than juxtaposed. The major concentration of marine shell and of the artifacts made from it lies to the south of the Ohio River and east of the Mississippi River (Goad 1980:5). Like many other researchers, Goad saw the source areas for the large marine gastropod *Busycon perversum* or *Busycon contrarium*, whose shell was fashioned into disk, tubular, barrel, columella, and wampum beads, as well as face masks, pins, containers, gorgets, spoons, atlatl weights, and undecipherable objects, to be the Gulf coastal waters along the Florida peninsula.

A recent project (Claassen and Sigmann 1993) to source the *Busycon* shell chemically included one shell lip specimen each from Indian Knoll and Ward, the former a Green River Archaic shell mound, the latter a Green River Archaic earthen mound. Elemental assay of *Busycon* shells from coastal middens of the Atlantic and Gulf coasts was conducted with the use of atomic absorption spectroscopy. A sample of 35 midden shells constituted the control set, used to establish the chemical parameters of the water bodies lying off-shore from the sites. Although the set is much smaller than the ideal control set, it was sufficient to confirm some geological provinces, particularly for magnesium, and to indicate useful differences in the shell chemistry of individuals grown in tropical and temperate waters, and in eastern, central, and western Gulf waters.

A few *Busycon* artifacts (or subject shells) were then assayed in the same manner for the same elements (iron, magnesium, strontium, and calcium), and their elemental ratios were compared with those of the control set. Cluster analysis was used to find the best fit of control shells with the subject shells. The lip specimen from Ward showed a close fit with shells that grew in tropical waters. The lip specimen from Indian Knoll clustered strongly with shells from Tampa Bay. Each time the control set is enlarged, as is planned, the clustering will be rerun. Statements about particular sections of coastline will no doubt be altered, but the chemical separation between tropical and temperate waters may endure and, thus, can be taken to indicate two different localities from which *Busycon* was drawn into the Green River valley cultural system.

Gastropod Beads

The earliest record of a shell bead in the eastern United States may be that found at the Archaic Tennessee Ervin site in a context dated to 7046 B.P. (Hofman 1985:1). It is fashioned not from a marine gastropod but from the locally available *Leptoxis* (*Anculosa*) riverine gastropod. *Leptoxis* appears to be the only freshwater gastropod used for bead manufacture. *Oxytrema* sp. shells are quite abundant in Green River and its shell middens, raising the question of why they were not thought suitable for beads. A date for the appearance of marine shell beads is not indicated in the literature.

There was a striking selection for small *Leptoxis* individuals to be made into beads in both western Tennessee River and Green River Archaic shell mounds. Unmodified *Leptoxis* recovered in two levels of a DeWeese column sample averaged 13.3 and 11.3 mm in height, respectively, and those ground on the transverse axis for stringing through different chambers around the columella and recovered from burials are considerably shorter in height. The maximum length of the Chiggerville *Leptoxis* beads that I have measured is 11.25 mm, and the average length in a set of 123 *Leptoxis* beads from Indian Knoll was 8.3 mm. The few ground *Leptoxis* beads found in shell mound sites in western Tennessee are even smaller, averaging 5.2 mm (Oak View Landing) and 10.6 mm (West Cuba Landing) in height. *Leptoxis* shell beads consistently are found at the neck and at the pelvis of burials, suggesting necklaces and belts in Indian Knoll costumes (although there are several lots with no body location indicated).

In a column sample taken from the DeWeese shell mound, *Leptoxis* shells constituted 21% to 68% of all gastropods in the lower 38 cm. From 55 cm to 225 cmbs *Leptoxis* never exceeds 12% of the inventory. Although both *Oxytrema* and *Leptoxis* fall off equally, the change may be indicating a change in the manufacturing of *Leptoxis* beads.

Leptoxis shells, locally available and abundant, were augmented in bead inventories of Green River folks by the acquisition of two types of comparably small marine gastropods, genera *Olivella* and *Marginella*. Both foreign species were ground only slightly to make a small hole in the upper wall of the shell, near the apex, and then were strung through that hole and the natural aperture, representing far less work than was expended on *Leptoxis* shells. Why these seemingly equivalent exotic species were acquired when the local riverine species was abundant and treated to greater (although unnecessary) grinding is a curiosity that may never be explained satisfactorily. Why the exotic small gastropods replaced *Leptoxis* entirely in Mississippian times is even more enigmatic. At what time do *Leptoxis* beads disappear as a bead style? Do they also disappear from the ecofact inventory at sites in the Green and Tennessee River valleys?

Fashion Provinces

Sharon Goad (1980:6) observed: "There is, probably due to lack of archaeological data, a peculiar distribution of shell in the Southeast. Shell is found near the coastal source areas and further to the north along the periphery of the region, but there is a gap of several hundred miles between the coast and these areas where shell occurs only sporadically."

Shell beads are the most common element of costume recovered in Green River shell mound burials, although more people were buried without them than with them. The Chiggerville collection housed at the University of Kentucky was examined for shell beads in January 1993 by the author. Thirty-two burials contained 1,905 cut and/or *Leptoxis* beads. An examination of the Indian Knoll collection revealed 112 graves with a total of 11,104 provenienced beads. There were no *Marginella* or *Olivella* beads at Chiggerville and only 141 in three graves at Indian Knoll.

The collection from the Archaic Ledbetter shell mound of the western Tennessee River valley, housed at the University of Tennessee, revealed that nine graves had a total of 327 shell beads and one grave had a string of shell diskbeads 3.35 m long. *Marginella* and/or *Olivella* beads were present in three graves (193 *Olivella* and 6 *Marginella* shells). The inventories of 12 other Archaic Tradition shell-bearing sites from the western Tennessee River valley were checked for beads, indicating that at only five sites—Bn 3, Bn 13, Bn 17, Bn 74 and Hy 13—were shell beads recovered from a total of seven graves. Neither shell-bearing component of Eva contained shell beads. (Both Anderson and Ervin sites do have shell beads, but I have not examined those collections.) None of the beads from these 12 sites were modified *Marginella* or *Olivella* shells.

The scarcity of shell beads made of either freshwater or marine shell in the western Tennessee River valley is striking in its contrast to Green River collections and would suggest that shell beads were rarely part of the costume of western Tennessee Archaic people. Does the Green River Archaic tradition use of shell beads mark a major difference in costume from Archaic cultures in surrounding areas? Does this use of shell beads form a fashion province?

Why Import Marine Shell?

The cut shell beads in these sites are made of the marine shell *Busycon* sp. The freshwater bivalve fauna of Green River is greatly varied in shell smoothness and thickness, yet there are numerous species which are prolific, pearly, more easily procured, and thicker than *Busycon*, that are large enough to serve as face masks for children. These shells could have been used for bead manufacture as well. Why did people of the Green and Tennessee river watersheds need or want to acquire marine shell when freshwater shell was readily available? The answer may lie in the structural differences in marine and freshwater shells.

John F. Boepple, a master craftsman and button turner in Ottesen, Germany, found hand-carving freshwater shell unrewarding because of a lack of exfoliation (Claassen 1994). Saltwater species have a crystalline structure that is conducive to their exfoliation in layers, which is not the case with freshwater species. In 1891, when Boepple initiated the freshwater shell button industry in Muscatine, Iowa, using shells harvested from the town's waterfront on the Mississippi River, his first challenge was to tailor the machinery used by the ocean shell button industry to the different cutting requirements of freshwater shell, which were not specified. Those different cutting requirements, once fully investigated, no doubt, will yield at least a partial answer.

Clearly there is much work to be done with the bead inventories of these sites and those in neighboring areas. The symbolism behind beads has rarely been explored or even problematized. Guy Prentice (1987a) sees them as a form of currency, and Robert Hall (1976) believes them to be symbolic of saliva or semen. Lynn Ceci (1988:66–67) cites sources indicating that gastropods commonly signify sun, rain, birth, fertility, and resurrection, that they provide hiding places for the soul and deities, and that "shell could hold the soul and help purify decaying flesh to permit entry into the spirit world." Their point of origin in both the social and physical environment may also be relevant aspects of the apparent preference for marine species.

Research Problems with Site Type

Perhaps the most interesting research questions associated with these shell mound sites is why people created mounds of shells and why they stopped mounding shell. The favored hypothesis until recently was that these sites were part of a larger geographical and temporal phenomenon of a broad subsistence base that exploited riverine resources from riverside villages. These sites were abandoned when people overharvested the molluscan resource about 3,500 years ago, but they moved to other localities and continued to exploit molluscan resources in lesser quantities. Why shellfish were added to the diet was frequently addressed with optimal foraging models that usually implied that shellfish were dropped from the diet when their inclusion violated optimal foraging tenets.

Several of the research problems already discussed coalesce to create a picture that is more complicated than the scenario typically held. The habitat reconstruction raises the possibility that the shells in the Carlston Annis and DeWeese mounds were not harvested from the adjacent Green River. The valve pairing contradicts the idea that these mounds were village sites. The striking change in the presence of freshwater gastropods suggests either a dietary change and/or an end of ornament production from local *Leptoxis* shells. In addition, this type of site—mounds of shells—was never again created by prehistoric peoples of the Green River or anywhere in the interior eastern United States. In many instances, not only in the Green River valley but also on the Ohio and the St. Johns rivers, shells were carried up inclines to be deposited at the top. Although freshwater shellfish inhabited all the rivers of the eastern United States, at only a few were shells mounded and burials placed in the mounds.

That shellfish were plentiful in other rivers in the Midsouth where shell mounds did not occur should not be doubted. Figures from the freshwater shell button industry of 1891 to 1950 indicate that there was a huge freshwater naiad population in the Mississippi River watershed that not even commercially motivated shell fishing could deplete (Claassen 1994). From Illinois rivers government figures record 15 to 20 tons of shells a season removed from the Fox River, totaling 353 tons by 1913, and 2,600 boats working the Illinois River daily from Pearl to Grand Island in 1907. One thousand tons of shells were shipped from the Kampsville area in 1910. By 1944 at least 32,603 tons of shell from rivers in Indiana, the principal river being the Wabash, had found a market.

The Mississippi, Ohio, Cumberland, and Tennessee rivers were quite important for button musseling. Two (of several) shell buyers working the Cumberland River from Paducah to Nashville purchased 7,008 tons of shells from 1907 to 1910. Other Kentucky rivers and streams that provided shells to the button industry were the Kentucky, Green, Clear Fork, Big South Fork, Beaver Creek, Goose Creek, and Obey. From 1932 until 1944, 35,448 tons of Kentucky shells were sold to button factories. The peak year was 1944. Yet of these rivers, it is only on Green River and the Tennessee River that we have found shell-bearing Archaic period sites. Why are shell mounds so geographically restricted in Kentucky and in the Midsouth?

Historically, the cessation of the Shell Mound Archaic, so vividly illustrated by the Green River site of Indian Knoll, has been explained as overexploitation of the mussel resource. However, the Mississippi, Tennessee, Cumberland, and Wabash rivers have sustained commercial musseling for over 100 years, during a period of dramatically increased water pollution, government engineering, and siltation. Fifty years after the industry began, 11,000 tons of shell were sold off the Tennessee River in western Tennessee alone in 1954–55. From 1965 through 1981 (no report for four years) 2,056.4 tons of shells were sold off the Wabash River. Overexploitation of the molluscan resource by the inhabitants of the Eva area, Pickwick, and Norris basins of the Tennessee River and by the inhabitants of the Riverton culture area on the Wabash cannot be the cause of the abandonment of the sites. It is hard to imagine the Archaic molluscan populations of the Green, Savannah, and St. Johns rivers, even though they are not commercially important sources of shell, being exhausted by the small human population when modern pollution, siltation, and the Corps of Engineers have not eliminated the molluscan populations there today.

Shells in the Maya world had various symbolic roles. Paired valves were the most common offering in building caches. Iconographically shells represented south, zero, death, completion, and fertility. Thousands of bodies in the shell mounds on Green River have been buried under mounded shell or in mounded shell. In fact, what ceases at the close of the Shell Mound Archaic on the St. Johns, Savannah, Tennessee, and Green rivers is a unique co-occurrence of flexed human and dog burials in association with mounded shell. Burials associated with dirt mounds continue into Woodland times along with shell bead grave inclusions. Adena and Hopewell mound centers are also inexplicably geographically restricted. Rather than thinking of them as simply shell midden villages sites, we should problematize the shell mounds of the Archaic tradition as burial sites in a symbolic complex that is a precursor to Adena-Hopewell, although differing in important ways from those Woodland complexes. There are non-shell-bearing sites, often in association with shell mounds that can carry · the function of "village," in the Green River valley.

Grave good evidence, bead styles, import of marine shell and copper, burial mounds, seasonal occupation, paired valves, an unexplained appearance and cessation of this type of site, even shell symbolism, all coalesce into a new perception of the Shell Mound Archaic as a far more complex cultural phenomenon than can be captured in optimal foraging models (Claassen 1991b; Hofman 1985). In recent years we have begun to uncover a tremendous amount of variation in Green River Archaic sites (Claassen 1992; Hensley 1991; Watson 1992); in the density of burials, in the location of burials, in the concept of cemetery, in grave goods, in dog burials, in bead inventories, in copper content, and in shell content, in topographic location. As we shed the normative conception of the Archaic in Kentucky forged by the natural environment, we are replacing it with images of a culture rich in human interactions and negotiations with a spirit world.

13 | Riverine Adaptation in the Midsouth

David H. Dye

Trends toward sedentism and increasing cultural complexity have been well documented in the Midsouth for Late Holocene (5000–2500 B.P.) hunters and gatherers (Brose 1979; Goad 1980), but key features of this adaptation, such as multiseasonal base camps, semipermanent habitations, multiregional exchange networks, and specialized plant gathering, are evident as early as the Middle Holocene (8000–5000 B.P.) in the Midwest (Brown and Vierra 1983:165) and Midsouth (B. Smith 1986:18–27). The emergence of cultural complexity and increasing sedentism during the Middle Holocene has been linked to an increase in the aquatic resource base, which in turn resulted in a sharp escalation in the kinds and amounts of riverine aquatic species available to Middle Archaic hunters and gatherers (Brown 1983:10; B. Smith 1986:22). A concomitant shift is recognized in the duration and intensity of settlement patterns as part of the narrowing focus on riverine-oriented resources. Smith notes that the nature, timing, and cultural consequences of the initial increase in utilization of floodplain aquatic species remain among the most interesting and most important general research topics concerning Middle Holocene hunting and gathering adaptations (1986:27). One result of the increased attention by midsouthern, Middle Holocene hunter-gatherers on riverine aquatic resources is the development of dense middens, particularly those composed of accumulations of mollusks (Dowd 1989; Futato 1989; Klippel and Morey 1986; Lewis and Lewis 1961; Walthall 1980; Webb and DeJarnette 1942).

Smith (1986:18–21) suggests that Middle Holocene midsouthern hunter-gatherers continued many of the cultural patterns established in the Early Holocene. Although temporal change in hafted biface morphology is well documented throughout the Southeast and Midwest, a general continuity in the Middle Holocene tool kit is evident for woodworking, plant food, and hide and carcass processing assemblages. In addition, the variety, range, and dietary significance of fundamental plant and animal taxa did not change substantially from the Early Holocene, with two exceptions: an increasing emphasis and orientation toward riverine aquatic species and the beginnings of plant cultivation. The Middle Holocene archaeological record is clear concerning the lack of increasing inventory of tool types or the advent of revolutionary technological innovations fostering significant socioeconomic impact from the Early Holocene (ibid.:18–22). Rather, a basic or primary adaptation to the temperate deciduous forest biome of eastern North America is evident throughout the Archaic tradition (Caldwell 1958), with the exception of an increasing reliance on riverine aquatic species and cultivated plants.

The basic dichotomous Middle Holocene seasonal scheduling of riverine and upland resources during the warm (dry) season and cool (wet) season is one aspect of the continuation of the early Holocene adaptation. Oriented primarily around riverine base camps from which small populations inhabited short-term, limited-activity sites in the upland and floodplain, the warm-season, cool-season settlement-subsistence strategy continued well into the historic period in various forms. The duration of warm/dry–season residential base camp occupation increased on elevated points in the floodplain, such as natural levees, point bars, or alluvial fans, in proximity to spatially or seasonally limited aquatic resources, with the appearance or enhancement of meander or shoal habitats as a result of floodplain stability around 7200 B.P. (B. Smith 1986:25; Waselkov 1982). By the Middle Holocene, hunter-gatherer settlement patterns shifted toward semipermanent, if not permanent, warm-season floodplain base camps and cool/wet–season upland and valley edge base camps or dispersed, short-term upland camps.

Paleoecology

Changes in solar radiation stemming from changes in the orientation of the earth's axis produced a pattern of midlatitude changes in climate during the Holocene (COHMAP 1988), which in turn brought about changes in ecological processes. During the Middle Holocene, white-tailed deer (*Odocoileus virginianus*) in central Illinois, for example, achieved only small body size because of changes in the quality of summer forage when climatic conditions were warmer and drier than present (Purdue 1989).

During the Early Holocene (12,500–8000 B.P.) cool temperatures dominated much of the Midsouth. Central Tennessee at this time, for example, was characterized by a mixed mesic forest and a vegetative pattern similar to the modern flora found on the Allegheny Plateau of Ohio and West Virginia. By 8000 B.P. warming and drying conditions resulted in a suite of flora similar to those found today in eastern Kentucky (H. Delcourt 1979).

By the Middle Holocene (8000–5000 B.P.) the onset of warm, dry summers was apparently brought on by the increased strength of the prevailing westerly winds (King and Allen 1977; Kutzbach 1987; MacMillan and Klippel 1981; Wright 1968, 1976). A wedge of warm, dry air produced a decrease in summer rainfall resulting in major vegetational changes in the midlatitudes (P. Delcourt and H. Delcourt 1981:150). This inferred warming and drying trend was characterized by changes in vegetation, landscape, and climate.

The warming/drying trend responsible for the eastward expansion of the prairies reached its maximum by 7000 B.P. (Wright 1974:10) in the Midwest. The warming episode extended into the midlatitudes of the Southeast west of the Appalachian Mountains, reaching its peak by 6000 B.P. More strongly zonal upper atmospheric circulation, accompanied by a decreased frequency of frontal storms and floods, brought about a stability in the Duck River floodplain from 7200 to 6400 B.P. at the same time that the maximum extension of xeric forest vegetation occurred in central Tennessee (Brakenridge 1984:25). By 5000 B.P. mixed Mesophytic forests had diminished across the central United States and were replaced by more xeric vegetation, dominated by ashes, hickories, and oaks (H. Delcourt 1979:277). In the northern Gulf Coastal Plain the Middle Holocene vegetation reflected a warm, but wet regional climate (H. Delcourt and P. Delcourt 1985:20; Kutzbach 1987:444).

Pollen records from the western Highland Rim in Middle Tennessee indicate that vegetation during the Middle Holocene was much like that of the Ozark Mountains of eastern Missouri today (Klippel and Parmalee 1982:456). By 5000 B.P. the dry conditions ameliorated, resulting in the return of mesic deciduous forest species in the Midsouth, although variation in the local environmental regimes are evident throughout the region. In northern Alabama, for example, a western Mesophytic oak-hickory forest was the dominant vegetative pattern. Meanwhile, in the sandy upland interfluves of the eastern Gulf Coastal Plain, the southeastern Evergreen Forest (southern pine forest) became dominant, reflecting a high fire frequency from lightning strikes and abundant precipitation throughout the year as a result of the influence of the tropical maritime air mass from the Gulf of Mexico and intensification of hurricane frequency (H. Delcourt and P. Delcourt 1985:20). Fires also may have been set by Middle Holocene hunters and gatherers on the Coastal Plain uplands to increase the carrying capacity of faunal resources (H. Delcourt 1979:277), inadvertently maintaining large tracts of open pine forest (H. Delcourt and P. Delcourt 1985:20) or prairies. Drought stress may have restricted the Coastal Plain southern pines from migrating northward (H. Delcourt 1979:277). In the Piedmont, oak-hickory southern pine forests dominated the landscape (P. Delcourt and H. Delcourt 1981:151).

In some areas of the Midsouth, such as the Upper Tombigbee valley in northeastern Mississippi (Bense 1983) and the Duck River valley in Central Tennessee (Turner and Klippel 1989:61), Middle Holocene climatic trends appear to have brought about the deterioration of upland resources and a concomitant restriction of important food resources for hunter-gatherers. At Old Field Swamp in southeastern Missouri, there was a xeric period between approximately 8500 and 5700 B.P. (King and Allen 1977). A return to more mesic conditions in southeastern Missouri took place approximately 5000 to 4500 B.P.

Initial Riverine Adaptation in the Midsouth

The Midsouth offers an ideal laboratory to evaluate the archaeological evidence of hunter-gatherer adaptation to landscapes, resource use, and social interaction. In this chapter I briefly outline evidence available for the initial orientation toward riverine aquatic resources and trends toward increasing cultural complexity at three Middle Holocene (Morrow Mountain) shell middens: Anderson (Dowd 1989; M. Moore et al. 1990), Eva (Lewis and Lewis 1961), and Mulberry Creek (Webb and DeJarnette 1942:235–66).

The Anderson Site

From March 1980 to early 1982 (Dowd 1989) and from August 25 to September 7, 1989 (M. Moore et al. 1990), excavations were conducted at the 0.3-ha Anderson site (40WM9) in Williamson County, Tennessee. The Anderson site is located in the immediate vicinity of the Central Basin and the Western Highland Rim at the confluence of Small Branch and Harpeth River on an arcuate ridge of a point bar in a meander of the Harpeth River (Hagee 1983:123–24). The Anderson site did not exhibit distinct, clear-cut stratigraphy; rapid midden buildup, attributed to the site's physiographic positioning on a point bar and apparently continuous occupation, resulted in various shades of dark black to dark brown midden.

Moore et al. (1990) defined four strata on the basis of their work at the Anderson site. Stratum I was a variably thin plowzone, ranging from 15 to 33 cm. Stratum II contained a moderate amount of mussel shell, limestone, and burned earth extending to a maximum depth of 60 cm below ground surface and ranging from approximately 13 to 33 cm in thickness. Stratum III, 1.16 m below ground surface and about 46 to 71 cm thick, contained a dense mass of gastropods that were not present in stratum II. Stratum IV represented the end of the primary midden and did not contain any artifactual material and held virtually no shell. Correlating the Moore et al. (1990) strata with Dowd's (1989) levels is difficult, not only because of differences in units of measure but also especially because of the difference in deposit thickness in the two site areas.

In the years preceding prehistoric site occupation, a warming and drying trend prevailed, leading to the emergence of a prairie-type vegetation in the immediate site vicinity and belts of brush and woods along the Harpeth River and its tributary streams. The woods were composed of mature, dense stands of beech, elm, hickory, oak, and other hardwoods (Parmalee and O'Hare 1983). Summer droughts may have been frequent (Hagee 1983:125). The Harpeth River at the time of initial site occupation was a shallow, fast-flowing, small- to medium-size river with a sand and gravel bottom; riffles and shoals were probably numerous (Parmalee and O'Hare 1983). Two periods of mesic conditions prevailed during the Anderson occupation (Hagee 1983:125). After about 5000 B.P. the Harpeth River appears to have risen and vegetation again shifted slightly toward a more mesic deciduous component, although much of the habitat remained open grassland (Hagee 1983:124–26).

The Anderson site occupational sequence indicates that midden accumulation began between 7200 to 7000 B.P., with an initial occupation by Morrow Mountain populations marked by intensive utilization of gastropods. Site use continued throughout the Morrow Mountain and Sykes-White Springs occupations, terminating in the initial stages of the Benton occupation around 4500 B.P.

On the basis of the frequency distributions of stylistic changes in hafted biface morphology, the Anderson site Morrow Mountain sequence may be subdivided into early, middle, and late temporal units, although there are no clear boundaries separating them. The frequency distribution of Morrow Mountain hafted bifaces indicates that several styles were employed at any one time during the period of site occupancy (Lindstrom and Steverson 1987:19). The association of Morrow Mountain Triangular, Morrow Mountain Straight-Stemmed, and Morrow Mountain Round Base points with burials 83, 84, and 85 from the Mulberry Creek site (Webb and DeJarnette 1942:2, Plate 289) further strengthens the observation that several projectile point or knife styles were contemporary with one another at Anderson, although specific styles may have predominated at any one time. Early Morrow Mountain (7000–6500 B.P.) is characterized by a predominance of Morrow Mountain Triangular forms as represented by levels 5 through 6. The Middle Morrow Mountain (6500–6000 B.P.) component, represented by level 4, contains a predominance of Morrow Mountain Straight-Stemmed projectile points. Late Morrow Mountain (6000–5500 B.P.) is characterized by Morrow Mountain Round Base/Eva hafted bifaces in levels 2 and 3. A late Middle Archaic Sykes/White Springs component is indicated by Sykes/White Springs and Anderson hafted bifaces. A terminal Middle Archaic Benton component is represented by a Benton blade cache. These latter two components are mixed with the late Morrow Mountain component in levels 1 and 2.

Some 25 burials may be assigned to the Early Morrow Mountain component, 22 burials are known from the Middle Morrow Mountain component, and 15 burials are assigned to the Late Morrow Mountain component (Joerschke 1983:132–33). Some 1,366 marine shell artifacts were recovered from burial contexts at the Anderson site. Almost one-quarter (22%) of the burials contained some form of shell bead, and 75% of these were in the upper three levels (Late Morrow Mountain, Sykes/White Springs, Benton); the other 25% was associated with the Middle Morrow Mountain component. Two possible Early or Middle Morrow Mountain burials, 17 and 56, contained shell beads (Dowd 1989:86, 106, Plate 67). The acquisition of marine shell developed gradually through the course of site occupation, possibly beginning in the early portion of the Middle Morrow Mountain component around 6500 B.P.

It is also noteworthy that burial 10, a twenty-year-old female, contained red ochre on the lower legs and feet and that burial 59, a twenty-one-year-old female, exhibited a Morrow Mountain Straight-Stemmed projectile point in the chest cavity (ibid.:106, Plate 21c). Dowd (ibid.:106) notes that the projectile point may have originated from the surrounding midden. Both of the individuals are attributed to the Middle Morrow component.

Forty-eight features were recorded at Anderson and were grouped into a variety of functional categories (ibid.:55–60). Nineteen features, including hearths or firepits, seem to be associated with general cooking activities; some were lined with limestone slabs. Some firepits contained heavy concentrations of ash. Each firepit was adjacent to a large, solid mass of mollusk shells, which suggests that these firepits were used to process mollusks for consumption. In the lower levels of the site, six concentrations of flat limestone rocks, arranged in circular patterns, appear to have been selected to fit together to form the flat floor surface of a structure (ibid.:53–57). Three groups of postmolds were identified, but a pattern could not be determined. Of particular interest are the features from the Early Morrow Mountain levels 6 and 7. In level 6 a cluster of large, nonlocal limestone slabs were found in an area approximately 1 × 1 m lying on the sterile subsoil. Several fire pits with rock-lined bottoms were noted, which also extended into the yellow subsoil. In level 7, 10 postmolds were found, and within this level in another area of the site, a 3.09 m^2 area contained a number of rock-lined features running in a linear pattern across the site. When the rocks were removed, the excavators found postmolds in the yellow subsoil.

Faunal analysis indicates that the Anderson site was occupied throughout the year (Breitburg 1993). The most important meat sources were deer, raccoon, and turkey. Deer and raccoon made up 90% of the mammal meat yield (82% by number of fragments), and deer, raccoon, and turkey comprised 90% of the total faunal meat yield (77% by number of fragments) (Dowd 1989:117). Through time there was a steady, but moderate, increase in the variety of faunal resources. Deer utilization declined, but raccoon use showed a steady increase throughout the occupation. The frequency of turkey remains indicates that their exploitation was approximately the same throughout the occupation. On the basis of the faunal assemblage, the site's inhabitants had access to a diversity of habitats: forest, forest edge/open woodland, grassland/brushland, and riparian/aquatic habitats.

The greatest concentration and variety of faunal remains, especially birds, was found in the Middle Morrow Mountain component. Through time the site occupants intensified their exploitative capabilities and the array of species taken became increasingly more diverse, steadily increasing in skeletal representation to the Middle Morrow Mountain zone, where there was a dramatic increase in skeletal elements of arboreal, terrestrial, aquatic, and semiaquatic birds. By the terminal phase of occupation (late Middle Archaic), the array of mammal, reptile, and fish species taken continued to remain the same, but the diversity of birds declined dramatically from that found in the previous occupation (Breitburg 1993).

A *Cucurbita* seed found in an Early Morrow Mountain context in level 7 represents one "of the earliest occurrences of *Cucurbita* in good archaeological context north of Mexico" (Crites 1991:80).

The Eva Site

The Eva site (40BN12) (Lewis and Lewis 1961) was excavated from September 11 to November 23, 1940, under the field supervision of Douglas Osborne as part of the federal work relief programs in conjunction with the Tennessee Valley Authority in what would become a part of the Kentucky Reservoir. Located in Benton County, Tennessee, on the western Highland Rim near the Gulf Coastal Plain to the west, the site lies atop a long, low knoll or natural levee. At the time of occupation, between 7200 and 7000 B.P., the Tennessee River flowed immediately west of the site. The original ground surface was covered with sand and gravel and was underlain by a thick deposit of clay. The site environment, based on recovered faunal remains suggests forest, forest edge, grassland/brushland, and riparian/aquatic habitats (Lewis and Lewis 1961:17–24).

Five strata were identified by Osborne on the basis of his excavations, not including the 12.7 to 20.3-cm plowzone. Stratum I, immediately below the plowzone, varied from a thin line to 80 cm. Much of this stratum, devoid of shell, had eroded, being washed from the higher elevations to the site's periphery. Lewis and Lewis (ibid.:9) interpreted the lack of shell as a result of the Tennessee River shifting position along with a change in climate, the higher precipitation reducing the accessibility of mussels by increasing the depth of the river (ibid.:9). Stratum I contained a mixed late Middle Archaic Sykes/White Springs and Benton component and Late Archaic Ledbetter and Little Bear Creek components.

Stratum II, some 90 cm thick, was characterized by its extensive mussel shell matrix and was designated the Three Mile component by Lewis and Lewis (1961:9). The upper 1 foot of stratum II, designated stratum II top, had the heaviest shell content of all the strata. The lower 61 cm had less shell but heavier ash content. The lower two-thirds of stratum II was bisected and designated stratum II middle and stratum II bottom. Stratum two represented the longest and most intensive occupation of the site and contained the greatest number of burials and artifacts, but there was comparatively less animal bone in this stratum than in the other strata. Stratum II appears to represent the later portion of the Morrow Mountain sequence based on comparison with hafted biface frequencies at the Anderson site.

Stratum III, a sand and silt deposit separating stratum II and stratum IV and varying from 45 to 75 cm, resulted from a flood of considerable duration that covered the site. This period of alluviation suggests that the Tennessee Valley may have returned briefly to more mesic conditions in the Middle Holocene as is also evident at the Anderson site between 6000 and 5700 B.P. (Hagee 1983:124–25).

Stratum IV, 45 cm thick at its maximum near the site's center, tapered at the periphery. Lewis and Lewis divided stratum IV into stratum IV top and stratum IV bottom, based on observable differences in the content of these divisions (1961:13). Stratum IV top contained abundant lithic debris, animal bone, heavy ash deposits, and numerous canine feces. Stratum IV bottom was composed of a heavier mussel shell content than stratum IV top. A radiocarbon determination of 7150 ± 167 B.P. (M-357) was obtained from white-tailed deer antler from the bottom of stratum IV (Crane 1956:666).

Stratum V was not a distinct midden deposit but, rather, represented a transition between the bottom of stratum IV and the original natural levee surface. Stratum V varied from a few centimeters to 30 cm thick and was characterized by charcoal and burned soil. A test unit excavated 3.3 m into the subsoil failed to locate evidence of buried components.

Lewis and Lewis (1961:13) defined three cultural complexes on the basis of Osborne's excavations and observations: the Eva component (strata IV and V), the Three Mile component (stratum II), and the Big Sandy component (stratum I and the plowzone). The Eva component is here considered an early Morrow Mountain component; Eva I projectile points and triangular biface blades, diagnostic markers for the Early Morrow Mountain component at Anderson, were virtually restricted to the Eva component (ibid.:30, 31, 40, 48), particularly in the top of stratum IV. The triangular bifaces at Eva were classified as "large and medium triangular biface blades" and resemble the Anderson site Morrow Mountain Triangular forms; for example, compare Lewis and Lewis (1961:51, 53, Plates 14 and 16a, b, c) with Dowd (1989:160, Plate 72b). In fact, Lewis and Lewis (1961:25) note that the percentage of projectile points appears to be lower in the Eva component than in later components; they suggest that the triangular bifaces at Eva may in fact be projectile points. Their contention is borne out by evidence from the Mulberry Creek site in Colbert County, Alabama, where Morrow Mountain Triangular projectile points were found wedged in the vertebrae of burials 84 and 85 (Webb and DeJarnette 1942:Plates 275:1, 290:1). Thus it appears that the Eva component (strata IV and V) at the Eva site is contemporary with the Morrow Mountain component at the Anderson site, as indicated by similarities in hafted biface morphology. The Eva I forms and the Morrow Mountain Triangular hafted bifaces appear to be contemporary, the Eva I forms being basally notched Morrow Mountain Triangular hafted bifaces. The radiocarbon date from Eva stratum IV bottom, 7150 ± 167 (Table 13.1) compares favorably with two dates from the Early Morrow Mountain component at Anderson, 7180 ± 230 B.P. and 6990 ± 120 B.P. (Crites 1991:72; Dowd 1989:179, Table 10).

The Three Mile component at Eva (stratum II) appears to be contemporary with the Middle and Late Morrow Mountain components at Anderson. Some of the triangular points at Anderson exhibit slight basal notches (Dowd 1989:157) reminiscent of Eva I and II hafted bifaces. These basally notched triangular forms and round base Morrow Mountain I points, most common at Eva in the Middle Morrow Mountain Three Mile component, were lumped together in the Anderson analysis in the Morrow Mountain Round Base category (ibid.:159; Lindstrom and Steverson 1987:8), thus making it difficult to compare Eva I and II forms at Eva with the Middle and Late Morrow Mountain components at Anderson.

The lower portion of the Three Mile component, stratum II bottom, was characterized by Cypress Creek II, Eva II, and Morrow Mountain I projectile points. Stratum II bottom seems to correlate well with the upper levels (2, 3, and 4) at Anderson. The Morrow Mountain I projectile points from Eva, termed Morrow Mountain Round Base at Anderson, seem to be associated with the Late Morrow Mountain component at Anderson. The Cypress Creek II forms at Eva are similar to Anderson Corner Notched, but on the basis of the Anderson site stratigraphy, these forms should postdate the Morrow Mountain component. However, the Morrow Mountain Straight-Stemmed point is not found at Eva; at Anderson it represents the middle portion of the Morrow Mountain sequence. Perhaps the Morrow Mountain Straight-Stemmed hafted bifaces were classified as Cypress Creek II projectile points at Eva. On the other hand the Middle Morrow Mountain component may be absent at Eva. On the basis of the stratigraphic occurrence of Cypress Creek II points in the middle and bottom of stratum II, it appears that they are most likely candidates for an equivalent hafted biface at Eva of the Anderson site Anderson Corner Notched.

No evidence of flooding was found within the Eva component at Eva, but the Eva component was separated from the Three Mile component by a blanket of alluvium (strata III), suggesting a brief return to more mesic conditions as seen at Anderson (Hagee 1983:124-25). This interpretation fits well with the change in hafted biface morphology from Early to Middle Morrow Mountain. Mesic conditions at Anderson appear to have occurred during the transition from Early to Middle Morrow Mountain.

The Three Mile component was devoid of flooding. Lewis and Lewis (1961:20) believe that the lack of evidence for flooding within the Eva and Three Mile components indicates drier than normal conditions with less annual precipitation. The resulting lowered Tennessee River would have afforded an extensive series of shoals. The absence of shells in the Big Sandy component indicates climatic change to the Lewis's (1961:9), namely, the onset of moister

Table 13.1. Radiocarbon Determinations for Anderson (40WM9) and
Eva (40BN12)[*]

Site Number	Lab Number[†]	Radiocarbon Age	Sigma	Maximum Age	Intercepts	Minimum Age
40WM9	GX-9900	5680	200	6729	6468	6299
40WM9	GX-8365	6495	205	7189	7373, 7386, 7422	7570
40WM9	URC-1940	6700	150	7429	7532, 7544, 7568	7669
40WM9	GX-8215	6720	220	7374	7575	7739
40WM9	AA-1182	6990	120	7679	7783	7929
40BN12	M-357	7150	167	7779	7983, 7976, 7940	8079
40WM9	URC-1941	7180	230	7739	7950, 7967, 7992, 8008, 8025	8170

*Radiocarbon dates were calibrated using Calib and Display Rev. 2.1, 1987, Quaternary Isotope Laboratory, University of Washington, Seattle.
†Lab numbers reported in Dowd (1989:178–81) and Crites (1991:72).

conditions, with increased annual, as well as seasonally high, precipitation, thus inundating the shoals.

The few features recorded for Eva include a blade cache and a flint knapping area in stratum IV bottom (Early Morrow Mountain) and several masses of shells and fire-cracked rock in strata II and IV (ibid.:15–17).

The frequency of mammal bones relative to other fauna was higher in the Eva component (94%) than in the Three Mile and Big Sandy components (83%). However, in the latter two components, birds, turtles, and fish comprise 17% of the faunal remains, in contrast to 6% in the Eva component. This distribution indicates an increase in variation in prey species in the Middle and Late Morrow Mountain components, as was also seen at the Anderson site, particularly the increase in aquatic species. However, any interpretation of the Eva faunal assemblage should be treated with caution because the lack of screening created severe sampling problems, especially a selection bias for large species.

In the Eva component, there was more than five times as much bone as that found in the Three Mile component, although the Three Mile occupation represented twice the depth of deposit and contained a dense mussel shell matrix that would have enhanced bone preservation. It is interesting to note that the frequency of bone and antler artifacts is not significantly different between the two components, with the exception that bone fishhooks were far more numerous in the Three Mile component than the Eva component (ibid.:81).

The Three Mile component showed a significant increase in mollusks, fish, and birds and a decline in frequency of deer. Lewis and Lewis (1961:20) believe that the difference in deer bone frequencies represents a decline in the deer population caused by a combination of increased Middle Holocene aridity and human predation. The reduction of the deer population was hypothesized to have been compensated by an increased utilization of riverine aquatic species and birds. The Lewises (ibid.) noted that the Eva populations turned to riverine aquatic species for a "stable, dependable food supply" during the Three Mile component.

One hundred and eighty human burials and 18 dog burials were excavated at the Eva site. Seventeen burials were attributed to the Eva component (Early Morrow Mountain), and 102 burials belonged to the Three Mile component (Middle and Late Morrow Mountain) (ibid.:104). Virtually all of the human burials were articulated, primary inhumations in a flexed or tightly flexed position (Magennis 1977:134), and appeared to have been tightly wrapped prior to burial (Lewis and Lewis 1961:105).

Less than half of the interments were afforded grave furniture, and most of the grave goods were utilitarian. The distribution of grave goods was random with respect to age, suggesting an egalitarian type of social system (Magennis 1977:135). The nine Middle Archaic burials accompanied by red or yellow ochre were found in the Three Mile component. Almost half were located in the middle zone of stratum II and, with one exception, were infants, a child, and adult females. Human burials accompanied by dog burials were also found only in the Three Mile component, in the middle and top strata. Dogs accompanied a child, two adult females, and an adult male. Bone beads were associated with an adult female in stratum IV bottom and with an adult male and female in stratum IV top. A child and an adult female contained bone beads in II top and bottom, respectively. Bone beads were somewhat predominant in the Eva component, but ochre and dog burials were restricted to the Three Mile component.

The skeletal sample was not representative of a true biological population but represented that portion of the group that inhabited and died at the site (Magennis 1977:138), suggesting that Eva was not occupied throughout the year. Lewis and Lewis (1961:17), on the other hand, believe that the Eva site inhabitants were sedentary hunters and gatherers.

Fifteen of the 18 dogs were found in the Three Mile component. None occurred in the Eva (Early Morrow Mountain) component (ibid.:144). Twelve of these were in stratum II top and middle (ibid.:102). Four dog burials were associated with human burials (ibid.:144); one was in the plowzone, one was in stratum II top, and two were in stratum II middle.

The Mulberry Creek Site

The Mulberry Creek site (1CT27), located in Colbert County, Alabama, was excavated under the field supervision of James R. Foster beginning in July 1936 as part of the federal work relief effort in Pickwick Reservoir (Webb and DeJarnette 1942:235–66). The shell midden was 5.4 m deep and was located at the confluence of Mulberry Creek and the Tennessee River in the Gulf Coastal Plain. Much of the Tennessee River and Mulberry Creek sides of the site, northeast and southeast, respectively, had undergone extensive erosion prior to excavation. Unfortunately, the site was almost completely inundated in February 1938, when the floodgates of Pickwick Lock and Dam were closed. No further excavations were carried out.

Foster (Webb and DeJarnette 1942:264) identified three broad occupational zones at Mulberry Creek. The earliest zone contained alternating layers of shell and sand. Several small shell lenses appear to represent the initial use of mollusks. The first large-scale use of shell was laid down on a sloping sandbar formed at the junction of Mulberry Creek and the Tennessee River. The shell accumulated to a depth of 60 cm, and the river then deposited about 1 m of clean yellow sand over the shell layer; this layer may correspond to the period of mesic conditions at Anderson and Eva. Only the lower portion of the shell layer sloping toward the river was covered with sand; the upper end of the site apparently was above the high watermark. More shell was deposited, forming a second layer of shell about 1 m in thickness, being thicker toward the river and fading out in the opposite direction. After the second shell deposit, the river once more deposited an almost level layer of clean sand about 50 cm thick over the whole area. After a deposit of nearly 0.9 m of shell had accumulated on the sand layer, a few centimeters of very fine-texture clay was laid down. After this point, shell continued to be added to the midden.

Foster's middle zone was 2.6 m thick and contained worked flint but no pottery. The upper zone contained pottery and was about 0.9 m thick.

Initial occupation of the Mulberry Creek site began with intermittent use, possibly on the original sandbar, marked by late Early Archaic Kirk-Stemmed projectile points. The Morrow Mountain occupation appears to be represented by a 15-cm layer of shell 6.9 m in length in the illustrated profile (Webb and DeJarnette 1942:Fig. 79). This shell midden was the first deposition of mollusks, and it rested on a natural levee or perhaps the alluvial fan resulting from the outwash of Mulberry Creek. Morrow Mountain Triangular hafted bifaces (WPA Type 1) are found in these early levels and perhaps point to an Early Morrow Mountain component in this area of the site (ibid.:256). The bone tools, antler points, bone awls, fishhooks, and an antler "shaft straightener" from Mulberry Creek bear a close resemblance to those from the Eva component at Eva (Walthall 1980:62) and the Early Morrow Mountain component at Anderson.

A sand layer rests on this initial midden. A Middle to Late Morrow Mountain shell midden appears to lie atop this sand layer. This second shell midden is the first major accumulation of mollusks at the site and forms a spoil pile down the bank of the Tennessee River (Webb and DeJarnette 1942:Fig. 79). Several Middle and Late Morrow Mountain burials were recovered from this sand layer on the Mulberry Creek side of the site.

A large circular grave containing three individuals, burials 83, 84, and 85, had been dug into the sand layer and rested directly on the initial 15 cm layer of shell, suggesting that these individuals were buried after the initial occupation of the site and after a subsequent flood. The rib cage of Burial 83, an adult male, had been penetrated by three projectile points. One of these points appears to be a Morrow Mountain Straight-Stemmed. The other two were fragmented on impact and could not be identified (ibid.:Plate 289.2, lower left). Another adult male, burial 84, contained seven Morrow Mountain projectile points. Four were found in the thoracic cavity, and one was in the mouth cavity. These five points include a Morrow Mountain Round Base, three Morrow Mountain Stemmed, and one that appears to be an Eva II projectile point (ibid.:Plate 289.2, upper row). Another point, a Morrow Mountain Triangular, entered the body from the front and lodged in a vertebral centrum (ibid.:Plate 275.1). A Morrow Mountain Round Base also had penetrated from the rear and became embedded between two neural processes (ibid.:245, Plate 275.2). In addition, the hands and forearms of this burial were missing, suggesting a pattern of dismemberment characteristic of the late prehistoric period. The third burial, 85, an adolescent male, was associated with a cache of artifacts placed between the left arm and the body (ibid.:Plate 274), including two deer ulna awls, a Morrow Mountain Triangular projectile point, and two Morrow Mountain Straight-Stemmed projectile points (ibid.:289.2, lower right). This individual also had a Morrow Mountain Triangular projectile point embedded in the spinal column (ibid.:Plates 290.1). These burials, containing a series of Morrow Mountain Triangular, Morrow Mountain Round Base, and Morrow Mountain Straight-Stemmed projectile points (ibid.:Plate 289:2), underscore some of the difficulties in using hafted bifaces for temporal controls.

Several interments in the immediate vicinity of burials 83, 84, and 85 appear to be contemporaneous. One in particular, burial 86, an adult of indeterminate gender, was 3 m southeast of burials 83, 84, 85. Buried with the individual was a cylindrical atlatl weight (ibid.:Plate 290.2) reminiscent of the three found in the Three Mile component at Eva (ibid.:66). At Eva, the atlatls clearly were associated with the Middle to Late Morrow Mountain component. At Anderson tubular or cylindrical atlatl weights were associated with the late component (Lindstrom and Steverson 1987:31). Burial 93 at Mulberry Creek was an adult male, who was found 3.9 m southwest of burials 83, 84, and 85 and had a Morrow Mountain Straight-Stemmed projectile point located in the abdominal area. Burial 94 was an infant buried with a conch shell cup 3 m northwest of burials 83, 84, and 85.

A Sykes/White Springs component appears to be mixed with much of the Middle and Late Morrow Mountain component at Mulberry Creek, making an accurate discrimination between Morrow Mountain and Sykes-White Springs components difficult. Walthall (1980:64) notes that the lower-level burials at

Mulberry Creek are similar to those of the Three Mile component at Eva. Both Anderson and Eva had Sykes-White Springs components mixed with later phases of the Morrow Mountain component.

Summary

In many parts of the Midsouth and Midwest, Middle Holocene populations adapted to changes in the resource base. Subsistence adjustments in the Midsouth involved increased emphasis on aquatic resources and increased use of floodplain settlements. Within the Central Basin and Lower and Middle Tennessee valleys, increased utilization of riverine aquatic resources and intensification of floodplain occupation began by approximately 7200 to 7000 B.P., following a warming trend that resulted in a stabilized fluvial regime (Brakenridge 1984:18). Shoal habitats emerged as stabilized water levels created or enhanced conditions favorable for increases in populations of riverine species. The higher biomass and increased carrying capacity of shoal habitats made available to local hunting and gathering populations a variety of abundant and easily obtainable riverine-dependent resources, including birds, fish, invertebrates, mammals, and turtles. Shoals are an attractive mosaic of habitats of interest to hunter-gatherer populations. Smith (1986:24) views the increased utilization of shoal or shallow area habitat aquatic species as an "opportunistic response to the advantageous emergence of a localized, seasonally abundant, dependable, and easily collected resource."

For example, fish that spawn in shoals, especially suckers such as redhorse, would be an attractive resource to midsouthern hunter-gatherers (Brietburg, personal communication). Spawning adult suckers often gather in streams and rivers in large schools over shallow, gravelly riffles above large pools. Suckers, each kind of which has its own particular habitat preference, spawn in shoals so shallow that their backs are exposed. During the spawning, the suckers do not show their customary timidity. In the Midsouth, eighteen species of suckers spawn between late March to early August. They could be taken easily by hand, with nets, spears, and traps, or with a variety of poisons such as black walnut hulls (*Juglans nigra*), Carolina moonseed berries (*Cocculus carolinus*), devil's shoestring roots (*Tephrosia virginiana*), and Ohio buckeye seeds (*Aesculus glabra*). Suckers are one of the dominant groups of large fishes in the Midsouth. Their total poundage in streams commonly exceeds that of all other fishes combined. Some suckers, such as the bigmouth buffalo (*Ictiobus cyprinellus*) average 2 to 14 pounds, although it is not uncommon for some individuals to reach 30 pounds (Pflieger 1975:178–201). Their flesh has a sweet, delicate flavor that ranks with some of the finest food fishes in the Midsouth (ibid.:195). The food energy of the silver redhorse (*Mosoxtoma anisurum*), 98 calories, is comparable to venison with 128 calories, and the protein value is even closer with 18 grams for redhorse and

21 grams for venison (Watt and Merrill 1975:Table 1). Unfortunately for archaeologists, when redhorse suckers are subjected to high heat, their numerous small bones disappear. At the Anderson site the most numerous fish recovered were redhorse, albeit in low numbers. The rarity of fish remains appears to have been due in part to the recovery techniques and to the position of the site at the headwaters of the Harpeth River where suckers are less likely to be found (Breitburg 1993; Dowd 1989:125–26).

Concomitant with the shift in subsistence strategies is decreased residential mobility resulting in a pattern of strategically located base camps associated with a logistically organized settlement strategy (Binford 1980). When a few primary resources, or a bundled set of favored resources, such as aquatic species, nuts, and deer, become more abundant, some settlement locales, because of their proximity to strategic resources, become preferred habitation areas for longer periods (Brown and Vierra 1983; Christenson 1981; Ford 1977; Neusius 1986; Stafford 1991; Styles et al. 1991, 1993). These strategic locations indicate an increased investment in more lasting facilities such as housing, storage facilities, and prepared hearths. For example, trash will be cleaned from certain areas (Brown and Vierra 1983:170). Storage pits, an increase in number of human burials, and prepared domestic platforms, perhaps indicating long-term habitation locales, have been cited as evidence of increasing trends toward sedentism (B. Smith 1986:26). Subterranean storage pits may serve as an archaeological indicator of prolonged food storage, perhaps suggesting storage for times when food resources become scarce, such as winter and spring.

Prepared domestic platforms provide convincing evidence of increasing sedentism. Sites with prepared habitation floors may have been "annually reoccupied by kin groups during the summer-fall dry season" (B. Smith 1986:27). In the Midsouth, prepared habitation platforms are best known for their association with Sykes-White Springs and Benton components (6000–5000 B.P.) (B. Smith 1986:26–27), but habitation areas with prepared floors have been securely associated with the Morrow Mountain component at the Walnut site (22IT539) between 7200 to 7000 B.P. in the Upper Tombigbee drainage (Ensor and Studer 1983:5.88). At the Walnut site, a Morrow Mountain, prepared habitation platform was associated with a variety of activities, including the reduction of local cobbles into finished tools and the use of those tools for fishing, hunting, and turtling. The habitation platforms appear to have been swept clean of debris (ibid.:5.276–5.288), suggesting repeated and perhaps long-term use. Associated with the Morrow Mountain occupation at Walnut was the presence of two cemeteries, suggesting a community plan involving secular and ritualistic activities.

Beginning around 6500 B.P. evidence of increasing cultural complexity appears in the Midsouth among hunter-gatherers. Residential mobility had begun to be replaced around 7000 B.P. with the appearance of permanent shelter at base camps near shoal areas along the major rivers and in upland drainages based on a greater focus on optimal species such as deer, fish, turkey, raccoon, and nuts. Brown and Vierra (1983) suggest that the pull of aquatic resources was inadequate to compensate for the significant noneconomic problems that the loss of mobility and the adoption of complete sedentism brought. Decision making associated with risk management under the constraints of environmental change and population growth promoted shifts away from residential mobility to complete sedentism. This process took place over a period of several thousand years. This line of reasoning suggests the early use of tokens of intergroup exchange, such as native copper, galena, exotic flints, red ochre, and carved bone pins. Shifts in behavioral strategies toward investment in institutions of intergroup cooperation was one response to giving up the security and the risk-averting features associated with mobility. Tokens of intergroup exchange are evident at Anderson (ochre and marine shell beads), Eva (ochre and bone beads), and Mulberry Creek (marine shell). At Anderson reliance on tokens of exchange appears to increase through time.

Additional lines of evidence suggest that many of these features emerged during Morrow Mountain times in the Midsouth in Middle Holocene sites that contain an increased number of primary and secondary burials, including cremations. An increase in the number of human burials found in Early Morrow Mountain components over earlier cultures may reflect longer and more consistent seasonal reoccupation of specific settlement locales (Ensor and Studer 1983:5.89; Hofman 1986; B. Smith 1986:26).

Subsistence economies became more broad-based during the Middle Archaic than they were during the Early Archaic (Christenson 1981:52). Aquatic resources in the Middle Archaic began to play a significant role in subsistence (Royer and Roper 1980:19; B. Smith 1986:22; Stoltman and Baerreis 1983:256; Styles 1986:168). For example, there is substantial evidence at this time for aquatic resource utilization along Duck River (Hofman 1984; Klippel and Morey 1986; Turner 1982), especially in the Duck River floodplain where it was flanked by uplands characterized by patchy vegetation (Turner and Klippel 1989:64).

Unfortunately, there is virtually no evidence of botanical remains from the sites discussed here (Anderson, Eva, Mulberry Creek) because appropriate recovery methods were not used when the sites were excavated (see also Hensley, this volume). However, at the Walnut site, large amounts of hickory nuts were recovered (Ensor and Studer 1983:5.89). Middle Archaic studies from the Midwest indicate increased opportunistic nut utilization, particularly hickory nuts, with bulk extraction and processing at both base camps and extractive camps (Stafford 1991:228). The importance of nuts and other upland/tributary resources points to the complexity of factors that structured the Middle Archaic settlement-subsistence system (Anslinger 1988; Jefferies and Lynch 1983; Lewis 1983; Stafford 1991). The Morrow Mountain subsistence strategies based on faunal analysis alone, particularly early Morrow Mountain populations, indicate that a wide variety of environments was utilized.

By the end of the Middle Archaic, around 5000 B.P., there is evidence for increased use of *Cucurbita* gourds, perhaps as containers and as a source of edible seeds (Watson 1989:559). In central Tennessee domesticated sumpweed has been dated to the third century B.C., domesticated *Chenopodium* has been recovered from the seventh century B.C., and maygrass has been dated to 4300 B.P. (B. Smith 1989). The earliest evidence for sumpweed use is 4300 B.P. (Crites 1991). Crites has obtained a 4200 B.P. age determination on sunflower (Crites 1993:147). He believes that the "initial domestication of sunflower may have occurred by the middle of the fifth millennium B.P." (ibid.).

The emergence of native cultigens was a result of a "complex mosaic of occasionally linked, generally parallel, but distinct coevolutionary histories of different areas of the mid-latitude Eastern Woodlands" (B. Smith 1987:37). With the continued occupation of specific locales adjacent to enriched, fixed-place resource concentrations, such as shoal area aquatic habitats, continually disturbed anthropogenic habitats were created. In this environment increased sunlight, soil fertility, and soil exposure brought about a favorable environment for seed germination, especially those intentionally harvested and planted, eventually resulting in plants with larger seeds or more seeds per plant. Increased competition among seedlings provided selective advantage to rapidly germinating and growing plants (Fritz 1990:413; B. Smith 1987).

At both Anderson and Eva there is a decline in the amount of deer represented in the recovered faunal remains and a concomitant increase in birds and small game. Especially noteworthy is the increase in fishhooks in the Three Mile phase at Eva and its association with the general demise of animal bone compared with the Eva component. However, the lack of bone may be a factor of recovery techniques. Perhaps a greater dependence on fish and other small fauna resulted in lower overall numbers of faunal elements where they were recovered through manual selection as opposed to systematic screening. At the Anderson site, 75% of all fishhooks were associated with the Early and Middle Morrow Mountain components.

Projectile points appear to decrease in size through time. At Eva, the Eva II projectile point is a continuation of the Eva I form, but on a smaller scale. Morrow Mountain Triangular projectile points at Anderson "were made smaller as time passed" (Dowd 1989:157). Cypress Creek projectile points also became smaller through time at Eva (Lewis and Lewis 1961:37–40). This decrease in projectile point size may be a reflection of greater reliance on smaller game, a greater variety of game, or both.

Archaeological evidence from Anderson, Eva, and Mulberry Creek are all clear concerning the presence of light-density Early Archaic occupations preceding the initial Morrow Mountain components. After 7200 B.P., multiseason base camps, characterized by structures at Anderson and storage pits at Mulberry Creek, become evident during the Early Morrow Mountain components. During the succeeding Middle and Late Morrow Mountain occupations, substantial increases are indicated at each site in terms of numbers of burials and accumulated trash indicating reduced residential mobility. On the basis of faunal evidence, for example, Breitburg (1993; see also Dowd 1989:126) suggests that Anderson was probably occupied during most of the year. Most burials occurred in the Middle and Late Morrow Mountain components (Joerschke 1983:132–33). Lewis and Lewis (1961) also believed that Eva was occupied throughout the year. The Middle to Late Morrow Mountain component, in particular, was the "longest and most intense occupation of the site, containing the greatest number of burials and artifacts" (Lewis and Lewis 1961:9). Austin (40BR82), a Middle Archaic site comparable in intensity of occupation to Anderson and Eva, is also believed to have been occupied throughout the year based on faunal analysis (Barker and Breitburg 1992). In addition, the Walnut site was believed to have been used as a permanent or semipermanent base camp (Ensor and Studer 1983:5.89).

Trends toward sedentism and cultural complexity in the Midsouth span several thousand years and seem generally to have been a product of dynamic cultural processes involving a series of behavioral choices concerning subsistence risk and stress by localized groups adjusting to changing demographic, ecological, and social organizational settings (Brown 1985:209; Doershuk 1989:16).

Territorial hunters and gatherers define rights of access to critical resources for social groups and form intercamp alliances through ad hoc ceremonies (A. Johnson and Earle 1987:61), often using tokens to compensate for regional differences in the availability of foods and to forge intergroup alliances that may have served to mediate hostilities. Evidence of warfare was not noted for Eva, but four apparent victims of violence have been noted at Mulberry Creek. This violence may have been the result of intercommunity hostilities (Walthall 1980:64). Evidence is increasing that Archaic populations were aggressive. This evidence includes perimortem violent trauma including decapitation, dismemberment, human bone grave goods, scalping, and trophy taking (M. Smith 1992). Mulberry Creek and, to a lesser extent, Anderson exhibit some of the earliest evidence of warfare in the Midsouth. Narrow-spectrum harvesting economies often exhibit increased conflict resulting from efforts to restrict access to critical resources in favored localities through territorial control (Walthall 1980:65–67; Winters 1974:xi).

Intergroup exchange as an avenue for prestige enhancement and alliance formation was well established by 5600 B.P. (Johnson and Brookes 1989). The appearance of objects manufactured from exotic material, such as marine shell, testifies to the use of tokens in intergroup exchange by 6500 B.P. at Anderson and Mulberry Creek. It is interesting to note that Eva did not exhibit evidence of conflict and likewise did not reveal evidence of intergroup exchange.

Data presented herein indicate that an increased exploitation of riverine aquatic species led to an intensive occupation of floodplain habitats, especially shoal environments, as early as 7000 B.P. in selected areas of the Midsouth. In other areas reduced mobility may have resulted from factors not associated with shoal habitats, such as patchy environments or prairie areas. In the three shell middens examined in this chapter, increased emphasis on riverine aquatic species is roughly contemporary with the Middle Holocene warming trend (H. Delcourt 1979) and associated midlatitude river aggradation and stabilization (Brackenridge 1984; P. Delcourt 1985; B. Smith 1986:24). Increased utilization of riverine habitats, especially the shoal areas, resulted in widespread availability and eventual accumulation of aquatic mussels in middens and is seen as a response to the emergence of a suite of dependable aquatic species that became seasonally abundant and easily collected (B. Smith 1986:24). Thus, initial trends toward decreased mobility, territoriality, warfare, and tokens of intergroup exchange apparently had their beginnings around 7000 B.P. in the Midsouth.

14 | Of Caves and Shell Mounds in West-Central Kentucky

Patty Jo Watson

Beginnings and Early Development

My INVOLVEMENT WITH cave archaeology began in the summer of 1955 when I married a caver—Red Watson—who became a founding member of the Cave Research Foundation (CRF), the governing body of which encouraged me to initiate investigations in Salts Cave, Mammoth Cave National Park, Kentucky, in the early 1960s (even though I was specializing in Old World prehistory at the time). Ultimately I did so because first Douglas Schwartz (at the University of Kentucky) and then Joe Caldwell (at the Illinois State Museum) declined to undertake long-term research on the prehistoric remains strewn throughout Salts Cave. Joe, in fact—although he was very clear in stating his disinclination to spend any more time in that cave, *ever*, than the generous tour CRF personnel afforded him in 1962—obtained $300 from the Illinois State Museum Society in support of Salts Cave archaeology and sent his cheerful and capable curatorial assistant, Bob Hall (who turned out to be a natural-born caver), to aid us in our first campaign: summer 1963.

Our initial goals were simple and straightforward, focusing on time–space systematics. How old was the archaeological material in Salts Cave? Where was it distributed within the cave? Why did prehistoric people explore the deep interior of this world-class cave, and what did they do there?

At first our approach was largely speleological and highly particularistic in documenting where the ancient cavers went and in accumulating radiocarbon determinations on their leavings, but by 1969 we had begun to realize some of the archaeobotanical potential in the plant and dietary remains from the dry cave passages (Yarnell 1969), something Joe Caldwell had remarked on after his one and only trip underground. By the early 1970s we were carrying out flotation as well as analyzing macroplant and microplant remains in the paleofeces abundantly preserved in both Salts Cave and Mammoth Cave. Preliminary results from Dick Yarnell's analysis of Salts Cave Vestibule flotation samples seemed to contain empirical evidence for the independent origin of native North American cultigens predating the introduction of domestic plants from Mexico.

In search of charcoal-bearing sediments antedating those in Salts Cave Vestibule, we turned to the Archaic shell mounds on Green River, 40 to 50 miles west of Mammoth Cave National Park, near Logansport, Kentucky. Extensive CWA/Works Progress Administration–subsidized excavation of several shell mounds during the 1930s and early 1940s had retrieved a massive amount of artifactual and human osteological material, but we did not know whether plant charcoal was either present or abundant there. Hence, as soon as Bill Marquardt had located a suitable site (15Bt5, Carlston Annis) and we had obtained permission from the landowner (Mr. Waldemar Annis) to work there, we excavated a 1- × 1- × 2-m test pit to premound sediment, saving the deposit for flotation. There was plenty of plant charcoal all right, but most of it was hickory nutshell and none of it from native North American cultigens. Moreover, after we spent another season (1974) of digging and floating, Charles Miksicek, Clark Erickson, and Gary Crawford found 11 small fragments of charred *Cucurbita* shell. *Cucurbita* rind in a third-millennium B.C. context was quite exciting, and in 1976 when we reported it, it was assumed to be the same genus and species, *Cucurbita pepo ovifera*, as that from the caves and to have derived ultimately from Mexico. We settled down to long-term research in the Big Bend of Green River to elucidate the nature of the Late Archaic shell mound subsistence system that seemingly included domestic gourdlike squash but no other cultigens. From 1976 to 1982 we examined this one mound (15Bt5) intensively from a variety of site-formation perspectives: geoarchaeological, malacological, macrobotanical, and microstratigraphical. Bill Marquardt's survey crews also began investigating the surrounding region. That survey was subsequently extended and continued by Charles Hockensmith and the Kentucky Heritage Council, who have recently documented shell middens in several counties of western Kentucky, and by Christine Hensley, whose M. A. thesis fieldwork on the Read site (15Bt10) chipped stone material is described in this volume (see also Hensley 1994).

During the final phases of our first decade of research Tom Gatus mapped the chert sources nearest the Big Bend, and Cheryl Claassen joined us to investigate seasonality in the mussel shells from the mounds and to advance innovative explanations for shell accumulation in mounds.

Meanwhile back in Mammoth Cave National Park, Ken Carstens carried out a study of surface archaeology (i.e., above-ground open sites and rock shelters) to produce preliminary culture historical sequences for the Central Kentucky Karst area around Salts Cave and Mammoth Cave. His mid-1970s research built on Schwartz's 1950s work, just as Guy Prentice's built on Carstens's.

A new phase of cave archaeology in the Mammoth Cave system was also launched when Cheryl and Patrick Munson with their graduate student, Ken Tankersley, and geological consultants John Bassett and Sam Frushour alerted us to new information on crystal mining and crystal use by the prehistoric cavers (Munson et al. 1989).

Just prior to initiating the crystal-mining project in Mammoth Cave, the Munsons carried out research in Wyandotte Cave near Corydon in southern Indiana that greatly expanded the preliminary findings and radiocarbon dates we reported from there in 1974 and also heralded the dawn of expanding interest in caves by archaeologists in the Midwest and Southeast. Until about 10 years ago the CRF Archaeological Project was the only long-term investigation in the United States focused on describing and explaining archaeological remains in a big cave. But several archaeologists are now going below ground in search of evidence applicable to a variety of problems, some of them ranging far beyond the specific subterranean data repositories themselves (Crothers and Watson 1993). There is a growing list of cave sites providing information on topics ranging from specific historical events such as the death of Floyd Collins in Sand Cave in 1925 (Crothers 1983) to protohistoric and earlier iconography and cave ceremonialism (Faulkner 1988; Faulkner, ed., 1986); systematic and intensive prehistoric crystal, chert, and speleothem mining (Ferguson 1983; P. Munson and C. Munson 1990; Munson et al. 1989); prehistoric mortuary patterns (Crothers 1989; Haskins 1988; Sneed and Sneed 1989; P. Willey 1989); as well as very impressive Archaic and Woodland period cave exploration well beyond the Central Kentucky Karst (Crothers 1987; Ferguson 1983; Robbins, Wilson, and Watson 1981).

It is clear from this brief overview that the work begun in 1963 in Salts Cave has ramified in various directions and is embedded within an expanding research matrix reaching well beyond Mammoth Cave National Park and the middle Green River region. In summing up, I refer to the major results emerging from these cave and shell mound studies under three headings: cave archaeology, shell mound archaeology, and origins of plant domestication in the Eastern Woodlands.

Cave Archaeology

Prehistoric people in the midcontinental karst region of the Eastern Woodlands entered big caves—including the world's longest, the Mammoth Cave System—as early as the third millennium B.C. and skillfully exploited a variety of materials they found there, some of this work necessitating long trips and sojourns of many hours several kilometers from the cave entrance.

At some times and places, beginning at least as far back as the Late Archaic, prehistoric people in this karst region also used the caves themselves for ceremonial or ritual purposes.

The use of caves as burial places, a phenomenon recognized several decades ago in the Copena area, is now known to include deposition of human remains in vertical shafts and fissures starting at least as early as the Late Archaic period.

Analysis of plant remains from dry caves has provided and is continuing to produce a considerable volume of information as well as some amazing detail about plant use in general and early cultigens in particular.

Shell Mound Archaeology

Chronologies for two of the Kentucky Green River shell mounds have been preliminarily blocked out radiometrically. Bt5 was apparently occupied (seasonally and perhaps intermittently) for some two millennia beginning no later than 3000 B.C.; at least part of Oh13 is seemingly somewhat later, 1000 B.C. and after.

However, even basic chronology for individual sites is a difficult question because the mounds (or at least Bt5) are very complex and very dynamic entities. Bioturbation is continuous (Stein 1980, 1983), and the original site-formation processes were manifold and intricate (Claassen 1982, and this volume; Stein 1980).

Knowledge of at least three kinds of non-shell-mound sites is essential to understanding the nature and function of the shell mounds themselves: upland rock shelters and lithic scatters, river bottom or low-terrace "burned-rock middens," and dirt middens or sheet middens with a high percentage of fire-cracked rock (nearly always sandstone in the middle Green River region of Kentucky) (Hensley 1991, 1994). Information on rock shelters is severely limited because of widespread, intensive vandalism; information on lithic scatters and burnt-rock middens is severely limited because they are inconspicuous, sometimes buried, and were virtually ignored by archaeology in favor of the richer, more obvious shell middens. Our comprehension of the shell mound settlement system is rudimentary, but upland lithic scatters and floodplain "dirt," or "burned-rock," middens probably played vital roles in that system, hence Hensley's recent focus on them (Hensley 1989, 1994).

Origins of Plant Domestication in the Midwest and Midsouth

The initial indications of pre–*Cucurbita* cultivar use in Salts Cave Vestibule were not borne out, partly because the chronology there has been revised downward (Gardner 1987; Kennedy 1990, and this volume). The general pattern of cultigen appearance in midcontinental North America is now fairly well defined, however, at least in broad outline. The Salts Cave–Mammoth Cave horticultural complex is one of several known for the Early Woodland period. The others are in the Ozarks, eastern Kentucky, and the Duck River and Little Tennessee River valleys of Tennessee (Chapman and Shea 1981; Cowan 1985; Fritz 1990; Gremillion 1993, 1994; Smith 1987, 1992a, b; Watson 1985a, 1988, 1989; Yarnell 1986, 1994). The primary data from Salts Cave and Mammoth Cave are more varied, abundant, and detailed than elsewhere but are confined chronologically to the Early Woodland. Evidence from Middle and Late Archaic sites is available from some of the Green River shell mounds (Crawford 1978), Cloudsplitter shelter (Cowan 1985), Cold Oak and other shelters in eastern Kentucky, Phillips Spring in Missouri, Russell Cave in Alabama, the Hays and

Higgs sites in Tennessee (Crites 1993), and open sites in the lower Illinois River valley of west central Illinois (see Fritz 1990 for a detailed summary). It appears that sunflower, sumpweed (*Iva annua*), and *Chenopodium* were domesticated between 2500 and 1000 B.C. and that maygrass was taken into cultivation soon after that if not earlier. A species of *Cucurbita* was present much earlier in west central Illinois (by 5000–4000 B.C.), but the exact identity and status of this cucurbit is still under discussion. There is also a circa 5000 B.C. occurrence of bottlegourd (*Lagenaria siceraria*) in an Archaic Florida burial (Doran and Newsom 1990), but the relations of this bottlegourd with the fifth-millennium B.C. gourdlike squash (*pepo*-gourd) and the Terminal Archaic–Early Woodland cultigens in the Midwest and Midsouth are also unclear (Newsom 1988, 1992). Some (Asch 1994) remain skeptical of the north-of-the-border hypothesis regarding the origins of domestic cucurbits. The recent discovery of *Cucurbita pepo* seeds in a Paleoindian context at the Page-Ladson site in Florida, however, demonstrates the presence of some form of presumably wild *Cucurbita pepo* north of Mexico at 12,000 B.P. (Newsom, Webb, and Dunbar 1993).

Conclusions

Although I like to think that what we have begun in the cave and shell mound precincts along Kentucky's Green River has been *well* begun, it is certainly no more than a beginning. Future research directions in both the cave and the shell mound areas are legion. In conclusion I touch briefly on a few of them.

Cave Archaeology

In terms of the big picture, evidence to date indicates that every dry cave with a negotiable opening to the surface was explored by Native Americans and probably made use of in one or more ways. We are very far from anything resembling a representative inventory of these cave sites, let alone documentation of the archaeological remains in them.

In terms of more specific issues, there are now some bioarchaeological data on mortuary activity in caves, but there is wide scope for a great deal more work on both synchronic and diachronic aspects of such activity.

Nonmortuary ritual and ceremonial use of caves—especially that resulting in pictographs, including "mud glyphs,"—is poorly understood, although data are slowly accumulating (DiBlasi this volume; Faulkner 1988). The logistical problems of adequate documentation are often very severe, but the potential for obtaining rare or otherwise inaccessible information is so great that much more work should be conducted on this topic.

We know something about mining or quarrying in two caves (the Mammoth Cave System and Wyandotte [Munson et al. 1989]) and have an inkling of it elsewhere (e.g., Big Bone Cave [Crothers 1987], Saltpeter Cave [Ferguson 1983]). There is surely much more to be learned. In the Mammoth Cave System there is also more to be done at the simple documentation level for crystal mining. Other avenues of research are awaiting attention with regard to the paleofecal remains: a detailed study of food processing, for example. In the Mammoth Cave area above ground, Carstens's and Prentice's work has amplified our knowledge of the cultural historical sequence that precedes and succeeds the deep cave period. But there is certainly more to be learned both in rock shelters and in open sites within the Park and—even more pressing—outside it.

Shell Mound Archaeology

In the shell mound area, several crucial issues remain to be investigated. We know something about chronology and formation processes at one shell mound (Bt5) and much less, but still something, about four others (Bt6, Bt10, Bt11, Oh13). Comparative information of the most fundamental kind (dates, basic site stratigraphy, archaeobotany, bioarchaeology, zooarchaeology) is essential from at least a sample of the remaining presumably more or less contemporaneous mounds.

We also need fundamental contextual data for these shell mounds. They were seasonally used: where were the shell mound people in the winter and early spring? What is the relation of the burned-rock middens to either the shell middens or the shell-free middens? The general cultural history of the Big Bend is poorly understood for the horizons before and after the shell midden era. No comprehensive research has even been conducted on time-space systematics; we are almost entirely ignorant of this basic information except in the most preliminary way.

Hence, it appears that as is so often the case with work in data-rich territories, we have learned just enough to define some really interesting and significant questions. I look forward to the next two decades of research along the middle Green River—above ground and below.

References

Adkins, Audrey M.
  1988   Diet and Dental Health in Archaic and Fort Ancient Populations in Kentucky. In *New Deal Era Archaeology and Current Research in Kentucky*, edited by D. Pollack and M. L. Powell, pp. 97–104. Kentucky Heritage Council, Frankfort.

Aitken, Melvin J.
  1974   Radiocarbon Dating. In *Physics and Archaeology*, pp. 26–84. Clarendon Press, Oxford.

Allaway, Elizabeth B.
  1980   Is There Sex after Death? An Investigation into the Meaning of Skeletal Sexual Dimorphism. Master's thesis, Department of Anthropology, University of Kentucky, Lexington.

Anslinger, C. Michael
  1988   Bluegrass: A Middle-Late Archaic Site in Southwestern Indiana. Paper presented at the 1988 Midwest Archaeological Conference, Urbana.

Armelagos, George J., David S. Carlson, and Dennis P. van Gerven
  1982   The Theoretical Foundations and Development of Skeletal Biology. In *A History of American Physical Anthropology, 1930–1980*, edited by F. Spenser, pp. 305–28. Academic Press, New York.

Asch, David L.
  1994   Aboriginal Specialty Plant Cultivation in Eastern North America: Illinois Prehistory and a Post-Contact Perspective. In *Agricultural Origins and Development in the Midcontinent*, edited by William Green, pp. 25–86. Office of the State Archaeologist, Report No. 19, University of Iowa, Iowa City.

Asch, David L., and Nancy Asch Sidell
  1988   Archaeological Plant Remains: Applications to Stratigraphic Analysis. In *Current Paleoethnobotany: Analytical Methods and Cultural Interpretations of Archeological Plant Remains*, edited by Christine A. Hastorf and Virginia S. Popper, pp. 86–96. University of Chicago Press, Chicago.

Barker, Gary, and Emanuel Breitburg
  1992   Archaic Occupations at the Austin Site (40RB82). Paper presented at the 49th Annual Meeting of the Southeastern Archaeological Conference, Little Rock.

Barker, H.
  1953   Radiocarbon Dating: Large-Scale Preparation of Acetylene from Organic Material. *Nature* 172:631–32.

Baxter, M. S., and A. Walton
  1971   Fluctuations of Atmospheric Carbon-14 Concentrations during the Past Century. *Proceedings of the Royal Society of London* (Section A), 321:105–27.
Beditz, Lindsay C.
  1981   Mammoth Cave National Park, Kentucky: Bluffline Survey of the Childress Farm/Grant Onyx Job Corps Civilian Conservation Center Property. Ms. on file, Southeast Archeological Center, Tallahassee.
  1979   Archeological Reconnaissance and Testing of Alternative JCCCC Sites in Mammoth Cave National Park. Ms. on file, Southeast Archeological Center, Tallahassee.
Belovich, Stephanie
  1993   Fracture Patterns in the Carlston Annis (Bt5) Late Archaic Shell Mound Population. Paper presented at the American Association of Physical Anthropologists, Toronto.
  n.d.   Vertebral Pathology at Bt5. Master's thesis, Department of Anthropology, Cleveland State University, Cleveland.
Bender, Margaret M.
  1971   Variations in the $^{13}C/^{12}C$ Ratio of Plants in Relation to the Pathway of Photosynthetic Carbon Dioxide Fixation. *Phytochemistry* 10:1239–44.
  1968   Mass Spectrometric Studies of Carbon 13 Variations in Corn and Other Grasses. *Radiocarbon* 10:468–72.
Benington, Federick, Carl Melton, and Patty Jo Watson
  1962   Carbon Dating Prehistoric Soot from Salts Cave, Kentucky. *American Antiquity* 28(2):238–41.
Bense, Judith A.
  1983   Early Holocene Cultural Adaptation in the Upper Tombigbee Valley of Northeast Mississippi: Results of Geoarchaeology. Paper presented at the 48th Annual Meeting of the Society for American Archaeology, Pittsburgh.
Berger, Rainer, N. Evans, J. Abell, and M. Resnik
  1972   Radiocarbon Dating of Parchment. *Nature* 235:160–61.
Binford, Lewis R.
  1980   Willow Smoke and Dog's Tails: Hunter-Gatherer Settlement Systems and Archaeological Site Formation. *American Antiquity* 45:4–20.
Blakely, Robert L.
  1971   Comparison of the Mortality Profiles of the Archaic, Middle Woodland, and Middle Mississippian Skeletal Populations. *American Journal of Physical Anthropology* 34(1):43–54.
Boas, Franz
  1910   *Changes in Bodily Form in Descendants of Immigrants.* The Immigrant Commission, Senate Document No. 208. Government Printing Office, Washington, D.C.
Boisvert, Richard
  1979   Mortuary Practices, Modes of Exchange and Cultural Change: Archaeological Evidence from the Lower Ohio Valley. *Kentucky Archaeological Association Bulletin* 12:1–16.
Brackenridge, G. Robert
  1984   Alluvial Stratigraphy and Radiocarbon Dating along the Duck River, Ten-

nessee: Implications Regarding Floodplain Origin. *Geological Society of America, Bulletin* 95:9–25.

Braun, E. Lucy
1950   *Deciduous Forests of Eastern North America.* Blakiston Company, Philadelphia.

Breitburg, Emanuel
1993   The Anderson Site (40WM9): An Analysis of Faunal Remains Recovered from a Tennessee Central Basin Middle Archaic Site. Ms. in possession of David H. Dye, Memphis State University.

Bridges, Patricia S.
1989a   Changes in Activities with the Shift to Agriculture in the Southeastern United States. *Current Anthropology* 30(3):385–94.
1989b   Spondylolysis and Its Relationship to Degenerative Joint Disease in the Prehistoric Southeastern United States. *American Journal of Physical Anthropology* 79(3):321–29.

Bridwell, Margaret
1952   *The Story of Mammoth Cave National Park, Kentucky.* Eleventh edition 1971. Mammoth Cave National Park, Kentucky.

Brose, David S.
1979   A Speculative Model of the Role of Exchange in the Prehistory of the Eastern Woodlands. In *Hopewell Archaeology,* edited by David S. Brose and N'omi Greber, pp. 3–8. Kent State University Press, Kent.

Brothwell, Don
1970   The Real History of Syphilis. *Science Journal* 6(9):27–33.

Brothwell, Don, and R. Burleigh
1975   Radiocarbon Dates and the History of Treponematoses in Man. *Journal of Archaeological Science* 2:393–96.

Browman, David L.
1981   Isotopic Discrimination and Correction Factors in Radiocarbon Dating. In *Advances in Archaeological Method and Theory,* edited by Michael B. Schiffer, pp. 241–96. Academic Press, New York.

Brown, James A.
1986   Early Ceramics and Culture: A Review of Interpretations. In *Early Woodland Archeology,* edited by K. Farnsworth and T. Emerson, pp. 598–608. Kampsville Seminars in Archeology, No. 2. Center for American Archeology, Kampsville, Ill.
1985   Long-Term Trends to Sedentism and the Emergence of Complexity in the American Midwest. In *Prehistoric Hunter-Gatherers: The Emergence of Cultural Complexity,* edited by T. Douglas Price and James A. Brown, pp. 201–31. Academic Press, New York.
1983   Summary. In *Archaic Hunters and Gatherers in the American Midwest,* edited by James L. Phillips and James A. Brown, pp. 5–10. Academic Press, New York.

Brown, James A., and Robert K. Vierra
1983   What Happened in the Middle Archaic? Introduction to an Ecological Approach to Koster Site Archaeology. In *Archaic Hunters and Gatherers in the American Midwest,* edited by James L. Phillips and James A. Brown, pp. 165–95. Academic Press, New York.

Brown, Ralph D.
  1939   Field Report on the Excavation of Bt10, Butler County, KY. Ms. on file, University of Kentucky Museum of Anthropology, Lexington.
Brucker, Roger W., and Richard A. Watson
  1976   *The Longest Cave.* Knopf, New York.
Bullitt, Alexander Clark
  1985   *Rambles in the Mammoth Cave during the Year 1844 by a Visiter* [sic]. Cave Books, St. Louis.
Burleigh, Richard, Keith Mathews, and Morven Leese
  1984   Consensus 6δ^{13}C Values. *Radiocarbon* 26:46–53.
Bushnell, David I., Jr.
  1920   Native Cemeteries and Forms of Burial East of the Mississippi. *Bureau of American Ethnology, Bulletin 71.*
Butler, Brian M., and Richard W. Jefferies
  1986   Crab Orchard and Early Woodland Cultures in the Middle South. In *Early Woodland Archeology,* edited by Ken Farnsworth and Tom Emerson, pp. 523–34. Kampsville Seminars in Archeology No. 2. Center for American Archeology, Kampsville, Ill.
Caldwell, Joseph R.
  1958   *Trend and Tradition in the Prehistory of the Eastern United States.* Memoir No. 88. American Anthropological Association.
Cantwell, Anne-Marie, James B. Griffin, and Nan A. Rothschild (editors)
  1981   The Research Potential of Anthropological Museum Collections. *Annals of the New York Academy of Sciences 376.*
Carstens, Kenneth C.
  1980   Archeological Investigations in the Central Kentucky Karst. Ph.D. dissertation, Department of Anthropology, Washington University, St. Louis.
  1976   Recent Investigations in the Central Kentucky Karst: A Preliminary Temporal Ordering of Several Surface Sites in the Mammoth Cave Area, Kentucky. Paper presented at the 55th Annual Meeting of the Central States Anthropological Society, St. Louis.
  1975a   Faunal, Ceramic, and Chipped Stone Coding Formats for the Mammoth Cave National Park Archeological Project. Ms. on file, Department of Anthropology, Washington University, St. Louis.
  1975b   Surface Archeology in Mammoth Cave National Park, Kentucky. Paper presented at the 40th Annual Meeting of the Society for American Archaeology, Dallas.
  1974   Archeological Surface Reconnaissance of Mammoth Cave National Park, Kentucky. Master's thesis, Department of Anthropology, Washington University, St. Louis.
Cassidy, Claire M.
  1984   Skeletal Evidence for Prehistoric Subsistence Adaptation in the Central Ohio River Valley. In *Paleopathology at the Origins of Agriculture,* edited by Mark Cohen and George J. Armelagos, pp. 307–38. Academic Press, New York.
  1980   Nutrition and Health in Agriculturalists and Hunter-Gatherers: A Case Study of Two Prehistoric Populations. In *Nutritional Anthropology: Contemporary Approaches to Diet and Culture,* edited by Norge W. Jerome, Randy F.

Kandel, and Gretel H. Pelto, pp. 117–45. Redgrave Publishing Co., New York.

1972　Comparison of Nutrition and Health in Preagricultural and Agricultural Amerindian Skeletal Populations. Ph.D. dissertation, Department of Anthropology, University of Wisconsin, Madison.

Ceci, Lynn

1988　Tracing Wampum's Origins: Shell Bead Evidence from Archaeological Sites in Western and Coastal New York. In *Proceedings of the 1986 Shell Bead Conference: Selected Papers*, edited by Charles Hayes, pp. 63–80. Research Records No. 20. Rochester Museum and Science Center, Rochester, N.Y.

Chapman, Jefferson, and A. B. Shea

1981　The Archaeobotanical Record: Early Archaic to Contact in the Lower Little Tennessee River Valley. *Tennessee Anthropologist* 6:64–84.

Chapman, Jefferson, and Patty Jo Watson

1993　The Archaic Period and the Flotation Revolution. In *Foraging and Farming in the Eastern Woodlands*, edited by C. Margaret Scarry, pp. 27–38. University Press of Florida, Gainesville.

Charles, Douglas K., and Jane E. Buikstra

1983　Archaic Mortuary Sites in the Central Mississippi Drainage: Distribution, Structure, and Behavioral Implications. In *Archaic Hunters and Gatherers in the American Midwest*, edited by James L. Phillips and James A. Brown, pp. 117–45. Academic Press, New York.

Christenson, Andrew

1981　*The Evolution of Subsistence in the Prehistoric Midwestern United States.* Ph.D. dissertation, Department of Anthropology, University of California, Los Angeles. University Microfilms, Ann Arbor.

Claassen, Cheryl

In Prep. An Analytical Study of Shells from DeWeese and Carlston Annis. In *The Archaeology of the Middle Green River, Kentucky*, edited by William H. Marquardt, Patty Jo Watson, and Mary C. Kennedy.

1994　Washboards, Pigtoes, and Muckets: Historic Musseling in the Mississippi River Watershed. *Historic Archaeology* 28(2):iii–145.

1992　Shell Mounds as Burial Mounds. In *Current Archaeological Research in Kentucky*, vol. 2, edited by David Pollack and A. Gwyn Henderson, pp. 1–11. Kentucky Heritage Council, Frankfort.

1991a　New Hypotheses for the Demise of the Shell Mound Archaic. In *The Archaic Period in the Mid-South*, edited by Charles H. McNutt, pp. 66–71. Archaeological Report No. 24, Mississippi Department of Archives and History and Occasional Papers No. 16. Anthropological Research Center, Memphis State University, Memphis.

1991b　Women, Shellfishing and the Shell Mound Archaic. In *Engendering Archaeology: Women and Production in Prehistory*, edited by Joan Gero and Margaret Conkey, pp. 276–300. Basil Blackwell, Oxford.

1986　Shellfishing Seasons in the Prehistoric Southeastern United States. *American Antiquity* 51:21–37.

1982　Shell Fishing Patterns: An Analytical Study of Prehistoric Shell from North Carolina Coastal Middens. Ph.D. dissertation, Department of Anthropology, Harvard University, Cambridge.

Claassen, Cheryl, and Samuella Sigmann
1993   Sourcing *Busycon* Artifacts of the Eastern United States. *American Antiquity* 58(2):333–47.
Clark, R. M.
1975   A Calibration Curve for Radiocarbon Dates. *Antiquity* 49:251–66.
Cleland, Charles E.
1976   The Focal-Diffuse Model: An Evolutionary Perspective on the Prehistoric Cultural Adaptations of the Eastern United States. *Midcontinental Journal of Archaeology* 1(1):59–76.
Cooperative Holocene Mapping Project COHMAP
1988   Climatic Changes of the Last 18,000 Years: Observations and Model Simulations. *Science* 241:1043–52.
Collins, Michael B. (editor)
1979   *Excavations at Four Archaic Sites in the Lower Ohio Valley Jefferson County, Kentucky*, vol. II. Occasional Papers in Anthropology No. 1. University of Kentucky, Lexington.
Cook, Della C.
1971   Patterns of Nutritional Stress in Some Illinois Woodland populations. Master's thesis, Department of Anthropology, University of Chicago, Chicago.
Cotter, John L.
1938   Report for quarter ending September 30, 1938 to the Works Progress Administration. Ms. on file, University of Kentucky Museum of Anthropology, Lexington.
Cowan, C. Wesley
1985   From Foraging to Incipient Food Production: Subsistence Change and Continuity on the Cumberland Plateau of Eastern Kentucky. Ph.D. dissertation, Department of Anthropology, University of Michigan, Ann Arbor.
Cowan, C. Wesley, and Bruce D. Smith
1993   New Perspectives on a Wild Gourd in Eastern North America. *Journal of Ethnobiology* 13:17–54.
Crabtree, Don E.
1972   *An Introduction to Flintworking*. Occasional Paper No. 28. Idaho State University Museum.
Craig, Harmon
1954   Carbon 13 in Plants and the Relationships between Carbon 13 and Carbon 14 Variations in Nature. *Journal of Geology* 62:115–49.
1953   The Geochemistry of the Stable Carbon Isotopes. *Geochimica et Cosmochimica Acta* 3:53–92.
Crane, H. R.
1956   University of Michigan Radiocarbon Dates I. *Science* 124:664–72.
Crawford, Gary
In Prep. Plant remains from Carlston Annis (1972, 1974), Bowles and Peter Cave. In *The Archeology of the Middle Green River, Kentucky*, edited by William H. Marquardt, Patty Jo Watson, and Mary C. Kennedy.
1982   Late Archaic Plant Remains from West-Central Kentucky: A Summary. *Midcontinental Journal of Archaeology* 7:(2)205–24.
1978   Analysis and Implications of Plant Remains from the Carlston Annis Site

and Bowles Site, Kentucky. Shell Mound Archeological Project Report. Ms. on file, Archeology Laboratory, Washington University, St. Louis.

Crites, Gary D.

1993 Domesticated Sunflower in Fifth Millennium B.P. Temporal Context: New Evidence from Middle Tennessee. *American Antiquity* 58(1):146–48.

1991 Investigations into Early Plant Domesticates and Food Production in Middle Tennessee: A Status Report. *Tennessee Anthropologist* 16(1):69–87.

Crothers, George

1989 Archaeology and Human Bone Context in Little Beaver Cave. Paper presented at the National Speleological Society Annual Meeting, Sewanee, Tenn.

1987 An Archaeological Survey of Big Bone Cave, Tennessee, and Diachronic Patterns of Cave Utilization in the Eastern Woodlands. Master's thesis, Department of Anthropology, University of Tennessee, Knoxville.

1983 Archaeological Investigations in Sand Cave, Kentucky. *National Speleological Society Bulletin* 45:19–33.

Crothers, George, and Patty Jo Watson

1993 Archaeological Contexts in Deep Cave Sites: Examples from the Eastern Woodlands of North America. In *Formation Processes in Archaeological Context*, edited by Paul Goldberg, David Nash, and Michael Petraglia. Prehistory Press Monographs in World Prehistory, vol. 17, pp. 53–60. Madison, WI.

Currie, Lloyd A.

1982 *Nuclear and Chemical Dating Techniques: Interpreting the Environmental Record*. ACS Symposium Series No. 176. American Chemical Society, Washington, D.C.

Currie, Lloyd A., and Henry A. Polach

1980 Exploratory Analysis of the International Radiocarbon Cross-Calibration Data: Consensus Values and Interlaboratory Error: Preliminary Note. *Radiocarbon* 22:933–35.

Dahlberg, Albert A.

1963 Analysis of the American Indian Dentition. In *Dental Anthropology*, edited by D. R. Brothwell, pp. 149–77. Pergamon Press, N.Y.

Damon, Paul E.

1982 Fluctuation of Atmospheric Radiocarbon and the Radiocarbon Time Scale. In *Nuclear and Chemical Dating Techniques: Interpreting the Environmental Record*, edited by Lloyd A. Currie, pp. 233–44. ACS Symposium Series No. 176. American Chemical Society, Washington, D.C.

Damon, Paul E., and Timothy W. Linick

1986 Geomagnetic-Heliomagnetic Modulation of Atmospheric Radiocarbon Production. *Radiocarbon* 28:266–78.

Dean, Jeffrey S.

1986 Dendrochronology. In *Dating and Age Determination of Biological Materials*, edited by Michael R. Zimmerman and J. Lawrence Angel, pp. 126–65. Croon Helm, London.

Delcourt, Hazel R.

1979 Late Quaternary Vegetation History of the Eastern Highland Rim and Adjacent Cumberland Plateau of Tennessee. *Ecological Monographs* 49:255–80.

Delcourt, Hazel R., and Paul A. Delcourt
1985   Quaternary Palynology and Vegetational History of the Southeastern United States. In *Pollen Records of Late-Quaternary North American Sediments*, edited by Vaughn M. Bryant, Jr., and R. G. Holloway, pp. 1–37. American Association of Stratigraphic Palynologists Foundation, Calgary.

Delcourt, Paul A.
1985   The Influence of Late-Quaternary Climatic and Vegetational Change on Paleohydrology in Unglaciated Eastern North America. *Ecologia Mediterranea* 11:17–26.

Delcourt, Paul A., and Hazel R. Delcourt
1981   Vegetation Maps for Eastern North America: 40,000 YR B.P. to the Present. *Geobotany* II:123–65.

de Vries, Hessel
1957   The Removal of Radon from CO_2 for Use in ^{14}C Measurements. *Applied Science Research, Section B* 6:461–70.

DeNiro, Michael J., and Samuel Epstein
1978   Influence of Diet on the Distribution of Carbon Isotopes in Animals. *Geochimica et Cosmochimica Acta* 42:495–506.

DiBlasi, Philip J.
1989   Prehistoric Grafitti and Self-Expression: Examples from the Central Kentucky Karst. Paper presented at the 46th Annual Meeting of the Southeastern Archaeological Conference, Tampa.
1986a   Kentucky Site Survey form, 15Ad70. Ms. on file, Kentucky Office of State Archaeologist, Lexington.
1986b   National Register of Historic Places form, 15Ad70. Ms. on file, Kentucky Heritage Council, Frankfort.

Doershuk, John F.
1989   *Hunter-Gatherer Site Structure and Sedentism: The Koster Site Middle Archaic.* University Microfilms International, Ann Arbor.

Doran, Glen H., and Lee A. Newsom
1990   A 7,290-Year-Old Bottle Gourd from the Windover Site, Florida. *American Antiquity* 55:354–60.

Dowd, John T.
1989   *The Anderson Site: Middle Archaic Adaptation in Tennessee's Central Basin.* Miscellaneous Paper No. 13. Tennessee Anthropological Association, Knoxville.

Downton, W. J. S.
1975   The Occurrence of C_4 Photosynthesis among Plants. *Photosynthetica* 9:96–105.

Droessler, Judith
1981   *Craniometry and Biological Distance: Biocultural Continuity and Change at the Late Woodland–Mississippian Interface.* Research Series, vol. 1. Center for American Archaeology at Northwestern University, Evanston, Ill.

Duffield, Lathel
1974   Nonhuman Vertebrate Remains from Salts Cave Vestibule. In *Archeology of the Mammoth Cave Area*, edited by Patty Jo Watson, pp. 123–33. Academic Press, New York.

Dunn, Frederick L.
1968   Epidemiological Factors: Health and Disease in Hunter-Gatherers. In *Man*

the Hunter, edited by Richard B. Lee and Irven Devore, pp. 221–28. Aldine, Chicago.

Edwards v. Sims
1929   *Edwards v. Sims,* December 3, 1929; 24 S. W.(2d) 619 and 232 Kentucky 791.

Ellsworth, Ivan J.
1934   The Forest Cover Type Map. Ms. on file, National Park Service, Southeast Archeological Center, Tallahassee, Fla.

Emerson, Thomas E.
1986   A Retrospective Look at the Earliest Woodland Cultures in the American Heartland. In *Early Woodland Archeology,* edited by Ken Farnsworth and Tom Emerson, pp. 621–33. Kampsville Seminars in Archeology No. 2. Center for American Archeology, Kampsville, Ill.

Ensor, H. Blaine, and Joseph M. Studer
1983   Excavations at the Walnut Site: 22IT539. In *Archaeological Investigations in the Upper Tombigbee Valley, Mississippi: Phase 1,* edited by Judith A. Bense. Report of Investigations 3. The University of West Florida, Office of Cultural and Archaeological Research, Pensacola.

Faller, Adolph
1975   The Plant Ecology of Mammoth Cave National Park, Kentucky. Ph.D. dissertation, Indiana State University, Terre Haute.

Faulkner, Charles H.
1988   A Study of Seven Southeastern Glyph Caves. *North American Archaeologist* 9:223–46.

Faulkner, Charles H. (editor)
1986   *The Prehistoric Native American Art of Mud Glyph Cave.* University of Tennessee Press, Knoxville.

Faulkner, Charles H., Bill Deane, and H. H. Earnest, Jr.
1984   A Mississippian Period Ritual Cave in Tennessee. *American Antiquity* 49(2):350–61.

Fenton, James P.
1993   Age and Sex Related Variation in Bilateral Skeletal Asymmetry at Indian Knoll (15-Oh-2), Kentucky. Paper presented at the Tenth Annual Kentucky Heritage Council Conference, Lexington.
1991   The Social Uses of Dead People: Problems and Solution in the Analysis of Post Mortem Body Processing in the Archaeological Record. Ph.D. dissertation, Department of Anthropology, Columbia University, New York.

Ferguson, Lee
1983   An Archaeological Investigation of a Cave in North Central Tennessee. Paper presented at the National Speleological Society Convention, Elkins, W. V.

Finkenstaedt, Elizabeth
1984   Age at First Pregnancy among Females at the Indian Knoll Oh-2 Site. *Transactions of the Kentucky Academy of Science* 45:51–54.

Ford, Richard I.
1988   The Intellectual Basis of Paleoethnobotany in the Southeast. Paper presented at Southeastern Archaeological Conference, New Orleans.
1977   Evolutionary Ecology and the Evolution of Human Ecosystems: A Case Study from the Midwestern U.S.A. In *Explanation of Prehistoric Change,* edited by James N. Hill, pp. 153–84. University of New Mexico Press, Albuquerque.

Fritz, Gayle J.
    1990   Multiple Pathways to Farming in Precontact Eastern North America. *Journal of World Prehistory* 4(4):387–435.

Funkhouser, William D., and William S. Webb
    1928   *Ancient Life in Kentucky.* The Kentucky Geological Survey, Series 6, vol. 34, Lexington.
    1932   *Archaeological Survey of Kentucky.* Reports in Anthropology and Archaeology 2. University of Kentucky, Lexington.

Futato, Eugene M.
    1989   *An Archaeological Overview of the Tombigbee River Basin, Alabama and Mississippi. Report of Investigations No. 59.* University of Alabama, State Museum of Natural History, Division of Archaeology, Tuscaloosa.

Gardner, Paul S.
    1987   New Evidence Concerning the Chronology and Paleoethnobotany of Salts Cave, Kentucky. *American Antiquity* 52:358–67.

Gatus, Thomas
    1984a   A Preliminary Reconnaissance of Some West Central Kentucky Chert Resources. In *Archaeology of the Middle Green River, Kentucky,* edited by William H. Marquardt, Patty Jo Watson, and Mary C. Kennedy. In prep.
    1984b   A Synopsis of Three Western Kentucky Chert Reconnaissance Studies. Paper presented at the 42nd Annual Meeting of the Southeastern Archaeological Conference, Pensacola.
    1983a   The Availability of Chert Resources in the Fort Campbell Vicinity. In *Archaeological Investigations in Fort Campbell, Kentucky-Tennessee,* edited by Nancy O'Malley, Jerod Funk, C. Jobe, Tom Gatus, and J. Reisenweber, pp. 339–58. Archaeological Report 67. Department of Anthropology, University of Kentucky, Lexington.
    1983b   Chert Availability in the Lower Cumberland and Lower Tennessee River Valleys in Western Kentucky. *Tennessee Anthropologist* 8(2):99–113.
    1980   Chert Resources in the Lower Cumberland and Lower Tennessee River Valleys in Western Kentucky. Paper presented at the Thirty-Seventh Southeastern Archaeological Conference, New Orleans.
    1979   *The Occurrence and Distribution of Chert Bearing Deposits in the Land between the Lakes Area of Western Kentucky.* Bulletin 12. Kentucky Archaeological Association, Scottsville.

George, Angelo I.
    1986   *Guide Book for the Kentucky Speleologist,* vol. 15. Louisville Speleopress, Louisville, Ky.

George, Angelo I. (editor)
    1990   *Prehistoric Mummies from the Mammoth Cave Area: Foundations and Concepts.* George Publishing Company, Louisville, Ky.

Gibbon, Guy
    1986   Does Minnesota Have an Early Woodland? In *Early Woodland Archeology,* edited by Ken Farnsworth and Tom Emerson, pp. 84–91. Kampsville Seminars in Archeology No. 2. Center for American Archeology, Kampsville, Ill.

Goad, Sharon
    1980   Patterns of Late Archaic Exchange. *Tennessee Anthropologist* 5:1–16.

Gremillion, Kristen J.
    1994   Evidence of Plant Domestication from Kentucky Caves and Rockshelters.

In *Agricultural Origins and Development in the Midcontinent*, edited by William Green, pp. 87–103. Office of the State Archaeologist, Report No. 19, University of Iowa, Iowa City.

1993   Plant Husbandry at the Archaic/Woodland Transition: Evidence from the Cold Oak Shelter, Kentucky. *Mid-Continental Journal of Archaeology* 18(2):161–89.

1990   Plant Remains from Ten Sites within Mammoth Cave National Park. In *Mammoth Cave Archeological Inventory Project Interim Report–1989 Investigations*, edited by Guy Prentice, pp. 76–96. National Park Service, Southeast Archeological Center, Tallahassee, Fla.

Gremillion, Kristen J., and Cecil Ison
1989   Terminal Archaic and Early Woodland Plant Utilization along the Cumberland Plateau. Paper presented at the 54th Annual Meeting of the Society for American Archaeology, Atlanta.

Griffin, James B.
1985   A Commentary on Some Archaeological Activities in the Mid-Continent, 1925–1975. *Mid-Continental Journal of Archaeology* 1(1):5–38.

1952a   *Archeology of the Eastern United States.* University of Chicago Press, Evanston.

1952b   Culture Periods in Eastern United States Archeology. In *Archeology of the Eastern United States*, edited by J. B. Griffin, pp. 352–64. University of Chicago Press, Evanston.

Guthe, Carl E.
1952   Twenty-Five Years in Archeology in the Eastern U.S. In *Archeology of the Eastern United States*, edited by J. B. Griffin, pp. 1–12. University of Chicago Press, Chicago.

Haag, William G.
1985   Federal Aid to Archeology in the Southeast, 1933–1942. *American Antiquity* 50:272–80.

1974   Pottery from Indian Knoll. In *Indian Knoll*, edited by William S. Webb, pp. 356–62. University of Tennessee Press, Knoxville.

1961   Twenty-Five Years of Eastern Archaeology. *American Antiquity* 27:16–23.

Hagee, Virginia L.
1983   Geoarchaeology of the Early- to Middle-Holocene Anderson Site, Williamson County, Tennessee. Master's thesis, Department of Geology, Vanderbilt University, Nashville.

Hall, Robert L.
1976   Pearls, Wampum, Sweat, and Tears. Ms. in possession of Cheryl Claassen, Boone, N. C.

Hamilton, Margaret E.
1975   *Variation among Five Groups of AmerIndians in the Magnitude of Sexual Dimorphism of Skeletal Size.* Ph.D. dissertation, University of Michigan. University Microfilms, Ann Arbor.

Hardy, Vernon Clayton
1974   The Effect of Size Variation on Statistical Assessments of Biological Distance between Human Skeletal Series. Master's thesis, Department of Anthropology, University of Kentucky, Lexington.

Haskins, Valerie A.
In Prep. Recent Dates from the Green River Shell Mound Region. In *Current Ar-*

chaeological Research in Kentucky, vol. 3, edited by Valerie A. Haskins and David Pollack. The Kentucky Heritage Council, Frankfort.

1995   Health and Disease of Prehistoric Inhabitants along the Green River, Kentucky. Ph.D. dissertation, Department of Anthropology, Washington University, St. Louis.

1988   The Prehistory of Prewitts Knob, Kentucky. Master's thesis, Department of Anthropology, Washington University, St. Louis.

Haskins, Valerie A., and Nicholas P. Herrmann

1989   Shell Mound Bioarchaeology: An Overview of Past Research from the Green River Region, and Preliminary Observations on New Data from the Reed Site, 15Bt10. Paper presented at the 46th Annual Meeting of the Southeastern Archaeological Conference, Tampa.

Hemberger, Jan Marie

1985   Preliminary Findings at the Pit of the Skulls (15Bn51). In *Woodland Period Research in Kentucky*, edited by David Pollack, Thomas Sanders, and Charles Hockensmith, pp. 188–202. The Kentucky Heritage Council, Frankfort.

1982   A Preliminary Report on the Pit of the Skulls (15Bn51). Ms. on file, Department of Anthropology, Washington University, St. Louis.

Hensley, Christine K.

1994   The Archaic Settlement System of the Middle Green River Valley, Kentucky. Ph.D. dissertation, Department of Anthropology, Washington University, St. Louis.

1992   Green River Archeological Study. In *Studies in Kentucky Archaeology*, edited by Charles D. Hockensmith, pp. 11–26. Kentucky Heritage Council, Frankfort.

1991   The Middle Green River Shell Mounds: Challenging Traditional Interpretations Using Internal Site Structure Analysis. In *The Human Landscape in Kentucky's Past: Site Structure and Settlement Patterns*, edited by Charles Stout and Christine K. Hensley, pp. 78–97. Kentucky Heritage Council, Frankfort.

1989   Green River Archaeological Study: A Preliminary Report. Paper presented at the 46th Annual Meeting of the Southeastern Archaeological Conference, Tampa.

1987   Late Archaic to Early Woodland Transitions in the Green River Shell Mound Region. A grant proposal. Ms. on file, The Kentucky Heritage Council, Frankfort.

Hensley-Martin, Christine K.

1986   A Reanalysis of the Lithic Industry from the Read Site, Butler County, Kentucky (15Bt10). Master's thesis, Department of Anthropology, Washington University, St. Louis.

Henson, B. Bart

1986   Art in Mud and Stone: Mud Glyphs and Petroglyphs in the Southeast. In *The Prehistoric Native American Art of Mud Glyph Cave*, edited by Charles B. Faulkner. University of Tennessee Press, Knoxville.

Herrmann, Nicholas P.

1993   Archaic Shell Mound Paleodemography: A Case Study from the Read Site, 15Bt10. Paper presented at the Tenth Annual Kentucky Heritage Council Conference, Lexington.

1990   The Paleopathology of the Read Shell Midden, 15Bt10. Master's thesis, Department of Anthropology, Washington University, St. Louis.

Higel, Thomas E.
1965   An Analysis of Ninety-one Indian Knoll Skeletons. Ms. on file, Office of State Archaeology, University of Kentucky, Lexington.

Hill, Carol A.
1976   *Cave Minerals.* National Speleological Society, Huntsville.

Hockensmith, Charles D., Thomas N. Sanders, and David Pollack
1985   The Green River Shell Middens of Kentucky. National Register of Historic Places Thematic Nomination Form. Ms. on file, Kentucky Heritage Council, Frankfort.

Hofman, Jack L.
1986   Hunter-Gatherer Mortuary Variability: Toward an Explanatory Model. Ph.D. dissertation, Department of Anthropology, University of Tennessee, Knoxville.
1985   Middle Archaic Ritual and Shell Midden Archaeology: Considering the Significance of Cremations. In *Exploring Tennessee Prehistory,* edited by T. Whyte, C. Boyd, and B. Riggs, pp. 1–22. Report of Investigations No. 42. Department of Anthropology, University of Tennessee, Knoxville.
1984   Radiocarbon dates from Ervin: A Mid-Holocene Shell Midden on the Duck River in Middle Tennessee. *Tennessee Anthropological Association Newsletter* 9:2–8.

Hooton, Earnest A.
1930   *The Indians of Pecos Pueblo, A Study of Their Skeletal Remains.* Papers of the Southwestern Expedition No. 4. Yale University Press, New Haven.

Howells, William W.
1960   Estimating Population Numbers through Archaeological and Skeletal Remains. In *The Application of Quantitative Methods in Archaeology,* edited by Robert F. Heizer and Sally Cook, pp. 158–76. Viking Fund Publications in Anthropology No. 28.

Hrdlička, Aleš
1927   Catalogue of Human Crania in the United States National Museum Collections. *Proceedings* (National Museum, Smithsonian Institution): 69(5).

Hunt, Geoffrey, and Robert R. Stitt
1981   *Cave Gating.* National Speleological Society, Huntsville, Alabama.

International Study Group
1982   An Inter-laboratory Comparison of Radiocarbon Measurements in Tree Rings. *Nature* 298:619–23.

Jefferies, Richard W.
1990   The Archaic Period in Kentucky: Past Accomplishments and Future Directions. In *Kentucky Archaeology State Plan,* edited by D. Pollack, pp. 143–246. Kentucky Heritage Council, Frankfort.
1988   The Archaic in Kentucky: New Deal Archaeological Investigations. In *New Deal Era Archaeology and Current Research in Kentucky,* edited by David Pollack and Mary Lucas Powell, pp. 14–25. Kentucky Heritage Council, Frankfort.
1982   Cultural Material. In *The Carrier Mills Archaeological Project: Human Adaptation in the Saline Valley, Illinois,* edited by Richard W. Jefferies and Brian

M. Butler, pp. 322–92. Research Papers No. 33. Center for Archaeological Investigations, Southern Illinois University, Carbondale.

Jefferies, Richard W., and B. Mark Lynch
1983   Dimensions of Middle Archaic Cultural Adaptation at the Black Earth Site, Saline County, Illinois. In *Archaic Hunters and Gatherers in the American Midwest*, edited by James L. Phillips and James A. Brown, pp. 299–322. Academic Press, New York.

Jenkins, Ned J., David H. Dye, and John A. Walthall
1986   Early Ceramic Development in the Gulf Coastal Plain. In *Early Woodland Archeology*, edited by Ken Farnsworth and Tom Emerson, pp. 546–63. Kampsville Seminars in Archeology No. 2. Center for American Archeology, Kampsville, Ill.

Jennings, Jesse D.
1977   Perspective. In *The Native Americans*, edited by Robert F. Spencer, et al., pp. 1–36. Harper & Row, New York.

Joerschke, Bonnie C.
1983   The Demography, Long Bone Growth, and Pathology of a Middle Archaic Skeletal Population from Middle Tennessee: The Anderson Site (40Mw9). Master's thesis, Department of Anthropology, University of Tennessee, Knoxville.

Johnson, Allen W., and Timothy Earle
1987   *The Evolution of Human Societies: From Foraging Group to Agrarian State.* Stanford University Press, Stanford.

Johnson, Jay
1981   *Yellow Creek Archaeological Project*, vol. 2. Archaeological Papers of the Center for Archaeological Research No. 2. Tennessee Valley Authority Publications in Anthropology No. 28, Knoxville.

Johnson, Jay, and Samuel O. Brookes
1989   Benton Points, Turkey Tails, and Cache Blades: Middle Archaic Exchange in the Midsouth. *Southeastern Archaeology* 8(2):134–45.

Johnston, Francis E.
1969   Approaches to the Study of Developmental Variability in Human Skeletal Populations. *American Journal of Physical Anthropology* 31:335–41.
1968   Growth of the Skeleton of Earlier Peoples. In *Skeletal Biology of Earlier Human Population*, edited by D. R. Brothwell, pp. 57–66. Pergamon Press, Oxford.
1962   Growth of the Long Bones of Infants and Young Children at Indian Knoll. *American Journal of Physical Anthropology* 20:249–54.
1961   Sequence of Epiphyseal Union in a Prehistoric Kentucky Population from Indian Knoll. *Human Biology* 33:66–81.

Johnston, Francis E., and Charles E. Snow
1961   The Reassessment of the Age and Sex of the Indian Knoll Skeletal Population: Demographic and Methodological Aspects. *American Journal of Physical Anthropology* 19(3):237–44.

Jones, J.
1876   *Exploration of the Aboriginal Remains of Tennessee.* Smithsonian Contributions to Knowledge No. 259, Washington.

Justice, Noel D.
1987   *Stone Age Spear and Arrow Points of the Midcontinental and Eastern United*

States: A Modern Survey and Reference. Indiana University Press, Bloomington.

Keegan, William (editor)
1987   *Emergent Horticultural Economies of the Eastern Woodlands.* Occasional Paper No. 7. Center for Archaeological Investigations, Southern Illinois University, Carbondale, Ill.

Kelley, Marc Allen
1982   Intervertebral Osteochondrosis in Ancient and Modern Populations. *American Journal of Physical Anthropology* 59:271–79.
1980   Disease and Environment: A Comparative Analysis of Three Early American Indian Skeletal Collections. Ph.D. dissertation, Department of Anthropology, Case Western Reserve University, Cleveland.

Kennedy, Mary C.
1990   Radiocarbon Dates from Salts and Mammoth Caves, Mammoth Cave National Park, Kentucky: An Analysis of the C-14 Process and the MCNP Dates. Master's thesis, Department of Anthropology, Washington University, St. Louis.

Kennedy, Mary C., Christine Hensley-Martin, and Patty Jo Watson
1983   Cave Research Foundation Archaeological Project—1983. In *Cave Research Foundation 1983 Annual Report,* pp. 22–23. Cave Research Foundation, Washington, D.C.

King, James E., and W. H. Allen
1977   A Holocene Vegetation Record from the Mississippi River Valley, Southeastern Missouri. *Quaternary Research* 8:307–23.

King, Mary Elizabeth
1974   The Salts Cave Textiles: A Preliminary Account. In *Archeology of the Mammoth Cave Area,* edited by Patty Jo Watson, pp. 31–40. Academic Press, New York.

Klein, Jeffrey, J. C. Lerman, Paul E. Damon, and Elizabeth K. Ralph
1982   Calibration of Radiocarbon Dates: Tables Based on the Consensus Data of the Workshop on Calibrating the Radiocarbon Time Scale. *Radiocarbon* 24:103–50.

Klippel, Walter E., and Darcy F. Morey
1986   Contextural and Nutritional Analysis of Freshwater Gastropods from Middle Archaic Deposits at the Hayes Site, Middle Tennessee. *American Antiquity* 51:700–813.

Klippel, Walter E., and Paul W. Parmalee
1982   Diachronic Variation in Insectivores from Cheek Bend Cave and Environmental Change in the Midsouth. *Paleobiology* 8(4):447–58.

Knutson, I. P.
1982   Multifactorial Contingency Table Analysis of Dental Disease in Osteological Populations. Ph.D. dissertation, Department of Anthropology, State University of New York, Buffalo.

Kromer, B., M. Rhein, M. Burns, H. Schoch-Fischer, K. O. Munnich, M. Stuiver, and B. Becker
1986   Radiocarbon Calibration Data for the 6th and 8th Millennia BC. *Radiocarbon* 28:954–60.

Kutzbach, John E.
1987   Model Simulations of the Climatic Patterns during the Deglaciation of

North America. In *North American and Adjacent Oceans during the Last Deglaciation*, edited by W. F. Ruddiman and Herbert E. Wright, Jr., pp. 425–46. *The Geology of North America*, Vol. K-3. Geological Society of America, Boulder.

Kwas, Mary L.

1981   Bannerstones as Chronological Markers in the Southeastern United States. *Tennessee Anthropologist* 6(2):144–71.

Latham, Earle E.

1969   *Soil Survey of Barren County, Kentucky.* United States Department of Agriculture, Soil Conservation Service, U.S. Government Printing Office, Washington, D.C.

Lee, Edmund F.

1835   *Map of Mammoth Cave, with Notes.* James and Gazley, Cincinnati.

Leigh, R. W.

1925   Dental Pathology of Indian Tribes of Varied Environmental and Food Conditions. *American Journal of Physical Anthropology* 8:179–99.

Leute, Ulrich

1987   *Archaeometry: An Introduction to Physical Methods in Archaeology and the History of Art.* VCH Verlagsgesellschaft, Weinheim, Germany.

Lewis, R. Barry

1990   The Mississippi Period in Kentucky. In *The Archaeology of Kentucky: Past Accomplishments and Future Directions*, edited by David Pollack, pp. 375–466. State Historic Preservation Comprehensive Plan Report No. 1. Kentucky Heritage Council, Frankfort.

1986   Early Woodland Adaptations to the Illinois Prairie. In *Early Woodland Archeology*, edited by K. Farnsworth and T. Emerson, pp. 171–78. Kampsville Seminars in Archeology No. 2. Center for American Archeology, Kampsville, Ill.

1983   Archaic Adaptations in the Illinois Prairie: The Salt Creek Region. In *Arhaic Hunters and Gatherers in the American Midwest*, edited by James L. Phillips and James A. Brown, pp. 99–116. Academic Press, New York.

Lewis, Thomas M. N., and Madeline K. Lewis

1961   *Eva: An Archaic Site.* University of Tennessee, Knoxville.

Libby, Willard F.

1970   Ruminations on Radiocarbon Dating. In *Radiocarbon Variations and Absolute Chronology*, edited by I. U. Olsson, pp. 629–40. Almqvist and Wiksell, Stockholm.

1952   *Radiocarbon Dating.* The University of Chicago Press, Chicago.

Lindstrom, Bruce, and Kenneth W. Steverson

1987   Lithic Artifacts from the Anderson Site, 40WM9. *Tennessee Anthropologist* 12(1):1–50.

Linick, Timothy W., Austin Long, Paul E. Damon, and C. W. Ferguson

1986   High-Precision Radiocarbon Dating of Bristlecone Pine from 6554 to 5350 B.C. *Radiocarbon* 28:943–53.

Linick, Timothy W., Hans E. Suess, and Bernd Becker

1985   La Jolla Measurements of Radiocarbon in South German Oak Tree-Ring Chronologies. *Radiocarbon* 27:20–32.

Long, Joseph K.

1966   A Test of Multiple-Discriminant Analysis as a Means of Determining Evolutionary Changes and Intergroup Relationships in Physical Anthropology. *American Anthropologist* 68:444–64.

1964   Multiple-Discriminant Analysis of Indian Crania of the Eastern United States. Master's thesis, Department of Anthropology, University of Kentucky, Lexington.

Lyon, Edwin A.

1982   New Deal Archaeology in the Southeast: WPA, TVA, NPS, 1934–1942. Ph.D. dissertation, Department of Anthropology, Louisiana State University, Baton Rouge.

Lyon, T. D. B., and M. S. Baxter

1978   Stable Carbon Isotopes in Human Tissues. *Nature* 273:750–51.

MacMillan, R. Bruce, and Walter E. Klippel

1981   Hunter-gatherer Adaptation to the Southern Prairie Peninsula. *Journal of Archaeological Science* 8:215–45.

Magennis, Ann L.

1977   Middle and Late Archaic Mortuary Patterning: An Example from the Western Tennessee Valley. Master's thesis, Department of Anthropology, University of Tennessee.

Manzano, Bruce

1990   Lithic Analysis. In *Mammoth Cave Archeological Inventory Project Interim Report—1989 Investigations*, edited by Guy Prentice, pp. 53–75. National Park Service, Southeastern Archeological Center, Tallahassee.

1989   Comparison of Lithic Assemblages from Two Upland Sites in Mammoth Cave National Park, Kentucky. Paper presented at the Southeastern Archaeological Conference, Tampa.

Marquardt, William H.

1974   A Statistical Analysis of Constituents in Human Paleofecal Specimens from Mammoth Cave. In *Archeology of the Mammoth Cave Area*, edited by Patty Jo Watson, pp. 193–202. Academic Press, New York.

1972a   Recent Investigations in a Western Kentucky Shell Mound. Paper presented at the Annual Meeting of the Society for American Archaeology, Miami.

1972b   Research Report on Excavations at the Carlston Annis Shellmound. Southeastern Archeological Conference *Newsletter* 16(2):45.

Marquardt, William H., and Patty Jo Watson

In Prep. Conclusion: In *Archaeology of the Middle Green River, Kentucky*. Edited by William H. Marquardt, Patty Jo Watson, and Mary C. Kennedy.

1983a   Excavation and Recovery of Biological Remains from Two Archaic Shell Middens in Western Kentucky. *Southeastern Archaeological Conference Bulletin* 20:112–29.

1983b   The Shell Mound Archaic of Western Kentucky. In *Archaic Hunters and Gatherers in the American Midwest*, edited by James L. Phillips and James A. Brown, pp. 323–39. Academic Press, New York.

1976   Excavation and Recovery of Biological Remains from Two Archaic Shell Middens in Western Kentucky. Paper presented at the Southeastern Archaeological Conference, Tuscaloosa.

1974   The Green River, Kentucky, Shellmound Archeological Project. Paper presented at the 73rd Annual Meeting of the American Anthropological Association, Mexico City.

Marquardt, William H., Patty Jo Watson, and Mary C. Kennedy
  In Prep. *Archaeology of the Middle Green River, Kentucky.*
May, J. Alan
  1982   Midden Formation Modeling Using Ethnographic and Archaeological
          Data: A Trend Surface Analysis of Midden Deposits at the Carlston Annis
          Site (15Bt5), Kentucky. Ph.D. dissertation, Department of Anthropology,
          University of Missouri, Columbia.
Meloy, Harold
  1971   *Mummies of Mammoth Cave.* Micron Publishing Company, Shelbyville, Ind.
Meloy, Harold, and Patty Jo Watson
  1969   Human Remains: "Little Alice" of Salts Cave and Other Mummies. In *The
          Prehistory of Salts Cave, Kentucky,* edited by Patty Jo Watson, pp. 65–69. Re-
          ports of Investigations No. 16. Illinois State Museum, Springfield.
Mensforth, Robert P.
  In Press The Pathogenesis and Paleoepidemiology of Periosteal Reactions in Lib-
          ben and Bt-5 Subadults. Ms. on file, Museum of Anthropology, University
          of Kentucky, Lexington.
  1990   Paleodemography of the Carlston Annis (Bt-5) Late Archaic Skeletal
          Population. *American Journal of Physical Anthropology* 80:81–99.
  1986   Paleodemography of the Carlston Annis (Bt-5) Skeletal Population. Ph.D.
          dissertation, Department of Sociology and Anthropology, Kent State Uni-
          versity, Kent, Ohio.
  1984   Paleodemography of the Carlston Annis Bt-5 Skeletal Population. Ms. on
          file, University of Kentucky, Museum of Anthropology, Lexington.
Michels, Joseph W.
  1973   *Dating Methods in Archaeology.* Seminar Press, New York.
Milner, George R., and Richard W. Jefferies
  1986   Mound Construction, Mortuary Practices and Paleodemography: A Reex-
          amination of an Adena Mound in Kentucky. Paper presented at the 43rd
          annual meeting of the Southeastern Archaeological Conference, Nash-
          ville.
Milner, George R., and Virginia G. Smith
  1988   Kentucky's New Deal Archaeological Excavations, Collections, and Re-
          search. In *New Deal Era Archaeology and Current Research in Kentucky,* edited
          by David Pollack and Mary Lucas Powell, pp. 1–13. Kentucky Heritage
          Council, Frankfort.
  1986a   Depression Era Federal Relief Programs and Kentucky Archaeology. Pa-
          per presented at a History Symposium, The Depression Decade in Ken-
          tucky, Part II, Eastern Kentucky University, Richmond.
  1986b   *New Deal Archaeology in Kentucky: Excavations, Collections, and Research.* Oc-
          casional Papers in Anthropology No. 5. Program for Cultural Resource
          Assessment, University of Kentucky, Lexington.
Molnar, Stephen, and Steven C. Ward
  1974   Dental Remains from the Salts Cave Vestibule. In *Archeology of the Mam-
          moth Cave Area,* edited by Patty Jo Watson, pp. 163–66. Academic Press,
          New York.
Moore, Clarence B.
  1916   *Some Aboriginal Sites on Green River, Kentucky: Certain Aboriginal Sites on
          Lower Ohio River.* Academy of Natural Sciences of Philadelphia, 2nd Series,
          vol. 16, No. 3, Philadelphia.

Moore, Michael C., C. Parris Stripling, John T. Dowd, and Richard Taylor, Jr.
　1990　The Anderson Site Revisited: Results of Recent Investigations at 40WM9, Williamson County, Tennessee. *Tennessee Anthropologist* 15(2):82–95.

Morrow, Carol
　1982　Analysis of Area A Middle Archaic Flaked Stone Technology. In *The Carrier Mills Archaeological Project*, edited by Richard W. Jefferies and Brian M. Butler, pp. 1289–1347. Research Paper No. 33. Center for Archaeological Investigations, Southern Illinois University, Carbondale.

Muller, Jon
　1986　Serpents and Dancers: Art of Mud Glyph Cave. In *The Prehistoric Native American Art of Mud Glyph Cave*, edited by Charles H. Faulkner. University of Tennessee Press, Knoxville.

Munson, Cheryl Ann, and Patrick J. Munson
　1981　*Archaeological Investigations, 1980, Wyandotte Cave, Indiana.* Report prepared for the Division of Forestry, Indiana Department of Natural Resources, Indianapolis.

Munson, Patrick J.
　1988　Late Woodland Settlement and Subsistence in Temporal Perspective. In *Interpretations of Cultural Change in the Eastern Woodlands during The Late Woodland Period*, edited by Richard W. Yerkes, pp. 7–16. Occasional Papers in Anthropology No. 3. Department of Anthropology, Ohio State University, Columbus.

　1986　Hickory Silviculture: A Subsistence Revolution in the Prehistory of Eastern North America. Paper presented at Emergent Horticultural Economies of the Eastern Woodlands Conference, Southern Illinois University, Carbondale.

Munson, Patrick J., and Cheryl A. Munson
　1990　*The Prehistoric and Early Historic Archaeology of Wyandotte Cave and Other Caves in Southern Indiana.* Indiana Historical Society, Indianapolis.

Munson, Patrick J., Kenneth B. Tankersley, Cheryl A. Munson, and Patty Jo Watson
　1989　Prehistoric Selenite and Satin Spar Mining in the Mammoth Cave System, Kentucky. *Midcontinental Journal of Archaeology* 14(2):119–45.

Nantz, Robert
　1972　Rogers Cave. In *Kentucky Underground* 1(4). Central Kentucky Grotto, National Speleological Society.

National Park Serivce
　1991　Engineering Report, Wastewater System, September 1991, Mammoth Cave National Park, Kentucky. Report on file, Mammoth Cave National Park, National Park Service, Kentucky.

Nelson, Nels C.
　1923　Kentucky: Mammoth Cave and Vicinity. Ms. on file, American Museum of Natural History, New York.

　1917　Contributions to the Archaeology of Mammoth Cave and Vicinity, Kentucky. *Anthropological Papers*, vol. 22, Part I. American Museum of Natural History, New York.

Neumann, Georg K.
　1952　Archaeology and Race in the American Indian. In *Archaeology of Eastern United States*, edited by J. B. Griffin, pp. 13–34. University of Chicago Press, Chicago.

1938   The Human Remains from Mammoth Cave, Kentucky. *American Antiquity*
         3:339–53.
Neusius, Sarah W.
1986   Generalized and Specialized Resource Utilization during the Archaic Pe-
         riod: Implications of the Koster Site Faunal Record. In *Foraging, Collecting,
         and Harvesting: Archaic Period Subsistence and Settlement in the Eastern Wood-
         lands*, edited by Sarah W. Neusius, pp. 117–44. Occasional Paper No. 6.
         Southern Illinois University, Center for Archaeological Investigations,
         Carbondale.
Neusius, Sarah W. (editor)
1986   *Foraging, Collecting, and Harvesting: Archaic Period Subsistence and Settlement
         in the Eastern Woodlands*. Occasional Paper No. 6. Southern Illinois Univer-
         sity, Center for Archaeological Investigations, Carbondale.
Neustupný, E.
1970   The Accuracy of Radiocarbon Dating. In *Radiocarbon Variations and Abso-
         lute Chronology*, edited by I. U. Olsson, pp. 23–34. Almqvist and Wiksell,
         Stockholm.
Newsom, Lee A.
1992   Early *Cucurbita pepo* from a Florida Wetsite. Paper presented at the Society
         for Ethnobiology Annual Meeting, Washington, D.C.
1988   Paleoethnobotanical Remains from a Waterlogged Archaic Period Site in
         Florida. Paper presented at the 53rd Annual Meeting of the Society for
         American Archaeology, Phoenix.
Newsom, Lee A., S. David Webb, and James S. Dunbar
1993   History and Geographic Distribution of *Cucurbita pepo* Gourds in Florida.
         Journal of Ethnobiology 13:75–97.
Niquette, Charles M.
1991   *Excavations at Andalex Village (15HK22), Hopkins County, Kentucky*. Contract
         Publication Series 91–03. Cultural Resource Analysts, Inc., Lexington,
         Kentucky.
1984   Lands Unsuitable for Mining: A Kentucky Example. *American Antiquity*
         49:834–41.
Nydal, Reidar
1983   The Radon Problem in ^{14}C Dating. *Radiocarbon* 25:501–10.
Olsson, Ingrid U.
1979   The Importance of the Pretreatment of Wood and Charcoal Samples. In
         Radiocarbon Dating, edited by R. Berger and H. Suess, pp. 135–46. Univer-
         sity of California Press, Berkeley.
1974   Some Problems in Connection with the Evaluation of ^{14}C Dates. *Geologiska
         Föreningens i Stockholm Förhandlingar* 96:311–20.
Ottesen, Ann
1979   *A Preliminary Study of Acquisition of Exotic Raw Materials by Late Woodland
         and Mississippian Groups*. Ph.D. dissertation, University Microfilms, Ann
         Arbor.
Palmer, Arthur N.
1981   *A Geological Guide to Mammoth Cave National Park*. Zephyrus Press,
         Teaneck, N.J.
Parmalee, Paul W., and Walter Klippel
1974   Freshwater Mussels as a Prehistoric Food Resource. *American Antiquity*
         39(3):421–34.

Parmalee, Paul W., and Constance O'Hare
1983   Snails and Freshwater Mussels from the Anderson Site. In *The Anderson Site: Middle Archaic Adaptation in Tennessee's Central Basin,* edited by John T. Dowd, pp. 37–42. Miscellaneous Paper No. 13. Tennessee Anthropological Association, Knoxville.

Patch, Diana
1976   An Analysis of the Archaeological Shell of Freshwater Mollusks from the Carlston Annis Shellmound West Central Kentucky. Bachelor's Honors thesis, Washington University, St. Louis.

Pearson, Gordon W., and Minze Stuiver
1986   High-Precision Calibration of the Radiocarbon Time-Scale, 500 B.C.–2500 BC. *Radiocarbon* 28:839–62.

Pearson, Gordon W., J. R. Pilcher, M. G. Baillie, D. M. Corbett, and F. Qua
1986   High-Precision ^{14}C Measurements of Irish Oaks to Show the Natural ^{14}C Variations from A.D. 1840–5210 B.C. *Radiocarbon* 28:911–34.

Perzigian, Anthony J.
1977a   Fluctuating Dental Asymmetry: Variation among Skeletal Populations. *American Journal of Physical Anthropology* 47:81–88.

1977b   Teeth as Tools for Prehistoric Studies. In *Biocultural Adaptation in Prehistoric America,* edited by Robert L. Blakely, pp. 101–14. Southern Anthropological Society Proceedings No. 11. The University of Georgia Press, Athens.

1973   Osteoporotic Bone Loss in Two Prehistoric Indian Populations. *American Journal of Physical Anthropology* 39:87–96.

1972   Bone Growth in Two Prehistoric Indian Populations. *Proceedings of the Indiana Academy of Sciences* 81:58–64.

1971   Gerontal Osteoporotic Bone Loss in Two Prehistoric Indian Populations. Ph.D. dissertation, Department of Anthropology, Indiana University, Bloomington.

Pflieger, William L.
1975   *The Fishes of Missouri.* Missouri Department of Conservation, Jefferson City.

Phillips, James L., and James A. Brown (editors)
1983   *Archaic Hunters and Gatherers in the American Midwest.* Academic Press, New York.

Pierce, Lorna K. C.
1987   A Comparison of the Pattern of Involvement of Degenerative Joint Disease between an Agricultural and Non-Agricultural Skeletal Series. Ph.D. dissertation, Department of Anthropology, University of Tennessee, Knoxville.

Polach, Henry A.
1979   Correlation of ^{14}C Activity of the NBS Oxalic Acid with Arizona 1850 Wood and ANU Sucrose Standard. In *Radiocarbon Dating,* edited by R. Berger and H. Suess, pp. 115–24. University of California Press, Berkeley.

1972   Cross Checking of NBS Oxalic Acid and Secondary Laboratory Radiocarbon Dating Standards. In Proceedings of the 8th International Conference on Radiocarbon Dating, edited by T. A. Rafter and T. Grant-Taylor. *Royal Society of New Zealand Bulletin* 14:688–717.

Polach, Henry A., and Lauri Kaihola
1988   Determination of Radon by Liquid Scintillation/Particle Spectrometry: Towards the Resolution of a ^{14}C Dating Problem. *Radiocarbon* 30:19–24.

Pond, Alonzo
    1937   Lost John of Mummy Ledge. *Natural History* 39:174–76.
    1935   Report of Preliminary Survey of Important Archaeological Discovery at Mammoth Cave, Kentucky. *Wisconsin Archeologist* 15:27–35.

Powell, Mary P.
    1992a   Endemic Treponematosis and Tuberculosis in the Prehistoric Southeastern United States: The Biological Costs of Chronic Endemic Disease. In *Human Paleopathology: Current Syntheses and Future Options*, edited by Donald J. Ortner and Arthur C. Aufderheide, pp. 173–80. Smithsonian Institution Press, Washington, D.C.
    1992b   Health and Disease in the Late Prehistoric Southeast: Regional and Social Variability. In *Disease and Demography in the Americas, Changing Patterns Before and After 1492*, edited by D. H. Ubelaker and J. Verano, pp. 41–53. Smithsonian Institution Press, Washington, D.C.
    1988   *Status and Health in Prehistory, A Case Study of the Moundville Chiefdom.* Smithsonian Institution Press, Washington, D.C.
    1985   The Analysis of Dental Wear and Caries for Dietary Reconstruction. In *The Analysis of Prehistoric Diets*, edited by R. I. Gilbert and J. H. Mielke, pp. 307–38. Academic Press, New York.

Prentice, Guy
    1994   A Settlement Pattern Analysis of Prehistoric Sites in Mammoth Cave National Park, Kentucky. Ph.D. dissertation, Department of Anthropology, University of Florida, Gainesville.
    1993   *Archeological Overview and Assessment of Mammoth Cave National Park.* National Park Service, Southeast Archeological Center, Tallahassee.
    1990   *Mammoth Cave Archeological Inventory Project Interim Report–1989 Investigations*, National Park Service, Southeast Archeological Center, Tallahassee.
    1989   *Archeological Overview and Assessment, Mammoth Cave National Park.* Southeast Archeological Center, National Park Serivce, Tallahassee.
    1988   *Mammoth Cave Archeological Inventory Project. Interim Report–1987 Investigations.* Southeast Archeological Center, National Park Service, Tallahassee.
    1987a   Marine Shells as Wealth Items in Mississippian Societies. *Midcontinental Journal of Archaeology* 12(2):193–223.
    1987b   Report on the First Year's Investigations of the Mammoth Cave National Park Archeological Inventory Project. Paper presented at the Southeastern Archaeological Conference, Charleston.

Prewett, David L., and David J. Wolf
    1979   The Biological Distance of Two Archaic Skeletal Groups: An Analysis of the Discrete Cranial Traits of 15Jf18 and Oh 2 Peoples. Paper presented at the 36th Annual Meeting of the Southeastern Archaeological Conference, Atlanta.

Price, T. Douglas, and James A. Brown (editors)
    1985   *Prehistoric Hunter-Gatherers: The Emergence of Cultural Complexity.* Academic Press, New York.

Protsch, Reiner
    1986   Radiocarbon Dating of Bones. In *Dating and Age Determination of Biological Materials*, edited by M. R. Zimmerman and J. L. Angel, pp. 3–38. Croon Helm, London.

Purdue, James R.
1989   Changes during the Holocene in the Size of White-Tailed Deer (*Odocoileus virginianus*) from Central Illinois. *Quaternary Research* 32(3):307–16.

Purdy, Barbara Ann
1974   Investigations Concerning the Thermal Alteration of Silica Minerals: An Archaeological Approach. *Tebiwa* 17:37–66.

Putnam, Frederick W.
1875   Archaeological Researches in Kentucky and Indiana. *Proceedings of the Boston Society of Natural History for 1874–1875* 17:314–32.

Quinlan, J. F.
1970   Central Kentucky Karst. In *Mediteranée, Etudes et Travaux* 7:235–53.

Rabkin, Samuel B.
1943   Dental Conditions among Prehistoric Indians of Kentucky. *Journal of Dental Research* 22:355–66.

Rafinesque, Constantine S.
1824   *Ancient History, or Annals of Kentucky: Introduction to the History and Antiquities of the State of Kentucky.* Author, Frankfort.

Rahavendra, A. S., and V. S. R. Das
1978   The Occurrence of C_4-photosynthesis: A Supplementary List of C_4 Plants Reported during Late 1974–Mid 1977. *Photosynthetica* 12:200–208.

Reidhead, Van A.
1981   *A Linear Programming Model of Prehistoric Subsistence Optimization: A Southeastern Indiana Example.* Indiana Historical Society, Indianapolis.

Renfrew, Colin
1973   *Before Civilization: The Radiocarbon Revolution and Prehistoric Europe.* Knopf, New York.

Robbins, Louise M.
1977   The Story of Life Revealed by the Dead. In *Biocultural Adaptation in Prehistoric America,* edited by R. L. Blakely, pp. 10–26. Southern Anthropological Society Proceedings No. 11. The University of Georgia Press, Athens.

1974   Prehistoric People of the Mammoth Cave Area. In *The Archeology of the Mammoth Cave Area,* edited by Patty Jo Watson, pp. 137–62. Academic Press, New York.

Robbins, Louise M., Ronald C. Wilson, and Patty Jo Watson
1981   Paleontology and Archeology of Jaguar Cave, Tennessee. In *Proceedings: VIIIth International Congress of Speleology, Bowling Green, Kentucky,* edited by Barry Beck, pp. 377–80. Atlanta, Georgia State University and the National Speleological Society.

Rolingson, Martha A.
1967   *Temporal Perspective on the Archaic Cultures of the Middle Green River Region, Kentucky.* Ph.D. dissertation, University of Michigan. University Microfilms, Ann Arbor.

Rothschild, Bruce M., Kenneth R. Turner, and Michael A. DeLucca
1988   Symmetrical Erosive Peripheral Polyarthritis in the Late Archaic Period of Alabama. *Science* 241:1498–1501.

Rothschild, Bruce M., and Robert J. Woods
1990   Symmetrical Erosive Disease in Archaic Indians: The Origin of Rheumatoid Arthritis in the New World? *Seminars in Arthritis and Rheumatism* 19(5):278–84.

Rothschild, Bruce M., Robert J. Woods, Christine Rothschild, and Jeno Sebes
1992   Geographic Distribution of Rheumatoid Arthritis in Ancient North America: Implications for Pathogenesis. *Seminars in Arthritis and Rheumatism* 22(3):181–87.

Rothschild, Nan A.
1979   Mortuary Behavior and Social Organization at Indian Knoll and Dickson Mounds. *American Antiquity* 44:658–75.
1975   *Age and Sex, Status and Role, in Prehistoric Societies of Eastern North America.* Ph.D. dissertation, New York University. University Microfilms, Ann Arbor.

Royer, J. E., and Donna C. Roper
1980   Archaic Adaptations in the Central Osage River Basin: A Preliminary Assessment. In *Archaic Prehistory on the Prairie-Plains Border*, edited by A. E. Johnson, pp. 13–23. Publications in Anthropology No. 12. University of Kansas, Lawrence.

Ruff, C. B.
1980   Age Differences in Craniofacial Dimensions among Adults from Indian Knoll, Kentucky. *American Journal of Physical Anthropology* 53:101–8.

Sarnas, Karl V.
1964   The Dentition of Indian Knoll Man. Dental Decay. *Odontologist Review* 15:424–44.
1957   Growth Changes in Skulls of Ancient Man in North America. *Acta Odontologica Scandinavica* 15:213–71.

Schenian, Pamela
1990   The Onionville Mine Complex. In *Studies in Kentucky Archaeology*, edited by Charles D. Hockensmith, pp. 196–210. The Kentucky Heritage Council, Frankfort.
1988   Report of the Archeological Mitigation of the Onionville Mine Complex, at Approximate Green River Mile 31.8, Henderson County, Kentucky. Archeology Service Center Report, Murray State University, Murray.
1987   There Was a Mine under Every Little Hill: An Archeological Reconnaissance of the Upland Area of Permit 851-0001 and the Investigation of the Onionville Mine Complex at Approximate Green River Mile 31.8, Henderson County, Kentucky. Archeology Service Center Report, Murray State University, Murray.

Schoenwetter, James
1974   Pollen Analysis of Sediments from Salts Cave Vestibule. In *Archeology of the Mammoth Cave Area*, edited by Patty Jo Watson, pp. 97–105. Academic Press, New York.

Schwartz, Douglas W.
1967   *Conceptions of Kentucky Prehistory: A Case Study in the History of Archeology.* Studies in Anthropology No. 6. University of Kentucky Press, Lexington.
1965   *Prehistoric Man in Mammoth Cave.* Interpretive Series No. 2. Eastern National Park and Monument Association, Mammoth Cave.
1960a Archaeological Survey of the Nolin River Reservoir. Ms. on file, Museum of Anthropology, University of Kentucky, Lexington.
1960b Prehistoric Man in Mammoth Cave. *Scientific American* 203:130–40.
1958a An Archaeological Report on Physical Remains from Mammoth Cave National Park. Ms. on file, Mammoth Cave National Park Library, Mammoth Cave National Park, Mammoth Cave.

1958b   Archaeological Report on Materials in the John M. Nelson Collection from Mammoth Cave National Park. Ms. on file, Mammoth Cave National Park Library, Mammoth Cave National Park, Mammoth Cave.

1958c   Archaeological Survey of Mammoth Cave National Park. Ms. on file, Mammoth Cave National Park Library, Mammoth Cave National Park, Mammoth Cave.

1958d   The Archaeology of Mammoth Cave National Park. Ms. on file, Mammoth Cave National Park Library, Mammoth Cave National Park, Mammoth Cave.

1958e   Description and Analysis of Museum Materials from Mammoth Cave National Park. Ms. on file, Mammoth Cave National Park Library, Mammoth Cave National Park, Mammoth Cave.

1958f   Report on Two Radiocarbon Dates from Mammoth Cave, Kentucky. Ms. on file, Mammoth Cave National Park Library, Mammoth Cave National Park, Mammoth Cave.

1958g   Sandals and Textiles from Mammoth Cave National Park. Ms. on file, Mammoth Cave National Park Library, Mammoth Cave National Park, Mammoth Cave.

1958h   Summary and Evaluation of the 1916 American Museum Archaeological Work in Mammoth Cave National Park. Ms. on file, Mammoth Cave National Park Library, Mammoth Cave National Park, Mammoth Cave.

Schwartz, Douglas W., and Lee Hanson
1961   Archaeological Excavation in the Nolin Basin—1961. Ms. on file, Office of State Archeology, University of Kentucky, Lexington.

Schwartz, Douglas W., and Tacoma G. Sloan
1960a   Archeological Survey of the Barren Reservoir. Ms. on file, Office of State Archeology, University of Kentucky, Lexington.

1960b   Archaeological Survey of Twenty-Two Small Federal Projects in Kentucky. Ms. on file, Office of State Archeology, University of Kentucky, Lexington.

1958   Excavations of the Rough River Site, Grayson County 12, Kentucky. Ms. on file, Office of State Archeology, University of Kentucky, Lexington.

Schwartz, Douglas W., Tacoma Sloan, and Lee Hanson
1960   Test Excavations in the Nolin Basin—1960. Ms. on file, Office of State Archeology, University of Kentucky, Lexington.

Scott, Eugenia C.
1979   Principal Axis Analysis of Dental Attrition Data. *American Journal of Physical Anthropology* 51:203–12.

Seeman, Mark F.
1986   Adena "Houses" and Their Implications for Early Woodland Settlement Models in the Ohio Valley. In *Early Woodland Archeology*, edited by K. B. Farnsworth and T. E. Emerson, pp. 564–80. Kampsville Seminars in Archeology No. 2. Center for American Archeology, Kampsville, Ill.

Shepard, Anna O.
1971   *Ceramics for the Archaeologist.* Carnegie Institution of Washington, Washington, D.C.

Skarland, Ivar
1939   The Skeletal Material. In *The Chiggerville Site, Site 1, Ohio County, Kentucky*, edited by W. S. Webb and W. G. Haag, pp. 28–49. University of Kentucky Reports in Anthropology No. 4. University of Kentucky, Lexington.

Smith, Bruce D.
1992a   Prehistoric Plant Husbandry in Eastern North America. In *Origins of Agriculture in World Prospective,* edited by C. Wesley Cowan and Patty Jo Watson. Smithsonian Institution Press, Washington, D.C.
1992b   *Rivers of Change; Essays on the Origins of Agriculture in Eastern North America.* Smithsonian Institution Press, Washington, D.C.
1989   Origins of Agriculture in Eastern North America. *Science* 246:1566–71.
1987   The Independent Domestication of Indigenous Seedbearing Plants in
Eastern North America. In *Emergent Horticultural Economies of the Eastern
Woodlands,* edited by W. Keegan, pp. 3–47. Occasional Paper No. 7. Center
for Archaeological Investigations, Southern Illinois University, Carbondale.
1986   The Archaeology of the Southeastern United States: From Dalton to de
Soto, 10,500–500 B.P. *Advances in World Archaeology* 5:1–92.
1975   *Middle Mississippian Exploitation of Animal Populations.* Museum of Anthropology, *Anthropological Papers* No. 57. University of Michigan, Ann
Arbor.
Smith, Maria
1992   Osteological Indications of Warfare in the Archaic Period of Western Tennessee. Paper Presented at the 49th Annual Meeting of the Southeastern
Archaeological Conference, Little Rock.
Sneed, Joel, and Carole Sneed
1989   Little Beaver Cave, Bartow County, Georgia. Paper presented at the National Speleological Annual Meeting, Sewanee.
Snow, Charles E.
1948   *Indian Knoll Skeletons of Site Oh2, Ohio County, Kentucky.* University of Ken-
tucky Reports on Anthropology and Archaeology No. 4. University of
Kentucky, Lexington.
Spence, Michael W., and William A. Fox
1986   The Early Woodland Occupations of Southern Ontario. In *Early Woodland
Archeology,* edited by K. Farnsworth and T. Emerson, pp. 4–46. Kampsville
Seminars in Archeology No. 2. Center for American Archeology, Kamps-
ville, Ill.
Stafford, C. Russell
1991   Archaic Period Logistical Foraging Strategies in West-Central Illinois.
Midcontinental Journal of Archaeology 16(2):212–46.
Stansbery, David
1965   The Naiad Fauna of the Green River at Munfordville, Kentucky. In *Annual
Report. American Malacological Union.*
Steadman, L. Ted, et al.
1959   Trace Elements in Ancient Indian Teeth. *Journal of Dental Research* 38:285–
92.
Steele, Dewey G.
1948   Homogenity in Indian Knoll. In *Indian Knoll Skeletons,* edited by Charles
E. Snow, pp. 492–509. University of Kentucky Reports in Anthropology
and Archaeology No. 4, part II. University of Kentucky, Lexington.
Stein, Julie K.
In Prep. Geoarchaeological Studies of the Green River Shell Middens. In *The Archeology of the Middle Green River, Kentucky,* edited by William H. Marquardt, Patty Jo Watson, and Mary C. Kennedy.

1983   Earthworm Activity: A Source of Potential Disturbance of Archaeological Sediments. *American Antiquity* 48:277–89.

1982   Geologic Analysis of the Green River Shell Middens. *Southeastern Archaeology* 1(1):22–39.

1980   Geoarchaeology of the Green River Shell Mounds, Kentucky. Ph.D. dissertation, Center for Ancient Studies, University of Minnesota, Minneapolis.

Stein, Julie K., Patty Jo Watson, and William B. White

1981   Geoarchaeology of the Flint Mammoth Cave System and the Green River, Western Kentucky. In *GSA Cincinnati '81 Field Trip Guidebooks, vol. III: Geomorphology, Hydrogeology, Geoarcheology, Engineering Geology*, edited by Thomas G. Roberts, pp. 507–42. American Geological Institute, Alexandria, Va.

Steponaitis, Vincas P.

1986   Prehistoric Archaeology in the Southeastern United States, 1970–1985. *Annual Review of Anthropology* 15:363–404.

Stewart, Robert B.

1974   Identification and Quantification of Components in Salts Cave Paleofeces. In *Archaeology of the Mammoth Cave Area*, edited by Patty Jo Watson, pp. 41–47. Academic Press, New York.

Stewart, T. Dale

1962   Comments on the Reassessment of the Indian Knoll Skeletons. *American Journal of Physical Anthropology* 20(2):143–48.

1957   Distortion of the Pubic Symphyseal Surface in Females and Its Effect on Age Determination. *American Journal of Physical Anthropology* 15:9–18.

Stoltman, James B.

1978   Temporal Models in Prehistory: An example from Eastern North America. *Current Anthropology* 19:703–46.

Stoltman, James B., and David A. Baerreis

1983   The Evolution of Human Ecosystems in the Eastern United States. In *Late-Quaternary Environments of the United States*, edited by Herbert E. Wright, Jr., pp. 252–68. University of Minnesota Press, Minneapolis.

Stuckenrath, Robert

1977   Radiocarbon: Some Notes from Merlin's Diary. *Annals of the New York Academy of Sciences* 288:181–88.

Stuiver, Minze, and Gordon W. Pearson

1986   High-Precision Calibration of the Radiocarbon Time Scale, AD 1950–500 BC. *Radiocarbon* 28:805–38.

Stuiver, Minze, and Henry A. Polach

1977   Discussion. Reporting of ^{14}C Data. *Radiocarbon* 19:355–63.

Stuiver, Minze, and P. J. Reimer

1986   A Computer Program for Radiocarbon Age Calibration. *Radiocarbon* 28:1022–30.

Stuiver, Minze, and Hans E. Suess

1966   On the Relationship between Radiocarbon Dates and True Sample Ages. *Radiocarbon* 8:534–40.

Stuiver, Minze, B. Kromer, B. Becker, and C. Ferguson

1986   Radiocarbon Age Calibration Back to 13,300 years BP and the ^{14}C Age Matching of the German Oak and U.S. Bristlecone Pine Chronologies. *Radiocarbon* 28:969–79.

Styles, Bonnie W.
 1986 Aquatic Exploitation in the Lower Illinois River Valley: The Role of Pa-
 leoecological Change. In *Foraging, Collecting, and Harvesting: Archaic Period
 Subsistence and Settlement in the Eastern Woodlands,* edited by Sarah W.
 Neusius, pp. 145–74. Occasional Paper No. 6. Southern Illinois University
 Center for Archaeological Investigations, Carbondale.

Styles, Bonnie W., Steven R. Ahler, and Melvin L. Fowler
 1993 Modoc Rock Shelter Revisited. In *Archaic Hunters and Gatherers in the
 American Midwest,* edited by James L. Phillips and James A. Brown, pp.
 261–97. Academic Press, New York.

Styles, Bonnie W., Karli White, and James R. Purdue
 1991 Shifts in Archaic Period Faunal Exploitation in the Mississippi River Valley: Modoc Rock Shelter Revisited. Paper presented at the 55th Annual
 Meeting of the Society for American Archaeology, New Orleans.

Suess, Hans E.
 1986 Secular Variations of Cogmogenic ^{14}C on Earth: Their Discovery and Interpretation. *Radiocarbon* 28:259–65.
 1967 Bristlecone-pine Calibration of the Radiocarbon Time-Scale from 4100 B.C.
 to 1500 B.C. In *Radioactive Dating and Methods of Low-level Counting,* pp. 143–
 51. International Atomic Energy Agency, Vienna.
 1954 Natural Radiocarbon Measurements by Acetylene Counting. *Science*
 120:5–7.

Sullivan, Norman C.
 1977 *The Physical Anthropology of Chiggerville: Demography and Pathology.* Master's thesis, Western Michigan University, Kalamazoo. University Microfilms, Ann Arbor.

Sundick, Robert I.
 1972a *Human Skeletal Growth and Dental Development as Observed in the Indian
 Knoll Population.* Ph.D. dissertation, University of Toronto. University Microfilms, Ann Arbor.
 1972b New Method for Assigning Ages to Immature Skeletons. Paper presented
 at the 41st annual meeting of the American Association of Physical Anthropologists, Kansas.
 1971 Skeletal Growth and Dental Eruption in the Indian Knoll Skeletons. Paper
 presented at the 40th annual meeting of the American Association of
 Physical Anthropologists, Boston.

Sussenbach, Thomas, Julie Morgan, and David Rotenizer with a contribution by
Pamela Schenian
 1990 *Cultural Resource Assessment of a 1355 Acre Mine Permit Area, Henderson
 County, Kentucky.* Program for Cultural Resource Assessment, Archeological Report 227. University of Kentucky, Lexington.

Swanton, John R.
 1946 *The Indians of the Southeastern United States.* Bureau of American Ethnology,
 Bulletin No. 137. Smithsonian Institution, Washington, D.C.

Tague, Robert G.
 1989 Variation in Pelvic Size between Males and Females. *American Journal of
 Physical Anthropology* 80:59–71.
 1988 Bone Resorption of the Pubis and Preauricular Area in Human and Nonhuman Mammals. *American Journal of Physical Anthropology* 76:251–67.

1986   Obstetric Adaptations of the Human Bony Pelvis. Ph.D. dissertation, Department of Anthropology, Kent State University, Kent, Ohio.

Tankersley, Kenneth B.
1989   Prehistoric Renewable Resource Mining in the Mammoth Cave System. Paper presented at the Southeastern Archaeological Conference, Tampa.

Tankersley, Kenneth B., Samuel S. Frushour, Frank Nagy, Stephen L. Tankersley, and Kevin Tankersley
1994   The Archaeology of Mummy Valley, Salts Cave, Mammoth Cave National Park, Kentucky. *North American Archaeologist* 15(2):129–46.

Tankersley, Kenneth B., J. L. Bassett, and Samuel S. Frushour
1985   A Gourd Bowl from Salts Cave, Kentucky. *Tennessee Anthropologist* 10:95–104.

Tappen, Nancy C.
1983   The Development of the Vermiculate Pattern in the Brow Region of Crania from Indian Knoll, Kentucky. *American Journal of Physical Anthropology* 60:523–37.

Taylor, R. E.
1987   *Radiocarbon Dating: An Archaeological Perspective.* Academic Press, Orlando.
1982   Problems in the Radiocarbon Dating of Bone. In *Nuclear and Chemical Dating Techniques: Interpreting the Environmental Record,* edited by Lloyd A. Currie, pp. 453–73. ACS Symposium Series No. 176. American Chemical Society, Washington, D.C.

Taylor, Walter
1971   *A Study of Archeology,* 3d ed. Southern Illinois University Press, Carbondale.

Thiel, Barbara
1972   The Distribution of Grave Goods with Infants and Children at Indian Knoll. Ms. on file, Office of State Archaeology, University of Kentucky, Lexington.

Thieme, Donald M.
1991   Season Specialization, Assemblage Diversity, and the Concept of a Subsistence-Settlement System: A Statistical Analysis of the Riverton Culture. *Midcontinental Journal of Archaeology* 16:85–117.

Tite, M. S.
1972   *Methods of Physical Examination in Archaeology.* Seminar Press, London.

Turner, William B.
1982   Initial Report of Testing at the Hayes Site. Paper Presented at the 39th Annual Meeting of the Southeastern Archaeological Conference, Memphis.

Turner, William B., and Walter E. Klippel
1989   Hunter-Gatherers in the Nashville Basin: Archeological and Geological Evidence for Variability in Prehistoric Land Use. *Geoarchaeology* 4(1):43–67.

Ubelaker, Douglas H.
1985   *Human Skeletal Remains: Excavation, Analysis, Interpretation,* 2nd ed. Taraxcum Press, Washington, D.C.

Van Gerven, Dennis
1972   Burial Sites in Kentucky with Bibliography Pertaining to Skeletal Collections Housed at Vine Street. Ms. on file, Office of State Archaeology, University of Kentucky, Lexington.

Virchow, Rudolf
   1950   Heredity and the Formation of Race. In *This Is Race,* edited by Earl W. Court, pp. 178–93. Originally published in 1896. Schuman, New York.

Von Bonin, G., and G. M. Morant
   1938   Indian Races in the United States. A Survey of Previously Published Cranial Measurements. *Biometrika* 30:94–139.

Wagner, Gail E.
   In Prep. Plant Remains from the Carlston Annis Site. In *The Archeology of the Middle Green River, Kentucky,* edited by William H. Marquardt, Patty Jo Watson, and Mary C. Kennedy.
   1988   Comparability among Recovery Techniques. In *Current Paleoethnobotany: Analytical Methods and Cultural Interpretations of Archaeological Plant Remains,* edited by Carl A. Hastorf and Virginia S. Popper, pp. 17–35. The University of Chicago Press, Chicago.
   1982   Testing Flotation Recovery Rates. *American Antiquity* 47(1):127–32.
   1979   The Green River Archaic: A Botanical Reconstruction II. Paper presented at the 36th Annual Meeting of the Southeastern Archaeological Conference, Atlanta.
   1978   An Archeobotanical Analysis of Five Sites in the Mammoth Cave Area. Master's thesis, Department of Anthropology, Washington University, St. Louis.
   1976   Aboriginal Plant Use in West-Central Kentucky. A Preliminary Report of Surface Sites in the Mammoth Cave Area. Paper presented at the 17th Annual Meeting of the Society for Economic Botany. University of Illinois, Urbana-Champaign.

Wainscott, Bob
   1965   Exploration into Rogers Cave. In *The Everlasting Darkness.* Central Kentucky Grotto, National Speleological Society, Huntsville, Ala.

Wakefield, Elmer G., and Samuel C. Dellinger
   1940   Diseases of Prehistoric Americans of South Central United States. *Ciba Symposia* 2:453–62.

Walthall, John A.
   1980   *Prehistoric Indians of the Southeast: Archaeology of Alabama and the Middle South.* University of Alabama Press, Tuscaloosa.

Ward, Steven C.
   In Prep. The Dental Anthropology of the Middle Green River Shell Middens. In *Archeology of the Middle Green River, Kentucky,* edited by William H. Marquardt, Patty Jo Watson, and Mary C. Kennedy.

Waselkov, Gregory
   1982   *Shellfish Gathering and Shell Midden Archaeology.* Ph.D. dissertation, University of North Carolina. University Microfilms International, Ann Arbor.

Waterbolk, H. T.
   1971   Working with Radiocarbon Dates. *Proceedings of the Prehistoric Society* 37(2):15–23.

Watson, Patty Jo
   1992   Discussant Comments. Archaic Mounds Symposium, Southeastern Archaeological Conference, Little Rock.
   1990   Trend and Tradition in Southeastern Archaeology. *Southeastern Archaeology* 9:43–54.

1989   Early Plant Cultivation in the Eastern Woodlands of North America. In *Foraging and Farming: The Evolution of Plant Exploitation*, edited by David R. Harris and Gordon C. Hillman, pp. 555–71. Unwin Hyman, London.

1988   Prehistoric Gardening and Agriculture in the Midwest and Midsouth. In *Interpretations of Culture Change in the Eastern Woodlands during the Late Woodland Period*, edited by R. Yerkes, pp. 39–67. Occasional Papers in Anthropology No. 3. Department of Anthropology, Ohio State University, Columbus.

1987   Cave Research Foundation Archeological Project—1986. In *Cave Research Foundation Annual Report, 1986*, pp. 31–33, 36–37. Cave Research Foundation, Columbus.

1986   Cave Archeology in the Eastern Woodlands. *Masterkey* 59:19–25.

1985a   Archeology. In *Caves and Karst of Kentucky*, edited by Percy H. Dougherty, pp. 176–86. Special Publication 12. Kentucky Geological Survey, University of Kentucky, Lexington.

1985b   The Impact of Early Horticulture in the Upland Drainages of the Midwest and Midsouth. In *Prehistoric Food Production in North America*, edited by Richard I. Ford, pp. 73–98. *Anthropological Papers* No. 75. Museum of Anthropology, Ann Arbor.

1983   Cave Research Foundation Archeological Project and Shellmound Archeological Project—1982. *Cave Research Foundation Annual Report, 1982*, pp. 13–15. Cave Research Foundation, Columbus.

1977   Prehistoric Miners of the Flint Mammoth Cave System. *Proceedings of the 6th International Congress of Speleology*. Vol. VI, subsec. Eb, pp. 147–49. Olomouc, Czechoslovakia.

1976   In Pursuit of Prehistoric Subsistence: A Comparative Account of Some Contemporary Flotation Techniques. *Midcontinental Journal of Archaeology* 1:77–100.

1974a   Excavations in the Vestibule of Salts Cave. In *Archeology of the Mammoth Cave Area*, edited by Patty Jo Watson, pp. 71–83. Academic Press, New York.

1974b   Lower Salts. In *Archeology of the Mammoth Cave Area*, edited by Patty Jo Watson, pp. 65–70. Academic Press, New York.

1974c   Mammoth Cave Archeology. In *Archeology of the Mammoth Cave Area*, edited by Patty Jo Watson, pp. 183–84. Academic Press, New York.

1974d   Prehistoric Cultural Debris from the Vestibule Trenches. In *Archeology of the Mammoth Cave Area*, edited by Patty Jo Watson, pp. 83–96. Academic Press, New York.

1974e   Prehistoric Horticulturalists. In *Archeology of the Mammoth Cave Area*, edited by Patty Jo Watson, pp. 233–41. Academic Press, New York.

1974f   Prehistoric Miners. In *Archeology of the Mammoth Cave Area*, edited by Patty Jo Watson, pp. 231–32. Academic Press, New York.

1974g   Recent History of Salts Cave. In *Archeology of the Mammoth Cave Area*, edited by Patty Jo Watson, pp. 21–23. Academic Press, New York.

1974h   Salts Cave (and Related) Material in East Coast Museum Collections. In *Archeology of the Mammoth Cave Area*, edited by Patty Jo Watson, pp. 167–82. Academic Press, New York.

1972   Archeological Activities in Mammoth Cave and Vicinity. In *Cave Research Foundation, Report 14*. Cave Research Foundation, Columbus.

1971 Excavations and Analysis in Salts Cave. In *Cave Research Foundation Thirteenth Annual Report*, pp. 21–25. Cave Research Foundation, Columbus.

1966 Prehistoric Miners of Salts Cave, Kentucky. *Archaeology* 19(4):237–43.

Watson, Patty Jo (editor)

1974 *The Archeology of the Mammoth Cave Area*. Academic Press, New York.

Watson, Patty Jo, and Kenneth C. Carstens

1982 Archaeological Survey and Testing in Mammoth Cave National Park, Ky. Ms. on file, Southeast Archeological Center, National Park Service, Tallahassee.

1975 Archaeological Resources of Mammoth Cave National Park: A Brief Summary. Report Prepared for the National Park Service. Ms. on file, Southeast Archeological Center, National Park Service, Tallahassee.

Watson, Patty Jo, and Richard K. Yarnell

1986 Lost John's Last Meal. *Missouri Archaeologist* 47:241–55.

1966 Archaeological and Paleoethnobotanical Investigations in Salts Cave, Mammoth Cave National Park, Kentucky. *American Antiquity* 31:842–49.

Watson, Patty Jo, Richard A. Yarnell, Harold Meloy, William Benninghoff, Eric Callen, Aidan Cockburn, Hugh Cutler, Paul Parmalee, Lionel Prescott, and William White

1969 *The Prehistory of Salts Cave, Kentucky*. Reports of Investigations No. 16. Illinois State Museum, Springfield.

Watt, Bernice K., and Annabel L. Merrill

1975 *Handbook of the Nutritional Contents of Foods*. Dover, New York.

Webb, William S.

1974 *Indian Knoll*, new ed. University of Tennessee Press, Knoxville.

1950a The Carlson [sic] Annis Mound, Site 5, Butler County, Kentucky. *University of Kentucky Reports in Anthropology* 7(4):267–54.

1950b The Read Shell Midden, Site 10, Butler County, Kentucky. *University of Kentucky Reports in Anthropology* 7(5).

1946 Indian Knoll, Site Oh2, Ohio County, Kentucky. *University of Kentucky Reports in Anthropology and Archaeology* 4(3):1–365.

1939 *An Archaeological Survey of Wheeler Basin on the Tennessee River in Northern Alabama*. Bureau of American Ethnology Bulletin No. 122. Smithsonian Institution, Washington, D.C.

1938 *An Archaeological Survey of the Norris Basin in Eastern Tennessee*. Bureau of American Ethnology Bulletin No. 118. Washington, D.C.

Webb, William S., and David L. DeJarnette

1942 *An Archeological Survey of Pickwick Basin in the Adjacent Portions of the States of Alabama, Mississippi and Tennessee*. Bureau of American Ethnology, Bulletin No. 129. Smithsonian Institution, Washington, D.C.

Webb, William S., and William D. Funkhouser

1930 *The Page Site in Logan County, Kentucky*. Reports in Anthropology and Archaeology 1(3). University of Kentucky, Lexington.

Webb, William S., and William G. Haag

1947 Archaic Sites in McLean County, Kentucky. *University of Kentucky Reports in Anthropology and Archaeology* 7(1)1–48.

1940 Cypress Creek Villages. *University of Kentucky Reports in Anthropology and Archaeology* 4(2)67–110.

1939   The Chiggerville Site. *University of Kentucky Reports in Anthropology and Archaeology* 4(1)1–62.

Weiss, Kenneth M.

1973   *Demographic Models for Anthropology.* Memoirs of the Society for American Archaeology No. 27. Society for American Archaeology, Washington, D.C.

1972   On the Systematic Bias in Skeletal Sexing. *American Journal of Physical Anthropology* 37:239–50.

White, William B.

1970   Sulfate Minerals in Central Kentucky Caves. In *Cave Research Foundation 1969 Annual Report*, pp. 10–11. Cave Research Foundation, Yellow Springs, Ohio.

1969   Mineralogy of the Salts Cave Archaeological Site. In *The Prehistory of Salts Cave, Kentucky*, by Patty Jo Watson et al., pp. 79–82. Report of Investigations No. 16. Illinois State Museum, Springfield.

Willey, Gordon R.

1966   *An Introduction to American Archaeology: North and Middle America*, vol 1. Prentice-Hall, Englewood Cliffs, N.J.

Willey, Patrick

1989   Excavated Human Skeleton from Little Beaver Cave. Paper presented at the Annual Meeting of the National Speleological Society, Sewanee.

Wilson, Ronald C.

1984   Archaeological Description of the Sinking Creek System. In *Central Kentucky Cave Survey, Bulletin*, edited by Gary Schindel, Sue Schindel, and Mary Tinker, pp. 27–33. The Center for Cave and Karst Studies, Department of Geography and Geology, Western Kentucky University, Bowling Green.

Winters, Howard

1974   Introduction to the New Edition. In *Indian Knoll* by William S. Webb. University of Tennessee Press, Knoxville.

1969   *The Riverton Culture: A Second Millennium Occupation in the Central Wabash Valley.* Reports of Investigations No. 13. Illinois State Museum, Springfield.

1968   Value Systems and Trade Cycles of the Late Archaic in the Midwest. In *New Perspectives in Archaeology*, edited by Sally R. Binford and Lewis R. Binford, pp. 175–221. Aldine, Chicago.

1963   An Archaeological Survey of the Wabash Valley in Illinois. Reports of Investigations No. 10. Illinois State Museum, Springfield.

Wright, Herbert E., Jr.

1976   The Dynamic Nature of Holocene Vegetation, a Problem in Paleoclimatology, Biogeography, and Stratigraphic Nomenclature. *Quaternary Research* 6:581–96.

1974   The Environment of Early Man in the Great Lakes Region. In *Aspects of Upper Great Lakes Anthropology*, edited by E. Johnson, pp. 8–14. Minnesota Historical Society, St. Paul.

1968   The Roles of Pine and Spruce in the Forest History of Minnesota and Adjacent Areas. *Ecology* 49:937–55.

Wyckoff, Larry M.

1977   The Physical Anthropology of Chiggerville: Biological Relationships and

Growth. Master's thesis, Western Michigan University. University Microfilms, Ann Arbor.

Yarnell, Richard A.

1994 Investigations Relevant to the Native Development of Plant Husbandry in Eastern North America: A Brief and Reasonably True Account. In *Agricultural Origins and Development in the Midcontinent*, edited by William Green, pp. 87–103. Office of the State Archaeologist, Report No. 19. University of Iowa, Iowa City.

1986 A Survey of Prehistoric Crop Plants in Eastern North America. *Missouri Archaeologist* 47:47–59.

1983 Prehistory of Plant Foods and Husbandry in North America. Paper presented at the 48th Annual Meeting for the Society for American Archaeology, Pittsburgh.

1974a Intestinal Contents of the Salts Cave Mummy and Analysis of the Initial Salts Cave Flotation Series. In *Archeology of the Mammoth Cave Area*, edited by Patty Jo Watson, pp. 109–12. Academic Press, New York.

1974b Plant Food and Cultivation of the Salts Cavers. In *Archeology of the Mammoth Cave Area*, edited by Patty Jo Watson, pp. 113–22. Academic Press, New York.

1969 Contents of Human Paleofeces. In *The Prehistory of Salts Cave, Kentucky*, edited by Patty Jo Watson, pp. 41–54. Reports of Investigations No. 16. Illinois State Museum, Springfield.

Young, Col. Bennett

1910 *The Prehistoric Men of Kentucky*. Filson Club Publications No. 25. John P. Morton, Louisville.

Zimmerman, Michael R., and J. Lawrence Angel

1986 *Dating and Age Determination of Biological Materials*. Croon Helm, London.

Contributors

Kenneth C. Carstens is professor of anthropology and director of the Murray State University Anthropology Program and Archeology Service Center in Murray, Kentucky. Between 1973 and 1980 he conducted archaeological research in Mammoth Cave National Park, and since 1980 he has been concentrating on archival and field studies of George Rogers Clark's 1780–1781 Fort Jefferson in extreme western Kentucky.

Cheryl Claassen is professor of anthropology at Appalachian State University, Boone, North Carolina, and a graduate student of the anthropology departments of the University of Arkansas and Harvard University. Her research focus for the past fifteen years has been shells and shell-bearing sites, particularly those in New York, North Carolina, and Kentucky. She is the author of a monograph on historic musseling industries in the Mississippi watershed and has edited two volumes on issues of gender in archaeology.

Philip J. DiBlasi is the staff archaeologist at the University of Louisville's Program of Archeology. Along with his wife, Jan Marie Hemberger, he became actively involved with cave archaeology through the Cave Research Foundation. His primary research interests are cave art, archaeological investigations of historic cemeteries, and cave resource management. He is active in the Kentucky Organization of Professional Archeologists and the Cave Research Foundation, serving on both as president and as a member of their board of directors.

David H. Dye is an associate professor of anthropology at Memphis University. His research has focused on the Archaic of the Tennessee River valley and the late prehistoric and protohistoric periods in the Mississippi River valley. Most recently he has edited, with Cheryl Anne Cox, *Towns and Temples along the Mississippi* and, with Ronald C. Brister, *The Protohistoric Period in the Mid-South: 1500–1700*. He is presently engaged in a study of Mississippian warfare.

Valerie A. Haskins is a Ph.D. candidate in anthropology at Washington University in St. Louis, where she earned her M.A. in 1988. She received her B.A. from DePauw University in 1979. She is presently an instructor of anthropology and archaeology at Western Kentucky University in Bowling Green, Kentucky. Her research has focused on the bioarchaeology and paleopathology of past populations, including those from Kentucky shell mound Archaic sites and mortuary caves, and the American Southeast, Greece, Jordan, and Guatemala.

Jan Marie Hemberger is an archaeologist for the U.S. Army Corps of Engineers, Louisville District. Her graduate studies at the University of Louisville focused on the management of cultural resources. She and her husband, Philip J. DiBlasi, are active in local and national cave archaeology through the Cave Research Foundation.

Christine K. Hensley recently received her doctoral degree from Washington University, St. Louis. Her dissertation research addressed the diversity of Archaic sites in the Middle Green River and outlined a preliminary settlement pattern for the Middle to Late Archaic. She is also involved in documenting caves and rockshelter sites in Honduras for the purpose of identifying preceramic occupations.

Nicholas P. Herrmann is a graduate student in the Ph.D. anthropology program at the University of Tennessee, Knoxville, where he also works in the Forensic Anthropology Center. He received his B.A. and M.A. at Washington University in St. Louis in 1988 and 1990, respectively. His research has focused on bioarchaeology with special interest in Kentucky shell mound Archaic, the American Southwest, and historic cemetery collections.

Mary C. Kennedy is a research associate at Washington University in St. Louis. In addition to the archaeology of the Central Kentucky Karst and radiocarbon dating, her research interests include method and theory and the archaeological manifestations of gender. She also specializes in the preparation of archaeological manuscripts for publication.

Cheryl Ann Munson is an assistant scientist in the Department of Anthropology at Indiana University-Bloomington. Her work has centered mainly on Indiana and the Ohio River valley and has included aspects of Mississippian settlement systems, public archaeology, and most recently geoarchaeological applications. She has directed numerous cultural resource management projects, including studies in caves and along Green River.

Mary Lucas Powell is director/curator of the William S. Webb Museum of Anthropology at the University of Kentucky. Since 1974 she has conducted bioarchaeological research on health and disease throughout the southeastern United States. Her current interests include patterns of association among rank, status, and health in late prehistoric Native American societies (her dissertation research at Northwestern University focused on the Mississippian chiefdom at Moundville, Alabama) and the natural history of infectious diseases indigenous to the Americas, particularly tuberculosis and treponematosis.

Guy Prentice has been employed as an archaeologist with the National Park Service, Southeast Archeological Center in Tallahassee, Florida, since 1986. Currently, he is acting as the principal investigator for the six-year Big South Fork National River and Recreation Area Archeological Resource Survey. His main archaeological interests include Eastern Woodland prehistory, economic theory, settlement pattern analysis and cartographic science, and Native American cosmology and religion.

Kenneth B. Tankersley is an assistant professor of anthropology at the State University of New York at Brockport. In addition to anthropological questions associated with prehistoric cave exploration and exploitation, his research interests include the geochronology of the peopling of the New World and the economic mechanisms of human adaptation, especially the procurement, use, and exchange of natural resources by Early Paleoindians.

Gail E. Wagner is an associate professor of anthropology at the University of South Carolina. Her research has centered on recovery techniques, comparability, and the paleoethnobotany of the late prehistoric crops of corn, beans, and tobacco, especially at Fort Ancient and other midwestern Mississippian sites. She has recreated Indian gardens for the public and continues to research and write about gardening practices. She is currently compiling a summary of paleoethnobotany in South Carolina.

Patty Jo Watson is Edward Mallinckrodt Distinguished University Professor of Anthropology at Washington University in St. Louis. Her primary scholarly interests are in agricultural origins in North America and the Near East, ethnoarchaeology, and archaeological theory. She participated in Oriental Institute/ University of Chicago projects in Iraq, Iran, and Turkey during the 1950s and 1960s. Since 1963 she has been carrying out fieldwork in Salts Cave and Mammoth Cave (Mammoth Cave National Park, Kentucky) and since 1972 at the Green River shell mounds in Butler and Ohio Counties, Kentucky.

Index

Adair Glyph Cave (15Ad70), 42, 82–84; foot-prints in, 83; inclusion in National Register of Historic Places, 83; mapping survey of, 82–83; mud drawings in, 83–84; photo-documentation in, 83–84; protection of glyphs in, 84; radiocarbon dates in, 43

American Museum of Natural History, 5, 6

Anderson site, 143–46; burials, 144–45; excavations at, 143; faunal assemblage, 145, 149, 156, 157; grave goods, 144–45; hearths, 145; intergroup exchange at, 157–58; lithics, 144–45, 148; living floors, 145; mesic conditions at, 143–44; occupational sequence, 144, 152, 156; ochre at, 145; post-molds, 145; projectile points, 144; radiocarbon dates at, 149; shell beads at, 136, 144; strata at, 143; structures at, 157; violence at, 157

Annis, Waldemar, 160

Annis Village site, 30

Appalachian Mountains, 142

Archaeological Resources Protection Act (ARPA), 85

Archaic hunter/gatherers, 119

Archaic period, 69, 106–7, 109, 110–11, 112, 119–20, 128, 132–33; adult mortality in, 120; adult sex ratios in, 122; as symbolic complex, 139; bioarchaeological data from, 118–19, 120; ceremonialism, 157; copper in, 139; Early, 156; environmental adaption in, 141; Late, 2–3, 48, 72, 92, 98, 114, 116, 130, 146, 160, 161, 162; lithic technology in, 104, 105; Middle, 3, 140, 144, 146, 162; mortuary practices in, 113–14, 139, 157; nut utilization in, 155; occupation of Read Shell Mound, 105, 116; subadult mortality in, 121, 129; subsistence, 6, 8, 9, 23, 27, 28, 29, 30, 80, 155, 160; technoeconomic culture history, 8; warfare in, 157, 158. *See also* Archaic/Woodland transition; Shell mounds

Archaic/Woodland transition, 50, 70, 71, 72, 79, 80, 163

Army Medical Museum, 108

Arrowhead Farm site, 133

Atlatls, 104; upper limb asymmetry and use of, 124; weights, 134, 152

Atomic absorption spectroscopy, 134

Austin site (40Br82) faunal analysis, 157

Averbuch site, 125

Barrett site, 111

Bassett, John, 160

Beaver Pond site, 25

Benton component, 144, 146, 154

Big Bend, 27, 28, 30, 92, 104, 132, 164; botanical analyses at, 89, 160

Big Bone Cave, 164

Big Sandy component, 147, 149

Bioarchaeology, 111–18

Biodistance studies, 112–13, 114

Blue Spring Hollow site (15Ed52, GRS-12), 7, 10, 29

Bluff City site, 109

Boepple, John F., 137

Bone beads, 150, 155

Bone pins, 155

Bone tools, 149, 151, 152; fishhooks, 152, 156

Botanical remains, 88, 89; sequencing of, 89

Bowles site (15Oh13), 2, 28, 29, 89, 111

Brown, Ralph D., 94, 98

Buckner site, 127

Burial mounds, 70

Butterfield site (15McL7), 111, 116

Button musseling, 136, 137

Caldwell, Joe, 159

Calhoun site, 109

Campbell site, 127

Carbon isotope ratios, 63. *See also* Radiocarbon dating

Carbonized wood remains, 89, 90

Carlston Annis Shell Mound site (15Bt5), 2, 28–29, 88–93, 131, 160; adult mortality at, 117; adult sex ratios at, 122, 124; bivalve density at, 132; charcoal dating, 28; com-